Sailing
A Beginner's Guide

Sailing
A Beginner's Guide

SECOND EDITION

Written and Designed by
David Seidman

Illustrated by
Kelly Mulford, with Jan Adkins

The McGraw·Hill Companies

This edition published 2011 by
Adlard Coles Nautical
an imprint of Bloomsbury Publishing Plc
36 Soho Square
London W1D 3QY
www.adlardcoles.com

Copyright © 2011 International Marine,
an imprint of McGraw-Hill, Inc.

First published in Great Britain by Adlard Coles Nautical 1995
Reissued 2001, 2004, 2007, 2011

First published in the USA, 1994, 1995 under the title
The Complete Sailor: Learning the Art of Sailing
by International Marine,
an imprint of the McGraw-Hill Companies

ISBN 978-1-4081-5379-6

A CIP catalogue record for this book is available from the British Library.

Printed and bound in Spain by GraphyCems.

Illustrations on pages 10-11, 20-21, 30-1, 62-3, 82-3, 98-9, 112-3, 118-9, 126-7, 136-7, 154-5,
164-5, 174-5, 200-1 are by Mark Whitcombe.

Note from the Publishers
This book is based on a US edition, altered where US rules conflict with European.
In particular, IALA buoyage and safety regulations which are compulsory in the USA,
but only advisable in Europe and the UK at present.

For Mom and Dad who, as usual, were right when they said that hanging around
the docks would get me into trouble. God bless you both.

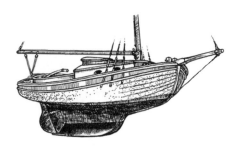

THE WATCH BELOW

While I stood my watch over this book, there have been others manning the
pumps below who have kept it afloat and must be thanked: Jon Eaton, whose
idea sent it down the ways; Molly Mulhern, who constantly tweaked the
autopilot to keep it on course; Kelly Mulford, for bringing life to my words; Jan
Adkins, who brought a fresh breeze; and Capt. Joe Friedman, the only hand I'd
trust at the wheel while I slept through a storm. You can stop pumping now;
we're there.

Contents

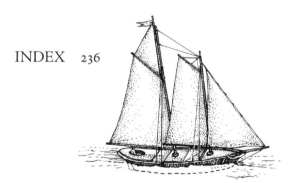

Becoming a Sailor

There are faster and more efficient and economical ways to travel on the water, but none as rewarding as travelling under sail. After decades of being blown about, soaked, awed, teased and satisfied, each time I set forth there is magic. For forty years it has stayed fresh and new, never failing to lighten my soul when I realise that through cunning and skill I have tricked the wind into moving my boat. There is nothing like it.

And that is what I hope to share with you in this book. Through these drawings and meagre words I hope to entice you into another world. The world of the sailor.

Anyone can learn to sail. That's easy enough. In fact there are books that will show you how to sail in a weekend. And I'm sure you're capable of doing it. But there is more to sailing than . . . well, than just sailing. By its very nature, sailing is slightly enigmatic and requires abstract thought. You can't just press a button and go wherever and whenever you like. It takes effort. Which in turn necessitates a certain amount of involvement. And this involvement is what being a sailor is all about.

After a few times out on the water you will see for yourself that there are many who sail but few who are sailors. You will also find that by the mere fact of commanding a boat, no matter how modest it may be, you will be hailed as Captain, or Cap'. It's a nice touch of nautical etiquette and a step up in station for most of us. But I'd rather be called Sailor any day.

A sailor is one who can handle a vessel of almost any type quietly and competently. He, or she, can read the water, the current, the waves, the clouds, and even the smells. The sailor, like any good craftsman, is at home with the tools of his trade and the elements he works in. Becoming a sailor takes time (more than a weekend, I can promise), and it takes work. But the time will pass all too swiftly, and the work will seem like pleasure.

Is it worth the effort? Years ago I read about an old man who enjoyed working his small sailing boat up and down a narrow river. His skill in handling the boat impressed the writer, who one day asked him why he sailed. The old man said that he first became a sailor for the pleasure it seemed to promise, but soon found it to be work mixed with small doses of fear. He almost gave it up right at the start. But before long the problems were overcome or in some manner dealt with. From then on, he said, the true rewards of sailing – patience, philosophy, self-respect, and the mastery of time – became evident. To him, these were the pleasures that becoming a sailor promised and eventually fulfilled.

Now it's your turn, and I envy the start of your adventure.

WIND SENSE

'To know the laws that govern the winds, and to know that you know them, will give you an easy mind . . . ; otherwise you may tremble at the appearance of every cloud.'

Joshua Slocum, *Sailing Alone Around the World*

S ailing is not a science that can be practised with precision. It is an art, or at the least a craft, with its own medium. As an artist uses and understands light, you must understand the wind. It is the sailor's medium.

In the beginning you need only know from where and how strong the wind is blowing. Without this you'll go nowhere. Literally. But the essence of sailing lies not just in reacting to the wind; if you would be a sailor, you must learn to read the wind and foretell what it will bring. It is a rare ability in the 21st century, but our marine forebears acquired a deep knowledge of the winds, and for good reason. Their lives depended on it. You will find some of this lore in the coming pages. To acquire a wind sense learn these few facts, and then start using your own natural abilities.

There is an old Irish saying that man's best friends and worst enemies are fire, rain and wind. We can't deny that wind possesses its share of riddles, but the better you under-stand the laws that govern it, the less a mystery the wind will be when you are on the water.

Direction

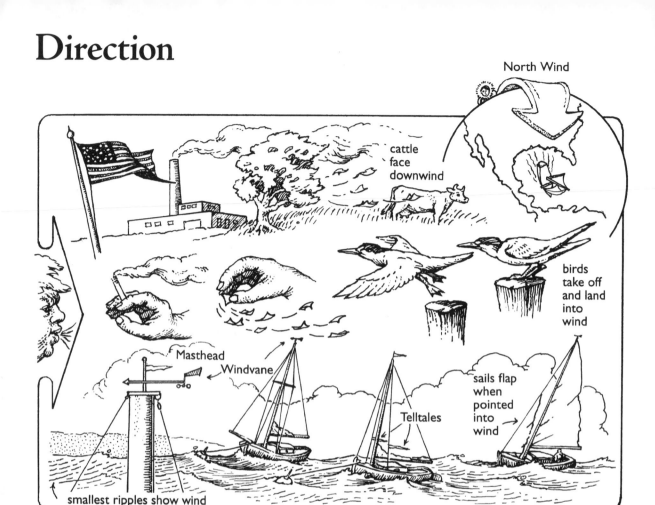

North Wind

cattle face downwind

birds take off and land into wind

Masthead Windvane

sails flap when pointed into wind

Telltales

smallest ripples show wind

By convention, winds are named for the quarter from which they blow. A wind blowing from the north towards the south is a north wind. But the wind's direction is never steady, and as you sail you'll need to keep track of what it is doing.

Clues to the wind are always around you. Waves are sculpted and pushed along by the wind, but only the ripples on the surface will show the wind's direction. Larger waves and swells may have been generated hours or days ago by distant forces. *Cat's-paws* – delicate, rapidly moving ripples that crest at right angles to the wind and chase it along the surface – reveal the direction of an approaching gust. Look for leaves, sand, or anything that can be blown. Boats at anchor or on moorings can give clues, for they will swing to point into the wind unless otherwise influenced by currents. Light shallow boats are the best indicators. Curiously, the sky is the last place to look, the movement of high clouds having little to do with the wind down here at the bottom of the atmosphere.

Make your own indicators on the boat. Install a flag or specially made *windvane* (better for light winds) at the top of the mast. Tie *telltales* (made from yarn) to the shrouds as high up as possible.

You are your own best indicator. Face the wind's general direction and turn your head slowly from side to side, noting the changing sensations on your skin and hair. There will be a difference in pressure, and temperature from evaporation, on each cheek until you are facing squarely into the breeze. Use your ears too. Even the slightest draught creates turbulence. Keep turning until the sound is the same in both.

If you practise sensing the wind on land as well as on the water, it will become second nature in a very short time.

Words of the Wind

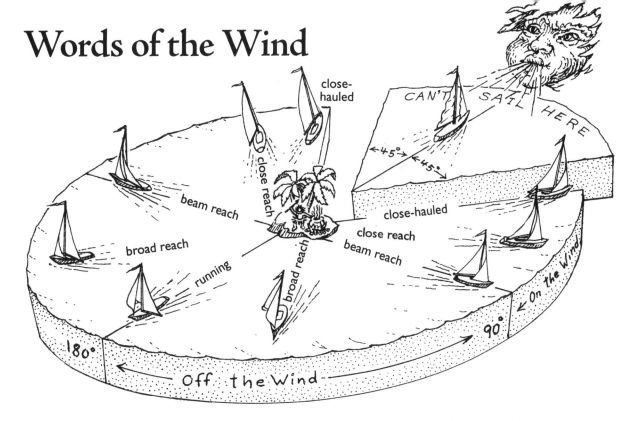

UP/DOWN: A sailor's world is divided into two halves: everything towards the wind and everything away from it. You face *upwind* by looking into the wind, and *downwind* by turning your back to it. Sailors shorten this to *up* or *down*. If you were told to 'bring her up', you would turn towards the wind; 'take her down' means to turn away.

WINDWARD/LEEWARD: This is another way of saying up or down. Anything upwind of you is to *windward*, anything downwind is to *leeward*, which is often pronounced 'loo'ard' by some traditional-minded sailors.

WEATHER/LEE: Anything upwind of you is prefaced by the word *weather*. A weather shore gives protection from the wind, but the weather side of a boat is exposed to it. Anything downwind of you is prefaced by the word *lee*. A gale can blow you onto a lee shore, and you can get out of the wind by anchoring in the lee of a bold shore.

ON/OFF: Sailing *on* the wind means your course is in a windward direction, and you are either close-hauled or on a close reach. Sailing *off* the wind means you are headed in a leeward direction, and you are on a beam reach, broad reach, or running with the wind.

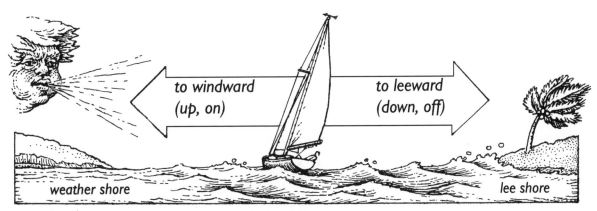

Land and the Wind

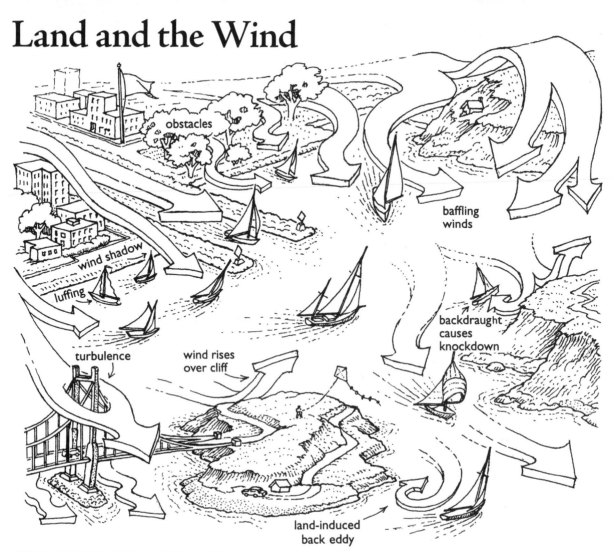

obstacles

baffling winds

wind shadow

luffing

turbulence

wind rises over cliff

backdraught causes knockdown

land-induced back eddy

THE EFFECTS OF LAND

Winds coming off the land will always be more capricious than those that have reached you over open water. New England's prevailing cool-weather northwesterlies can be maddeningly indecisive to a sailor used to the steadier southwesterlies of summer. And a blue-water ocean sailor may be at a loss to decipher wind directions on a lake, while the inland sailor may find the steadier winds of the open sea thoroughly uninteresting.

Large land features can produce their own wind systems. The notorious Santa Ana winds of Southern California are caused by inland desert air tumbling down the coastal mountains to the shore. Or winds can be funnelled by the banks of a river or down a narrow tree-lined lake.

More important to most sailors are the smaller land features that affect the wind. Looking at this illustration you may get some clues as to why the winds where you sail seem irrational. Try to find wind funnels that compress and accelerate winds. Islands cause eddies that whirl about for great distances downwind. Cliffs have only a minor effect on winds blowing along their face, but cause radical changes to those blowing towards or over them. Solid objects blocking a wind, such as buildings or another boat, make *wind shadows* – areas of reduced wind speed – that can extend downwind for up to thirty times the height of the object. Bridges and other open barriers create wind flaws with baffling shifts. The mere passage of a wind over or through something is enough to alter it.

PREVAILING WINDS

The difference in temperatures at the equator and the poles, with warm air rising to be replaced by colder air, is the foundation of the world's wind patterns. To this we add a deflecting effect from the Earth's eastward rotation, the presence of relatively stationary areas of high and low pressure, and landmasses with their own localised wind machines to produce the prevailing winds of the world.

Between 30 and 50 degrees north and south latitude is the home of the westerlies. Just south of 30 degrees north is the northern boundary of the northeast trade winds. This narrow buffer zone between two major wind systems is an area of calms and light variable winds known as the 'horse latitudes'. Here early explorers were forced to jettison their horses, as food ran low while they sat becalmed waiting to hitch a downwind ride on the trade winds to the New World.

Of course these global wind patterns are often obscured by local influences, such as land and sea breezes.

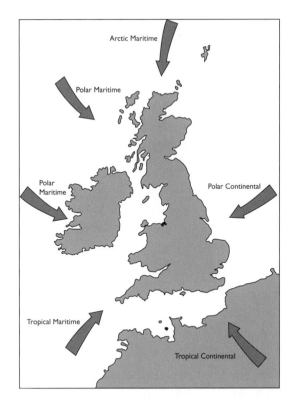

LAND & SEA BREEZES

As the land heats up during the day, warm air rises to be replaced by cooler air from over the water. This shoreward movement of air, called a *sea breeze*, creeps in around noon, becomes strongest (10 to 15 mph) by late afternoon, then tails off and dies around sunset.

At night the land cools rapidly. The air above it soon becomes comparatively colder than the air over the water, whose temperature is more stable. This causes a wind from the land towards the water, called a *land breeze*, that starts before midnight and continues until the land is once again heated. The temperature differences are not as great during the night, so land breezes are seldom more than 10 mph.

Sea breezes can work with or against a prevailing wind. On the South Coast of England, for example, the southwesterly is often augmented by a sea breeze which by mid afternoon can blow quite strongly on shore, dying away again at sunset. An easterly, associated with high pressure over England, can be cancelled out in a similar way.

Large water masses, such as lakes, can have their own wind systems as strong as any from the sea.

On smaller lakes, these breezes are weaker and do not extend far from shore. They can still be useful, though, and may even be dominant when the prevailing wind is light. Very often the only wind you'll find is near shore, with the centre as calm and flat as a mirror.

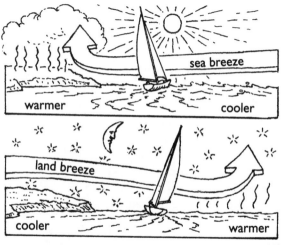

True & Apparent Winds

There are two winds in sailing, *true* and *apparent*. The wind direction and speed you feel when standing on the dock or sitting in your boat while it is moored is the true wind. All wind indicators on land show its direction and speed. As we've seen, wind's nature is fickle and rarely true to anything; but we'll call this wind true and let it go at that.

The wind you feel when moving is the apparent wind, a combination of the true wind and the wind you create for yourself by moving through the air. The wind indicators on your boat when it is underway show the apparent wind. This is handy because you adjust your sails to the apparent wind, not the true.

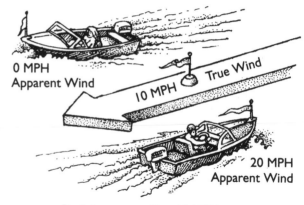

0 MPH
Apparent Wind

10 MPH True Wind

20 MPH
Apparent Wind

Both boats travelling 10 MPH

The true wind + the wind you make by moving = the Apparent Wind

For boats that rarely exceed 6 mph the distinction between true and apparent is not particularly important. Look to the boat's wind indicators, and trim sails accordingly.

Fast boats, however, make their own wind. If you're sailing a high-performance dinghy like a Laser, or a multihull like a Tornado catamaran, the apparent wind is *very* important. The faster the boat goes, the more it distorts the true wind. When a catamaran sailing on a beam reach gets hit with a strong gust, it immediately starts to accelerate. As the boat goes faster, the apparent wind shifts forward and increases in speed. The true wind's direction and the boat's course haven't changed, but suddenly you are trimming the sails in tight to their close-hauled position. After the gust passes, the boat slows down and you can ease the sails out until you are back on a beam reach again.

The most extreme examples of this are windsurfers and iceboats. Watch closely and you'll notice that in a strong breeze they are almost always trimmed as if close-hauled regardless of their course relative to the true wind, even if it is a broad reach.

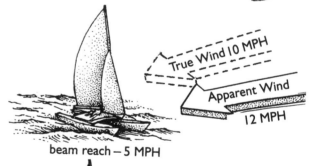

True Wind 10 MPH

Apparent Wind
12 MPH

beam reach – 5 MPH

GUST

boat accelerates

GUST

New Apparent Wind
24 MPH

close-hauled – 15 MPH

Wind Speed Tables

Before the 19th century there was no uniform way of describing wind and sea conditions. One sailor's fresh breeze was another's howling gale. In 1806 Admiral Sir Francis Beaufort devised a table that classified winds into groups called Forces. The system worked, and is still in use today.

The trouble is that his tables were devised for ships of the line and meant more to those on board the *Constitution* during the War of 1812 than the crew of a modern Catalina 22 trailer/sailer. So the tables below have been adapted to make them more relevant to a small coastal cruiser.

FORCE	MPH (KNOTS) *	PRESSURE LBS./ SQ. FT.	DESC.	WAVE PATTERN	WAVE HEIGHTS	EFFECTS ON LAND	SMALL CRUISER
Force 1	1–3 (1–3)	.004–.036	Light airs	Glassy calm, some ripples	Flat	Flag hangs limp, windvanes do not respond.	Use motor. Steerageway possible; full main and large drifter.
Force 2	4–7 (4–6)	.064–.196	Light breeze	Overall ripple pattern	0–.5'	Flag stirs, leaves rustle, wind felt on face, windvanes move.	Boat begins to heel, full main and drifter or #1 genoa.
Force 3	8–12 (7–10)	.256–.576	Gentle breeze	Small glassy waves	.5'–1'	Flag occasionally extends, leaves and twigs in constant motion.	Comfortable sailing. Noticeable heeling; full main and #1 genoa.
Force 4	13–18 (11–16)	.676–1.29	Moderate breeze	Longer waves	1'–1.5'	Flag flaps, small branches move, dust and paper raised.	Great sailing. Boat making speed. Full main and #1 genoa.
Force 5	19–24 (17–21)	1.44–2.30	Fresh breeze	Some whitecaps	1.5'–2.5'	Flag ripples, small leafy trees begin to sway.	Leeward rail near water. Single reef in main and #2 genoa.
Force 6	25–31 (22–27)	2.5–3.84	Strong breeze	Whitecaps, some spray	2.5'–4'	Flag snaps, large branches in motion, whistling in wires.	Sailing becomes strenuous. Second reef in main and working jib.
Force 7	32–38 (28–33)	4.09–5.77	Moderate gale	Swells form with whitecaps	4'–5.5'	Flag extended, whole trees in motion.	Progress to windward impossible. Three reefs in main and working jib.
Force 8	39–46 (34–40)	6.08–8.46	Fresh gale	Foam blown off wave tops in well-marked streaks	5.5'–7.5'	Twigs and small branches broken, difficult to walk.	Limit of boat's sailing ability. Use motor or seek shelter.
Force 9	47–54 (41–47)	8.83–11.6	Strong gale	Waves begin to heighten and roll	7.5'–10'	Slight structural damage occurs.	Run under bare poles, lie ahull, or sit to sea anchor.
Force 10	55–63 (48–55)	12.1–15.8	Whole gale	Very high rolling waves with long over-hanging crests	10'–13'	Trees broken or uprooted, considerable damage.	Swear oaths you will not keep once back on land.

Note: Wind pressure varies greatly according to the shape of an object; pressures indicated are only approximate. Wave patterns are described for large open lakes or oceans. Smaller bodies of water will have diminished wave patterns. Also, wave patterns will be different near abrupt shore features like cliffs, or when the wind is blowing against a current. When judging waves, look into the wind to estimate their size and power, not downwind.

*MPH: Statute miles (5,280 feet) per hour. Used on inland waters.
 KNOTS: Nautical miles (6,076 feet) per hour. Used at sea or on coastal waters.

Wind Strength

HOW HARD IS IT BLOWING?

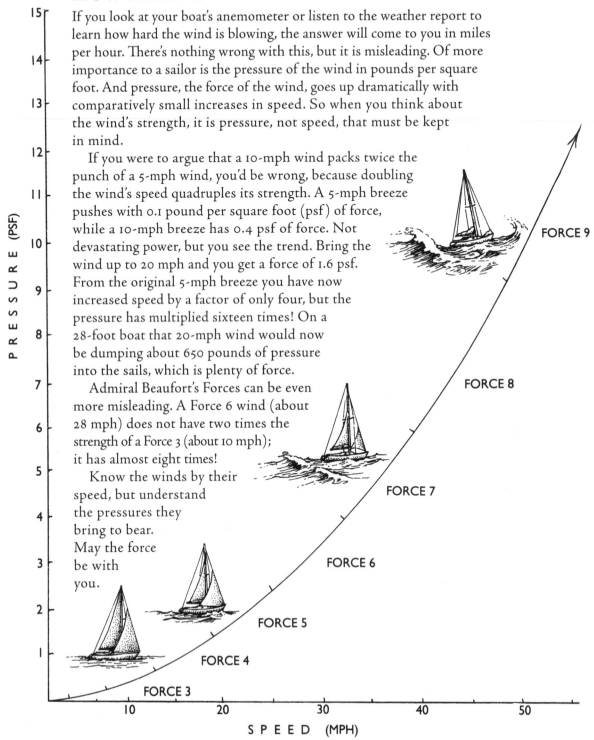

If you look at your boat's anemometer or listen to the weather report to learn how hard the wind is blowing, the answer will come to you in miles per hour. There's nothing wrong with this, but it is misleading. Of more importance to a sailor is the pressure of the wind in pounds per square foot. And pressure, the force of the wind, goes up dramatically with comparatively small increases in speed. So when you think about the wind's strength, it is pressure, not speed, that must be kept in mind.

If you were to argue that a 10-mph wind packs twice the punch of a 5-mph wind, you'd be wrong, because doubling the wind's speed quadruples its strength. A 5-mph breeze pushes with 0.1 pound per square foot (psf) of force, while a 10-mph breeze has 0.4 psf of force. Not devastating power, but you see the trend. Bring the wind up to 20 mph and you get a force of 1.6 psf. From the original 5-mph breeze you have now increased speed by a factor of only four, but the pressure has multiplied sixteen times! On a 28-foot boat that 20-mph wind would now be dumping about 650 pounds of pressure into the sails, which is plenty of force.

Admiral Beaufort's Forces can be even more misleading. A Force 6 wind (about 28 mph) does not have two times the strength of a Force 3 (about 10 mph); it has almost eight times!

Know the winds by their speed, but understand the pressures they bring to bear. May the force be with you.

PRESSURE (PSF)

SPEED (MPH)

FORCE 9

FORCE 8

FORCE 7

FORCE 6

FORCE 5

FORCE 4

FORCE 3

ONE BOAT'S GALE . . .

The ability of a boat to stand up to the wind and use the full power of its sails is directly related to its size. The smaller the boat, the stronger the wind feels. A bigger boat can almost always withstand more of a blow and carry more sail.

In a Force 7 wind a 20-foot keelboat can carry only a small jib with no mainsail, about 20% of its total sail area, and it will be hard-pressed to make progress into the wind. A 40-foot cruiser might be able to carry her working jib and a main with two reefs, about 40% of her sail area, and make her way slowly into the wind. An 80-foot ocean racer would have up its #2 genoa and a single-reefed main, about 60% of its sail area, and would step out to windward at a good clip.

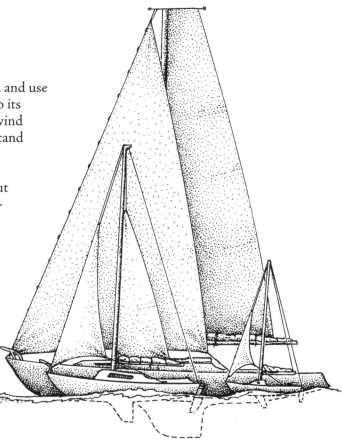

FORECASTS

British yachtsmen are well served by forecasts from the Met Office. The most useful are the succinct 5-minute shipping forecasts on BBC Radio 4. *Imminent* means within 6 hours, and *good* means visibility over 5 miles, while *quickly* signifies a barometer dropping up to 6.0 mb in 3 hours. Gale warnings are broadcast at the earliest opportunity, and both Radios 4 and 3 broadcast inshore waters forecasts. Many local

radio stations put out Small Craft Warnings for winds expected to exceed Force 6. British Telecom R/T coast radio stations broadcast twice daily, and HM Coastguard issue local forecasts of strong winds on Ch 67, or on request. And before setting off it's as well to phone BT's recorded Marinecall, which gives 54-hour forecasts for 15 areas as well as the outlook.

These reports are not gospel, because wind is an immediate and localized phenomenon. A voice coming out of a radio sounds authoritative, but what it is saying is, or was, true only where and when the data was gathered. Use radio reports, but trust what you see and feel even more.

Can we ever really know the wind? John Masefield, sailor and Poet Laureate of England, summed it up nicely:

> "A very queer thing is the wind.
> I don't know how it beginned,
> And nobody knows where it goes.
> It is the wind, it beginned and it blows."

WORKING WINDS

'Then they learned how to use the wind. For the first time they harnessed a force other than their own muscles, their servants', or their wives. It was a discovery whose effects reached down the ages . . .'
Lionel Casson, *The Ancient Mariners*

Taming wind as a motive power probably predates all other labour-saving mechanical devices. Long before a wheel rolled, some shaggy fellow straddled a log or sat on a raft and held up something to catch the wind. He could only go directly downwind, but it was certainly better than paddling. Like a man standing on ice holding out an umbrella, all he could do was follow where the wind took him. But in time hulls were devised that prevented slipping to leeward. Picture giving ice skates to the man with the umbrella; if his blades are sharp and his balance good, he could be pulled along with the wind off to one side. Now boats were just a little less at the wind's mercy.

Time passed and sails were made that allowed boats to head closer to the wind. The man on ice skates threw away his umbrella, picked up a sail, and flew across the face of the wind or even slightly into it. And ships began setting off into unknown waters, of which the ancient charts said only, 'There be dragons,' with a good chance they might even return.

The story of how sails evolved is a fascinating one and, until well into the 19th century, directly affected the advancement of mankind. But today we sail for pleasure. While the intent may be different, the principles of how a boat sails remain the same.

With the Wind

A small clay model of a Mesopotamian boat places the earliest provable date of sail power at more than five thousand years ago. And few marine archaeologists would argue the likelihood that sails were used at least two or three millennia before that.

It's an old and seemingly instinctive idea to catch the wind and travel along with it. The first purpose-built sail was probably nothing more than a flat sheet of woven fronds or linen hung from a *yard* (a horizontal pole). Untold centuries later, sails were woven or stitched together into a baggy shape. This full cut allowed the sail to grab as much wind as it could and to hold it, much like a modern spinnaker.

The principle of the square sail is simplicity itself. Moving air hits the sail, which is held at right angles to the breeze. As air piles up against the canvas, the pressure on the windward side increases, pushing the sail and thus the boat. It's effective but limited. A square-rigged boat is at its best when going downwind, which means going slowly. This is because the apparent wind diminishes as the boat goes faster, making downwind sailing in any boat one of the slowest of courses.

But the days of the square sail were slower times. From the ancient Egyptians off to explore the Land of Punt, to the Romans out on conquest, the square sail was good enough. When the wind was against them these coastal sailors would anchor or put slaves to the oars. Good upwind sailing ability was not important.

The Vikings were different. They carried no slaves and resisted being told where they could go, even by the wind. Their square sails, like the one shown here on a 9th-century longship, could be adjusted to make the sail fuller for going down-wind or flatter when sailing closer to the wind. The Vikings were among the first seafarers to sail successfully at an angle to the wind, a triumph due not so much to the sail they used as to the graceful hull with its shallow keel that gripped the water to prevent leeway. As we'll see, both hull and rig must work together to achieve good overall sailing qualities.

Across the Wind

While the Vikings were busy plundering their way through
Europe and voyaging towards the New World, Arab sailors were
trading from Zanzibar to the Malay peninsula and beyond to
fabled Cathay. They set forth from the Persian Gulf with a sail
that let them fly downwind for long ocean passages on the annual
monsoon winds, or reach across the wind among the Spice Islands
and along the coastlines of Asia. Seventh-century Europeans called
the sail *lateen* (Latin), for they knew it from the Mediterranean,
but it was born far to the east before the time of Christ.

A look at the lateen rig suggests a derivation from the square sail.
Tilt the square sail's yard so one end almost touches the deck, cut
off the excess cloth to make a triangle, and you have the lateen rig.
But unlike the square sail, only one side of which feels the wind, the
lateen splits the wind with its forward edge, directing air smoothly
over both sides. This establishes an airflow similar to that around
an aeroplane's wing, with the resultant forces *pulling* the boat
through the water towards the wind rather than *pushing* it away.

It was a stroke of brilliance, an intuitive experiment in aero-
dynamics giving sailors their first look into the eye of the wind.
But it was a teasing look. The far-ranging Arab dhow could sail
no closer than 70 degrees to the wind, and 90 degrees was more
common. It wasn't the rig's fault. The most popular class of sailing
boat in the world, the Sunfish, uses a lateen rig and can sail to
within 45 degrees of the true wind, like any other modern sailing
boat. The problem was with the clumsily shaped hulls, which did
not move easily through the water or resist making leeway.

So there we have it. The Vikings had refined the hull but not
the sail. The Arabs had refined the sail but not the hull. Not
until the 1800s were efficient hulls and sails brought together for
windward sailing, this time with a rig called the *lug*.

The lug rig had been around in different forms for a long time.
In the West it may have been derived from the earliest square
sail, which it resembles, or from the lateen. The classic sail of the
Chinese junk is a type of lug rig, and these go back well over two
thousand years. In the 15th century the Ming Dynasty dispatched a
spectacular armada of junks to Asia and Africa in a dazzling display
of sailing technology, navigation and force that no other power on
Earth could match. But in Europe the lug did not come into common use until the late 1700s, and then only on smaller craft.

It was the most powerful windward sail possible at the time.
The lugger shown here is a Yarmouth mackerel boat of about
1860 reaching in a stiff breeze with shortened sail. After thousands of years, by combining an aerodynamically efficient sail
with a sleek hull that resisted leeway, the builders of this little
hooker could finally say that they had mastered the wind.

YH932

7th-Century Lateen-Rigged Dhow

WIND

Working the Wind

MAKING THE SAIL PULL

The lateen and lug rigs were major steps forward because they let the wind blow across both sides of the sail. If the sail was made by a clever sailmaker, the divided wind would mould the cloth to a curved shape similar to that of an aeroplane's wing. These sails were, in effect, primitive airfoils that pulled a boat towards the source of the wind.

When the wind blows against one side of a sail, it can only push a boat in a down-wind direction.

When the wind blows equally on both sides, the sail becomes like a large flap.

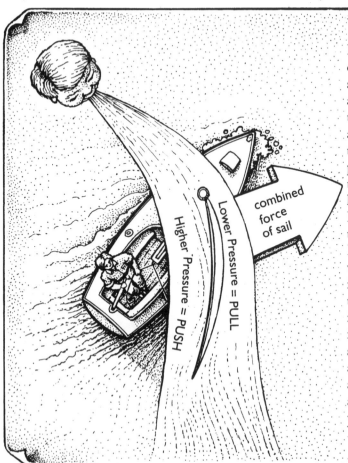

Higher Pressure = PUSH

Lower Pressure = PULL

combined force of sail

But if a sail splits the wind and takes a curved shape with air flowing over both sides, areas of higher and lower pressure are created. Higher pressure occurs on the windward side of the sail and pushes against it. Lower pressure occurs on the leeward side, creating a suction that pulls at the cloth and provides most of the sail's drive. The combined effect, like an aeroplane's wing, produces lift. But instead of supporting an aeroplane, this lift pulls a boat through the water. For maximum aerodynamic thrust when reaching or close-hauled, the sail is adjusted to trap just enough wind to hold its shape. Trim the sail too far in and you get only the lesser pushing force. Let it too far out and it loses its shape. By maintaining the proper sail angle you can make the wind take you almost anywhere, except to within about 45 degrees on either side of the wind's eye.

DIRECTING THE SAIL'S PULL

It would be nice if the sail's pull went entirely into making the boat go forward. Unfortunately it comes at an angle to the boat, with a large part of it drawing the boat sideways. If a tugboat were to pull a boat as a sail does, the boat would slip along on a diagonal course.

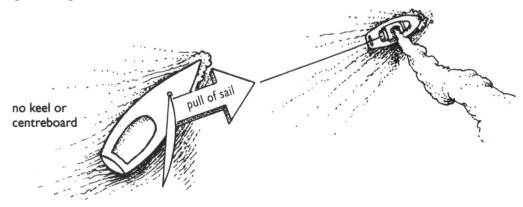

no keel or centreboard

pull of sail

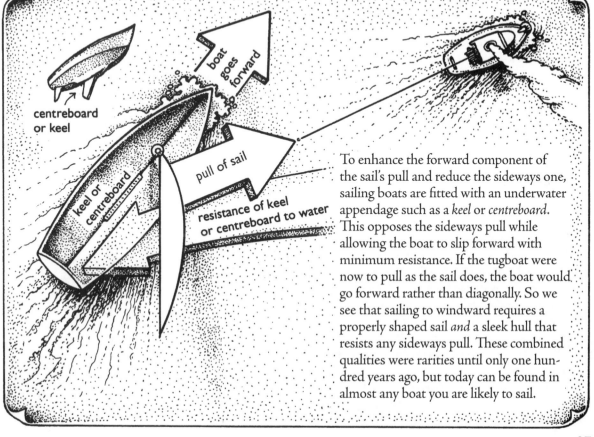

centreboard or keel

boat goes forward

keel or centreboard

pull of sail

resistance of keel or centreboard to water

To enhance the forward component of the sail's pull and reduce the sideways one, sailing boats are fitted with an underwater appendage such as a *keel* or *centreboard*. This opposes the sideways pull while allowing the boat to slip forward with minimum resistance. If the tugboat were now to pull as the sail does, the boat would go forward rather than diagonally. So we see that sailing to windward requires a properly shaped sail *and* a sleek hull that resists any sideways pull. These combined qualities were rarities until only one hundred years ago, but today can be found in almost any boat you are likely to sail.

Into the Wind

A sailing boat cannot sail directly into the wind, but it can get there indirectly. By sailing as close to the wind as possible in one direction (say, with the wind from your right side) and then changing course to sail as close to the wind as possible in the other direction (with the wind now from your left), you can zigzag your way to a destination lying straight to windward. The process is called *beating* or *working to windward*, and each time you change direction you are *tacking* or *coming about*.

Beating to windward in an early fore-and-aft boat (as non-square-rigged craft were once called) was tough work. Tacking a lateen or lug sail often required that the long yard be lowered and then raised on the opposite side. It was frequently dangerous, not always successful, and risky in close quarters.

A better way came from Holland in the 17th century with the advent of the *gaff sail*. The long yard was replaced by a shorter gaff that need not be lowered on each tack. After centuries of experimenting there were other improvements in efficiency. The sail's leading edge was now held taut against the mast to improve its qualities as an airfoil, and later a *boom* (a spar along the bottom of the sail) was added to draw the sail out into the flatter shapes needed for windward sailing. By the 1800s the gaff sail was the most common one in the world. It made oceanic and coastal trade profitable, as only small crews were needed to handle what had once been thought sizeable ships. The rig could also be fast. In 1905 the elegant gaff-rigged schooner yacht *Atlantic* set a transatlantic record that stood for 75 years. It took an all-out effort from a high-tech racing trimaran to finally improve on her speed.

The gaff rig is still around; here we see the enduring little Beetle Cat beating to windward. This 12-foot 6-inch catboat was a good performer when designed in the early 1920s and still is today, with hundreds actively sailing. But in our quest for rigs that are easier to handle and get us closer to the wind, the triangular Bermudian sail eventually displaced the four-cornered gaff sail in the position of pre-eminence.

The Bermudian rig came by its name from the traditional sail of that island, and it can still be seen today in island working craft. It was also known as the *marconi* rig, because its tall masts resembled the new wireless radio towers of the 1920s. These sails successfully imitated the shape of a bird's wing, giving rise to performance capabilities that would seem like witchcraft to the 19th-century fishermen in their Yarmouth lugger.

Today this form of sail, when mounted on a well-conceived hull, drives boats as close to the wind as is possible and at speeds over 50 mph. These are sails that truly work the wind.

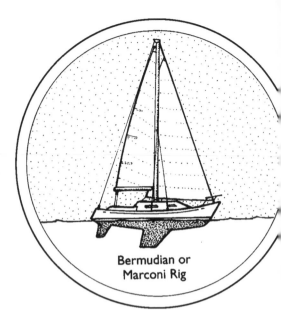

Bermudian or
Marconi Rig

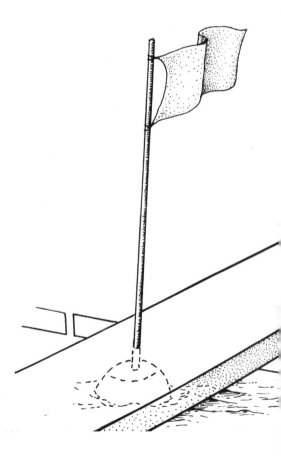

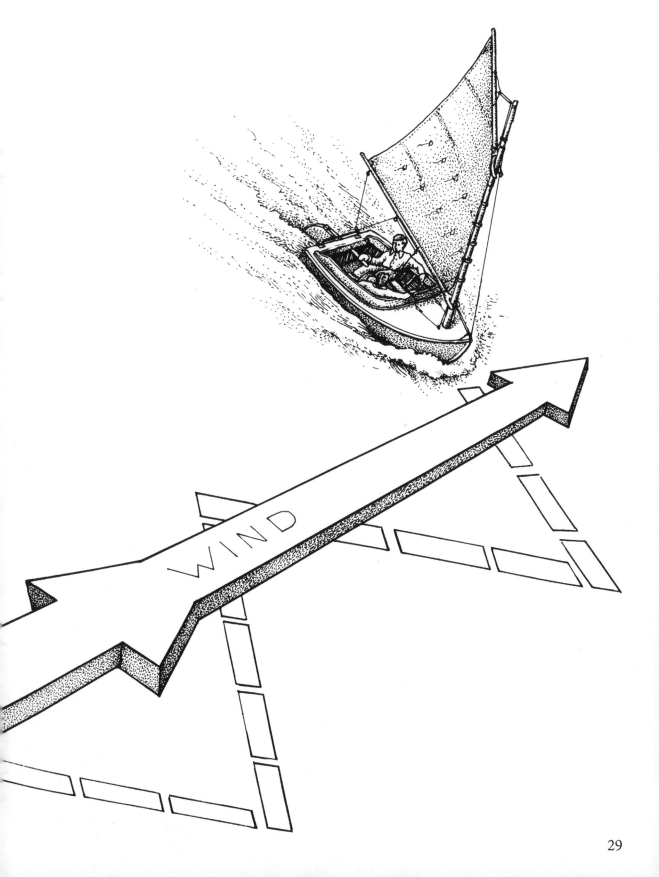

WIND

GETTING UNDERWAY

'Even now, with a thousand little voyages notched in my belt, I feel a memorial chill on casting off, as the gulls jeer and the empty mainsail claps.'
E. B. White, 'The Sea and the Wind that Blows', *Essays of E. B. White*

When you step aboard for the first time, a boat may appear to be a random collection of hazards waiting to pounce. That's why the best boat to learn on is often someone else's. If you can, find a friend to take you out and help you get past those first awkward moments. If you must learn on your own, start small, but not too small. The boat you choose should have room for you and a companion, and be stable enough so you feel secure. Boats with only one sail are good starters. But if your boat is a sloop, with a mainsail and jib, do not be tempted to sail with only the main up. This will only make the boat harder to handle.

Do things slowly. Think first. Learn to sail in a place with plenty of open water, and out of the way of large, expensive, solid objects – like docks or other boats. Make your first voyages modest ones. Keep a weather eye out for changes. Winds of 5 to 12 mph are ideal. Go easy on yourself. You are more important than the boat. Flop around, make mistakes, learn, and by all means enjoy. As Charles II, England's first yachtsman, said, 'God would not damn a man for a little irregular pleasure.'

Bending Sail

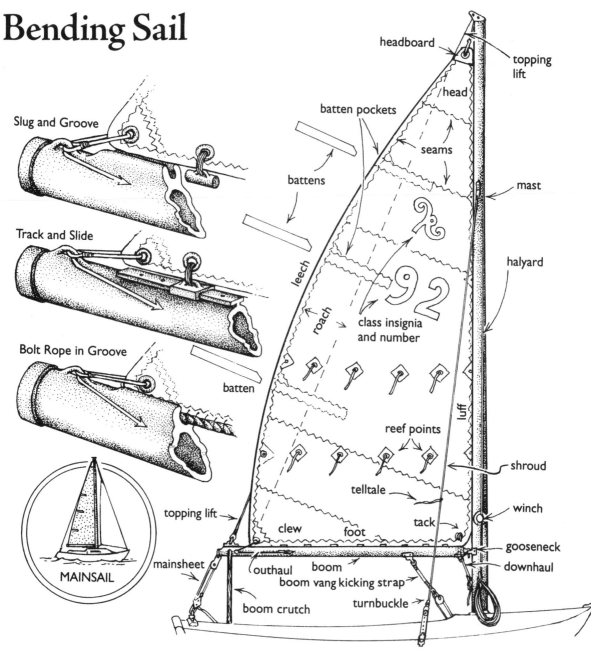

Slug and Groove

Track and Slide

Bolt Rope in Groove

MAINSAIL

headboard

topping lift

head

batten pockets

seams

battens

mast

halyard

leech

class insignia and number

roach

reef points

luff

shroud

telltale

winch

clew

foot

tack

gooseneck

topping lift

downhaul

mainsheet

outhaul

boom

boom vang kicking strap

turnbuckle

boom crutch

batten

To *bend on* sail is to fasten it in place for hoisting, starting with the *mainsail* (pronounced 'mains'l'). First attach the *foot* of the sail. Insert the *slugs* or *boltrope* (a rope sewn onto the edge of the sail) into the groove on the boom. Start with the *clew* at the *gooseneck*, then work the sail back towards the end of the boom. Secure the *tack*, then the clew, using the *outhaul* to pull the wrinkles from the foot. The free end of the boom is usually supported in a *crutch* or held up by a *topping lift*.

Thin wooden or fibreglass *battens* are used to extend the *leech* (from lee-edge) to increase sail area. This extra area is called the *roach*. Place the battens in their pockets, making sure they fit snugly without having to be forced into place. Some pockets require a *reef knot* (page 149) at their ends to secure the battens.

Attach the *luff* to the mast in the same manner as the foot. The *halyard* (from haul-yard, a line used to hoist the yard and its sail on a square-rigger) is then

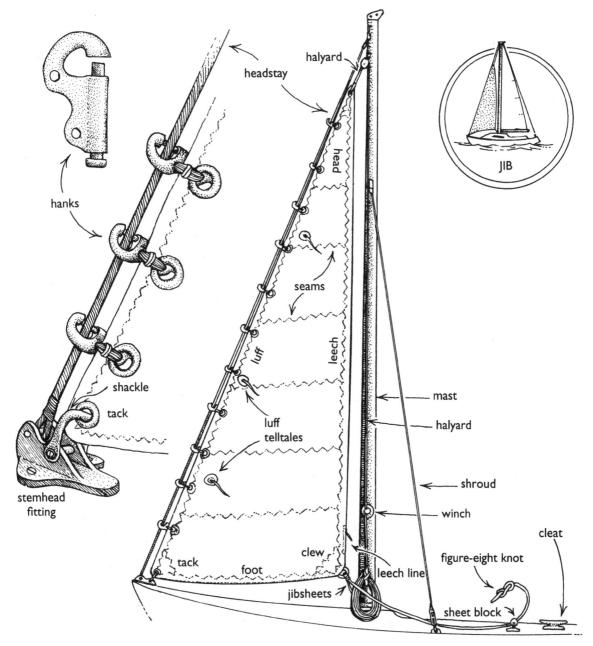

headstay

halyard

hanks

head

shackle

tack

luff

seams

leech

luff
telltales

mast

halyard

shroud

winch

stemhead
fitting

JIB

cleat

figure-eight knot

clew

tack

foot

leech line

sheet block

jibsheets

made *fast* (secure) to the *head* of the sail using a *shackle* or a *bowline* (page 147). The main halyard is always led to a *cleat* on the right side of the mast.

Since *hanks* are commonly used to hold the jib to the *headstay*, it is proper to say you are *hanking on*, as well as bending on, a jib. Make the tack fast to a shackle at the base of the stay. When coming out of a sailbag, the tack and head look very much alike. Labelling them will help you avoid hoisting the jib upside down. Snap on the hanks, lowest

one first, working towards the head. Keep all the hanks facing the same way to prevent twisting the luff. Secure one end of the halyard to the head and the other to a cleat on the left side of the mast. Make the *jibsheets* fast to the clew using bowlines. Their free ends will usually lead around the *shrouds*, through *sheet blocks*, and back to cleats near the cockpit. Tie a *figure-eight knot* (page 146) in their ends so they won't shake their way back through the blocks.

Steering

The rudder dates back to about 1200. Before that a steering oar, or board (from which we get the word *starboard*), was lashed to the boat's right side. Bringing that side of the boat against a dock would damage the oar, so the left side was always 'to *port*'. Port and starboard are not relative, like right and left. One side of the boat is always port, the other starboard, no matter which way you are facing.

Rudders controlled by a *tiller* seem to be a source of confusion since they must be moved opposite the direction of the boat's intended turn. When you swing the tiller to starboard the rudder moves to port, which deflects water moving past the hull, making the boat turn to port. Wheels are easier to understand. Turn the wheel to starboard and the boat goes to starboard. Whether steering with a tiller or wheel, move it in small increments. Large and frequent course corrections will only slow the boat down.

Turning the rudder forces the stern to slip sideways, making a wider arc than the bow. How much the stern slips depends on the boat's pivot point. With the centreboard down, or on boats with keels, the pivot point is just forward of midships, and the stern will not swing out as much. With no centreboard or keel, the pivot point is near the bow, and the stern will swing out in a much wider arc. You'll want to keep your centreboard down when manoeuvring.

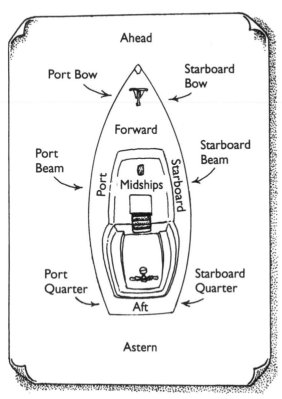

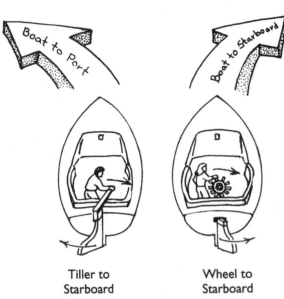

Tiller to Starboard

Wheel to Starboard

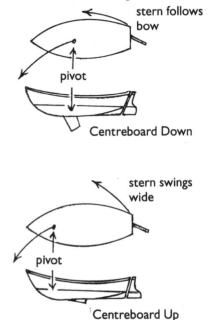

stern follows bow

pivot

Centreboard Down

stern swings wide

pivot

Centreboard Up

Making Sail

Upon coming aboard, stow all gear so it will stay in place when the boat *heels* (leans) to the wind. Bail her out, check that all necessary safety equipment is on board, and lower the centreboard for extra stability while getting ready.

The aftmost sail is always hoisted first so the boat will weathercock its bow into the wind. On two-masted boats (yawls and ketches) the mizzen is hoisted first and sheeted *flat* (pulled in all the way) to act as a windvane. The mainsail follows, and finally the jib, with plenty of slack in their sheets to keep them *luffing* (shaking) freely until you are ready to get underway.

On a sloop the main goes up first, with its sheet free so the boom will swing with the wind. If there is one, untie the *downhaul*. Look aloft to make sure the halyard is *clear* (not tangled) and then haul away. As you hoist, check that the sheet runs freely through its blocks so the boom swings to the breeze and the sail luffs rather than filling. Set the luff up firmly. If the gooseneck can slide, raise the sail as high as possible, then tension the luff by pulling down with the downhaul. Make the halyard fast to its cleat and coil the *fall* (unused length) so it can be let run in an emergency. *Ease off* (slacken) the topping lift and stow the boom crutch if there is one.

Next get the jib up. Make sure its halyard is clear and the sheets are free. Hoist away until its luff is absolutely straight, with no *scallops* (concave curves) between the hanks. There should be a slight crease parallel to the luff and a few inches back that will disappear when the sail fills. Make the halyard fast to its cleat and coil neatly (page 156).

Give a final check. Gear secure? Sheets free? Halyards coiled? Sails luffing? Good, you're ready to get underway.

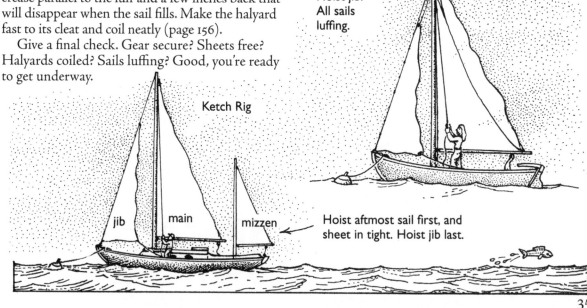

Ketch Rig

jib   main   mizzen

1 Attach halyards. Free sheets.   Sloop Rig

2 Hoist main and slack off topping lift.

3 Hoist jib. All sails luffing.

Hoist aftmost sail first, and sheet in tight. Hoist jib last.

Leaving a Mooring ...

With your sails luffing freely and the centreboard down, study your surroundings. Notice the wind's direction and force, and if it is steady or shifting. Pick a route out of the anchorage that is easy to sail and takes you away from docks, shoals and other boats.

All boats swing about their moorings. When your bow has swung in the desired direction, *slip* (let go) the mooring *pendant* (pronounced 'pennant') and the boat will start drifting backwards. To keep the bow swinging off the wind, turn the rudder so the stern backs towards the wind. You could also *backwind* the jib by holding its clew out to windward, or walk the mooring pendant aft, pulling the stern up to it.

Once you have fallen at least 45 degrees off the wind, you can begin sailing. To get the boat going, turn the rudder to point her away from the mooring, haul in the jibsheet on the leeward side,

wait a few seconds until the jib fills and is pulling, and then trim in the main. Until the boat gains *steerageway* (enough speed to respond to the rudder), head a little downwind of your intended course. Do not try to *pinch her* (sail too close to the wind) or trim the sails all the way in. Both will result in making a lot of *leeway* (sideslip) with very little forward progress. Bear off, gain speed, and then set your course.

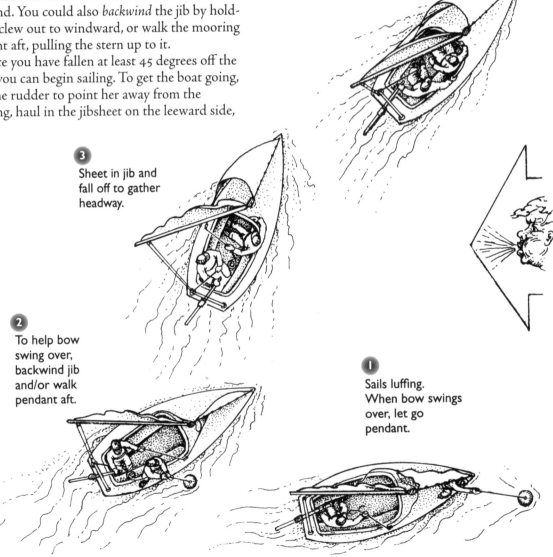

4 Trim main.

3 Sheet in jib and fall off to gather headway.

2 To help bow swing over, backwind jib and/or walk pendant aft.

1 Sails luffing. When bow swings over, let go pendant.

. . . or a Dock

It is hard to handle a sailing boat with any degree of precision in confined quarters. This is why sailing from a dock takes more thought and care than from a mooring. Docks are hard, unyielding, and take pleasure in fouling stray sheets or overhanging booms. Before making sail, think through each procedure and leave yourself an out, just in case.

1. If possible, hang off the dock's leeward side from your bow dockline. This will allow the boat to sit head to wind. Cast off the dockline and you're underway as though from a mooring.

2. Almost as good is to lie alongside the dock with the wind blowing on your nose. When you push the bow clear of the dock, the sails should fill. Take in on the jibsheet first, and be careful that the stern does not hit the dock as you turn outwards.

3. It is usually impossible to leave from the windward face of a dock with the wind pressing the boat against it. Walk the boat to a more favourable side and leave from there.

4. If you can't walk the boat around, paddle clear of the dock and anchor as far off as possible. Once the sails are up and the anchor retrieved, you must immediately gain headway so as not to drift back on the dock. On larger boats you may have to row out the anchor, and haul the boat out to it.

5. When the wind is over the stern, leave under jib alone with the main down. Once in open water, round up into the wind and hoist the main.

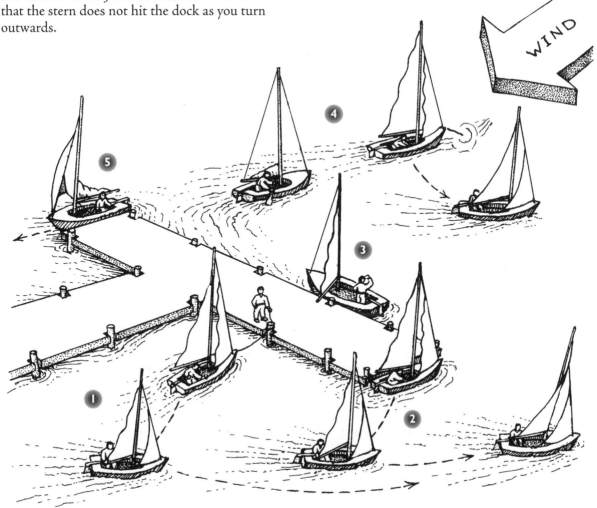

Reaching

In the old sailing navy a beam wind was called 'a soldier's breeze', implying that even a landlubber could handle the boat with the wind from this quarter. On anything from a close to a broad reach, all you have to do is pick your course and steer it. Even if your sails are not properly trimmed, you'll move out at a good clip. A reach is the fastest and most forgiving point of sailing – good reasons to spend as much of your first sail as possible on a reach.

Upon clearing the anchorage, set a course that keeps the apparent wind well off to the side. If you have a centreboard, pull it halfway up – a little higher for a broad reach, lower for a close reach. Now adjust the angle of your sails for maximum thrust, beginning with the jib. Slack off the sheet until the sail's luff starts to get *soft* (lose shape) or begins luffing. Then pull in slowly until the sail is drawing with its full curvature, but no further. That's the point of highest efficiency. Trim the main the same way, and finally, if you have one, the mizzen.

You may notice that as you work your way aft each sail wants to be trimmed in closer than the one ahead of it. This is due to the deflected wind from the leading sail. The *Thomas W. Lawson*, the only seven-masted schooner, was an extreme example of this with her aftmost sail almost always sheeted home.

Since the wind is never constant, you will occasionally have to retrim to keep her *footing* (going at speed). Keep your eye on the jib's luff, for it is there that a shift will first show itself. Every once in a while, *start* (pay out) the sheets and retrim just to be sure. Naturally, if you change course you will have to retrim.

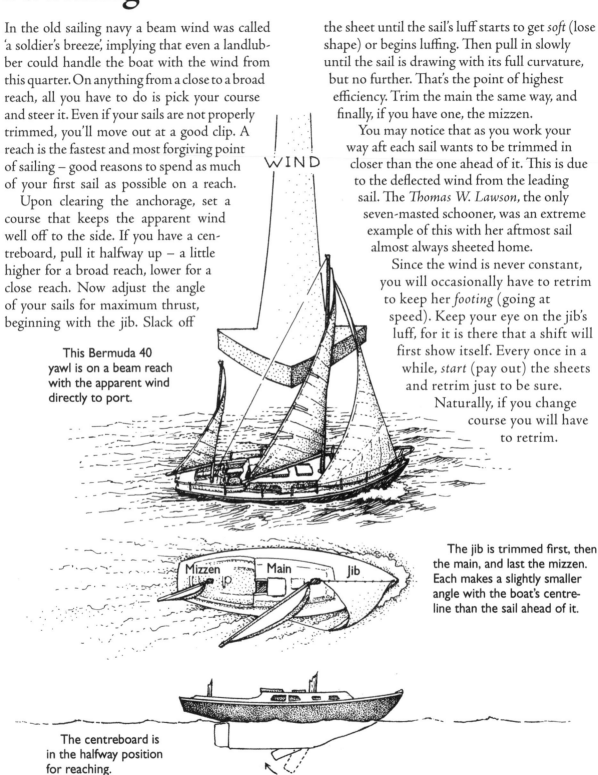

WIND

This Bermuda 40 yawl is on a beam reach with the apparent wind directly to port.

The jib is trimmed first, then the main, and last the mizzen. Each makes a slightly smaller angle with the boat's centreline than the sail ahead of it.

Mizzen Main Jib

The centreboard is in the halfway position for reaching.

Keeping a Course

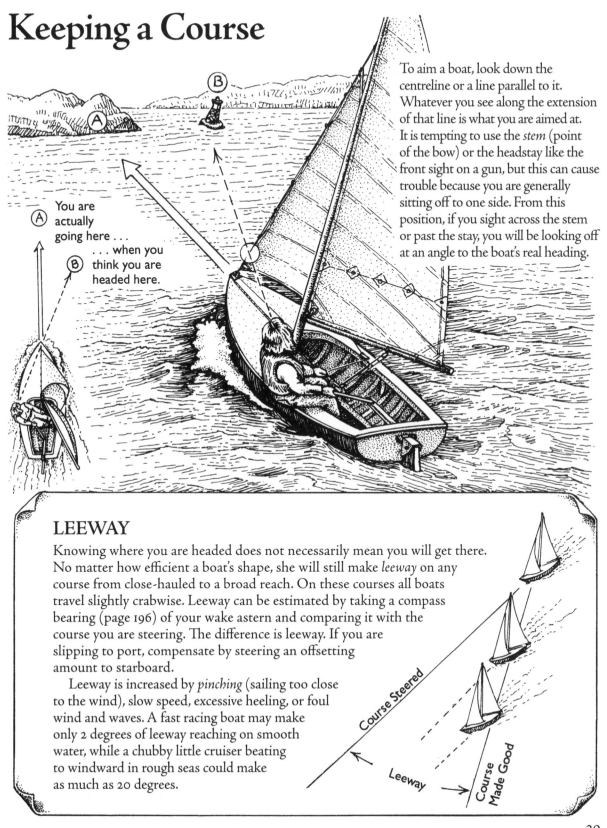

You are
actually
going here . . .

. . . when you
think you are
headed here.

To aim a boat, look down the centreline or a line parallel to it. Whatever you see along the extension of that line is what you are aimed at. It is tempting to use the *stem* (point of the bow) or the headstay like the front sight on a gun, but this can cause trouble because you are generally sitting off to one side. From this position, if you sight across the stem or past the stay, you will be looking off at an angle to the boat's real heading.

LEEWAY

Knowing where you are headed does not necessarily mean you will get there. No matter how efficient a boat's shape, she will still make *leeway* on any course from close-hauled to a broad reach. On these courses all boats travel slightly crabwise. Leeway can be estimated by taking a compass bearing (page 196) of your wake astern and comparing it with the course you are steering. The difference is leeway. If you are slipping to port, compensate by steering an offsetting amount to starboard.

Leeway is increased by *pinching* (sailing too close to the wind), slow speed, excessive heeling, or foul wind and waves. A fast racing boat may make only 2 degrees of leeway reaching on smooth water, while a chubby little cruiser beating to windward in rough seas could make as much as 20 degrees.

Course Steered

Leeway

Course Made Good

Close-Hauled

As you coax your boat closer to the wind, you have to pull in the sails to keep them from luffing. Eventually you reach a point where they are trimmed to their limits. You are then *close-hauled*, travelling as *close* to the wind as possible with the sails *hauled* in all the way.

No boat can sail directly into the wind. The best you can do is about 45 degrees to one side of the true wind, or about 30 degrees off your apparent wind when underway. To point this close you must fully lower the centreboard and sheet in the jib. Do not pull it in absolutely flat, but leave a slight arc in the foot so the sail can still act as an airfoil. On the wind, the jib's primary purpose is to funnel air through a *slot* between it and the main. If the slot is properly formed, air accelerates over the main's leeward side, greatly enhancing its pulling power.

To trim the main, sail close-hauled with the jib properly trimmed and the main boom all the way in. Then slowly ease the main until its luff loses shape from being *backwinded* (turbulence from too small a slot) by the jib. Sheet it back in until it regains its shape. The sails are now working together.

Once the sails are trimmed, leave them. On a larger boat the sheets can be made fast. But on smaller, capsizable boats, hold them for quick releasing if overpowered by a gust of wind. From now on you adjust the sails' angle to the wind through small corrections to the rudder. Keep an eye on the forwardmost sail's leading edge. If it starts to soften or shake, you are pointing too high. Bear off until the sail draws again, but no further. That's the heading of maximum efficiency.

While your goal is to point as high as possible, you must not sacrifice speed. Sailing too close (pinching) starves the sails of wind, slowing the boat and encouraging leeway. You'll make better progress to windward if you bear off a little to keep up your speed. Sail her *full and by* (sails full and drawing), and keep her footing. When she's in the groove, she'll heel, pick up speed, and seem to come alive.

Even the steadiest breeze shifts subtly, sometimes inviting you closer to your goal and other times pushing you away. A shift aft, which lets you point higher, is called a *lift* (it lifts you to windward). A shift forward, which forces you to bear away, is called a *header* (it heads you off). To gain ground to windward use lifts, and continually test the wind's direction by edging upwind until the jib begins to luff, then bearing off slightly. As the wind shifts, meet it, thereby gradually eating (in small nibbles) your way into the wind.

A Well-Formed Slot between Jib and Main

Slot Effect

Backwinded Mainsail

40

THE EVER-CHANGING WIND

The wind can change in strength as well as direction. In a puff you may have to sit further to windward, or even *hike out* (lean out over the windward rail), to keep her from heeling too much. Heeling more than 20 degrees, or letting the lee deck drag in the water, will slow you down and impede handling. If a gust is too strong, dump some wind by quickly freeing the sheets or *rounding up* (turning into the wind). A gust will feel like a lift, shifting the apparent wind aft and allowing you to point higher. A momentary lull will feel like a header, moving the apparent wind towards the bow and forcing you to bear off.

To know if you're getting the most from your boat, maintain a clear view of the forward sail's luff, keep your senses alert, and try to stay in touch with how the boat is reacting.

+ Feel the wind's force and direction on your face.
+ Watch how the headstay sags when the jib is trimmed.
+ Listen and look for the jib luffing.
+ Watch the telltales and windvane.
+ Feel how much she is heeling.
+ Listen to the bow wave and look at the wake.
+ Feel the pull of the sheets and tug of the tiller.
+ Listen to the hum of the rudder and centreboard.

All these signs give clues as to how she is going. Like a good equestrian, the helmsman controls his mount as much by his senses as by his mind. Think of your boat as something alive, taking the time to develop a feel for it.

Tacking

On page 28 we saw that a destination lying straight into the wind must be approached indirectly by tacking. Like switchbacks on a mountain slope too steep to ascend directly, tacking makes the seemingly impossible possible.

Tacking swings the boat's bow 90 degrees through the wind. Each close-hauled leg of this zigzag is called a *tack*. You are on *starboard tack* when the wind is from your starboard side. When you change directions by coming about, the wind is from your port side, and you are on a *port tack*.

When it's time to tack, the skipper says 'Ready about' and bears off slightly (5 to 10 degrees) to pick up momentum for the turn. The crew makes sure the jibsheets are *clear* (not tangled) and ready to run out. With the command 'Hard a'lee', the boat is turned so it rounds up into the wind. When the jib starts to luff, release the leeward sheet, move to the opposite side of the boat, and take hold of the other sheet.

Try for a smooth turn through the wind, not an abrupt pirouette. By *shooting* (using momentum to coast ahead), you gain a few boat lengths to windward each time you come about. With the helm *down* (tiller to leeward or wheel to windward) and the turn well started, the coasting boat will take care of itself for a few moments so you can let go of the helm and attend to other tasks.

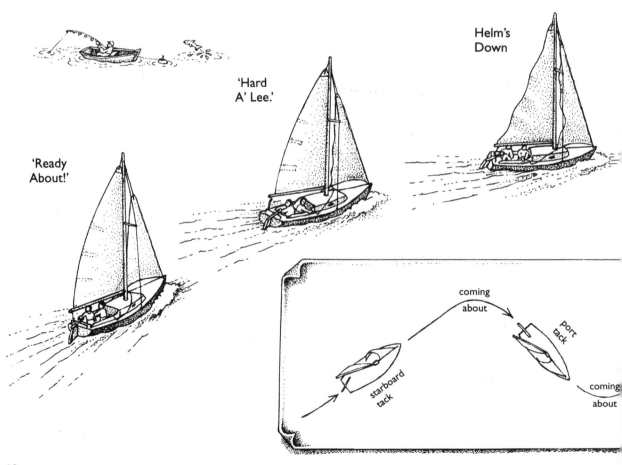

After the bow passes through the wind, the sails will luff until the boat approaches its new tack. As the jib begins to fill, start trimming it in. You need not bother with the main, as it tacks by itself, but watch out for the boom as it swings across. While coming about the boat will lose headway and needs to regain speed before settling into the new tack. Briefly fall off until she's back to speed and footing, then start edging up and testing the wind once again.

It is often best to work to windward in a series of many short tacks, rather than a few long ones. This way you can tack whenever the wind heads you, thereby sailing a shorter course. To tell where your next tack will take you, sight directly *abeam* (perpendicular to your present heading) from your windward side. Use an *athwartship* ('across-ship') line like the back side of a cabin, or mentally adjust your present compass course by 90 degrees. Allow for current and leeway to be sure you will *fetch* (reach) your mark.

Some boats are unusually *weatherly* (sail closer to the wind) and can tack in less than 90 degrees. The best of the 12-metre America's Cup boats could tack within 64 degrees of the true wind. Others need more, sometimes up to 110 degrees for slower boats in rough seas. Learn what your boat can do.

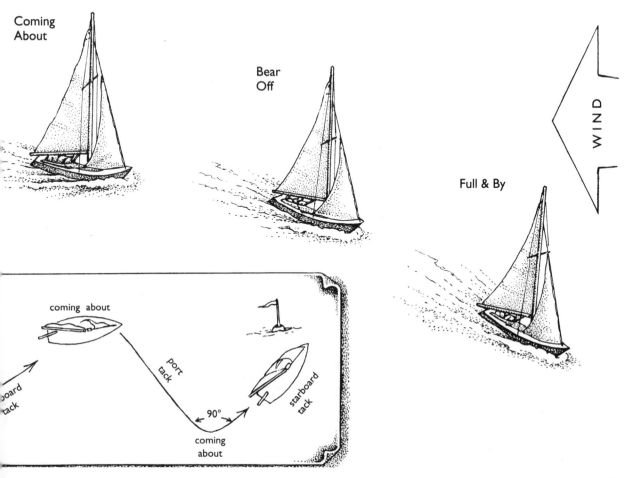

Coming About

Bear Off

Full & By

WIND

coming about

port tack

starboard tack

90°

coming about

board tack

Other Tacks

TACKING A CLIPPER

With the trade winds at their backs, clipper ships were majestic grey-hounds, but when close-hauled or tacking they could be incorrigible dogs. The best clippers could point no higher than about 60 degrees off the wind. On this course, with plenty of momentum to see her through, the helmsman gently turns into the wind with the jibsheets free and the *spanker* (aftmost sail) hauled to weather. With every-thing luffing, she gradually comes about. To help her pass through the wind, the spanker is let go, jibs sheeted in, the main yards hauled over, and the sails on the foremast held *aback* (wind on their forward faces). With almost no headway, the sails slowly spin her around. Once on the new tack the yards of the foremast are brought around, and all sails are trimmed. Square-riggers often lost ground when tacking, or missed coming about altogether. A slow laborious process from which the phrase 'backing and filling' was derived.

Full and by

Let go and haul

WIND

Mainsail haul

Ready about!

Helm's a'lee

THE PROA

Centuries before the Christian era, canoes of Oceania crossed thousands of sea miles to colonise the Pacific, and almost all of them were to windward. These deceptively frail craft were safe, sophisticated and extremely seaworthy. The fastest was the Micronesian proa. Capable of speeds up to 20 mph, it carried its *ama* (outrigger) to windward, and its double-ended hull sailed equally well in both directions. To come about, the wind is brought abeam, and the sheet released so the sail luffs and the boat stops. The tack of the sail is untied from the bow and walked to the other end of the boat, which becomes the new bow. At the same time, the helmsman takes his steering paddle from the stern and moves it to what will be the new stern. The sail's tack is then retied near the new bow, sheets hauled in, and you're off on the new tack.

Tack!

WIND

44

In Irons

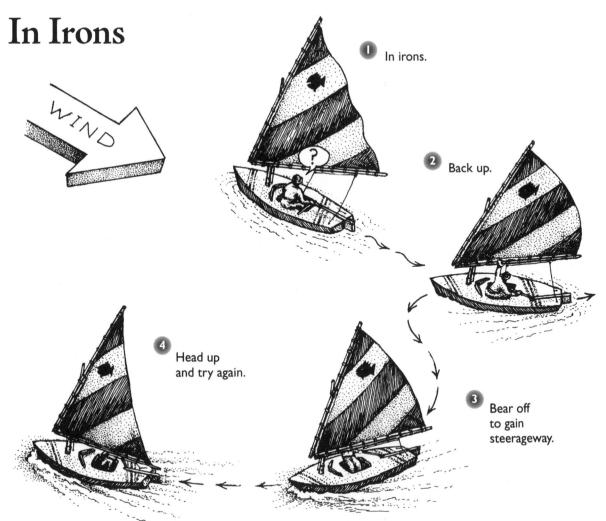

WIND

1 In irons.

2 Back up.

3 Bear off to gain steerageway.

4 Head up and try again.

When trying to tack, you may find that the boat will round up into the wind and then just sit there with sails luffing. It won't come about or go back on the old tack. You're trapped, and very appropriately said to be *in irons*.

The most common way of getting into this predicament is by trying to tack without enough momentum to carry you through. Heavier keelboats can shoot for long distances when luffing, but lighter centreboard boats tend to slow down (and some catamarans even stop) the moment their sails lose drive. Always have plenty of headway as you begin to tack. If your boat is reluctant to tack, keep your jib sheeted for the old tack as you pass through the wind so it will be backwinded and push the bow around. Easing the main will also help.

Once in irons, the only way out is backwards, as if getting underway from a mooring. Leave the jib and mainsheets free to run so there is no chance of the sails catching the wind prematurely. When the boat begins to drift backwards, use the rudder to turn the stern so the bow falls off on the desired tack. You may have to help the bow around by holding the jib aback. On boats with no jibs, push the main boom all the way out on the side opposite the one you want to turn towards.

Once the boat is pointing in the right direction do not retrim for close-hauled sailing until you build up some speed. Sheeting in too early will either bring the boat back into irons, or *stall* (lose aerodynamic lift with the wind on only one side) the sails so you are blown sideways, with a good chance of being capsized. So bear off and accelerate for a few moments. Then come to close-hauled, and with plenty of *way on* (momentum), try to tack again.

Downwind

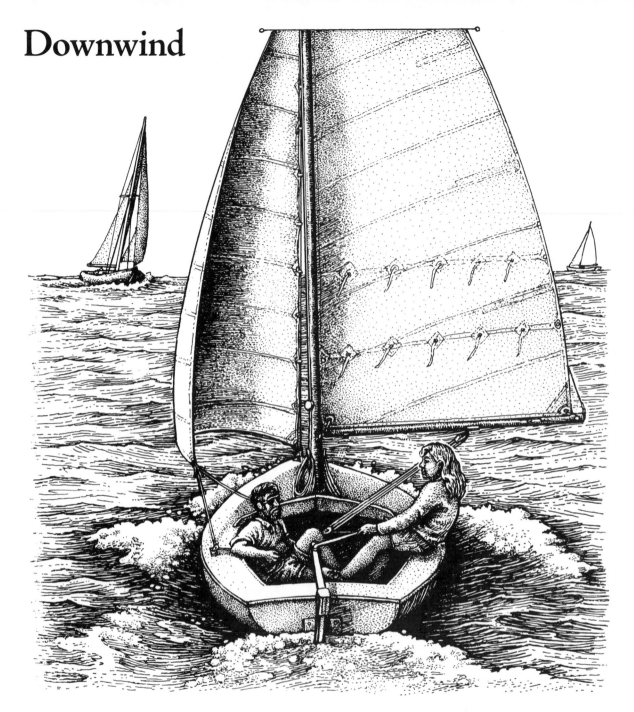

As you turn further off the wind, from close-hauled to a reach and then to a broad reach, you continually ease out your sails to keep them working as efficient airfoils. With the wind on each side of it, the sail generates both pushing and pulling forces. But beyond a broad reach, with the wind more than 150 degrees off your bow, there is a change. The sails lose their aerodynamic lift and begin acting only as wind catchers to push the boat along. This is downwind sailing; you're *running free*.

This is also the slowest of all courses. Since you are being driven by your apparent wind, the faster you go the less wind there is to push you. Even on a breezy day the wind seems to drop as you turn downwind, until on a *dead run* it may feel as if wind has abandoned you. But don't be fooled. When you head back up into the wind that same boisterous breeze will still be there waiting for you.

To get the most drive from the sails, keep them square to the apparent wind. This is simple enough when you are sailing just below a broad reach, but when you head further downwind the jib becomes *blanketed* (cut off from the wind) by the main and goes limp. When this happens, pull the jib out from behind the main and get it to *draw* (fill) on the opposite side. Now you are sailing *wing and wing* or, as the 19th-century schoonermen used to say, 'reading both pages'. You'll need to concentrate at the helm to keep both sails full, especially when the winds are variable or waves make it hard to hold a course. Make sure the main is out all the way, but not so far as to press the boom against the shrouds or the sail against the spreaders.

If the wind passes over to the other quarter you are sailing *by the lee*. The wind and the main are now on the same side, and if the wind gets around to the forward side of the mainsail, WHAM! The main, boom and all, gets violently slammed across the boat. The jib may flop back and forth, but this is not dangerous. It is the main's boom that you, and the rigging, have to watch out for.

The changing of the wind over the stern from one side to the other, and the resultant swinging over of sails, is called a *gybe*. A controlled gybe, as we'll see in the following pages, is a good thing to know. An uncontrolled gybe, like those caused when sailing by the lee, is a good thing to avoid.

Watch your masthead telltale. If the wind crosses your stern, or the end of the boom begins to lift, or the main's leech starts to flop around, a gybe is imminent. To prevent this, turn upwind quickly – away from the side the main is on.

Since there is no sideways push from the wind when running, you can raise the centreboard all the way to reduce underwater drag. On some boats keeping it lowered slightly can improve steering or add stability. Experiment. Try to keep the boat level while running, and in windy going shift your weight aft to make steering easier.

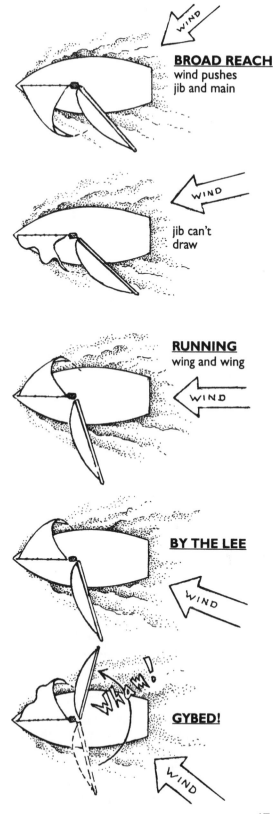

BROAD REACH
wind pushes jib and main

jib can't draw

RUNNING
wing and wing

BY THE LEE

GYBED!

WHAM!

Gybing

A gybe brings the wind from one side of the boat to the other by turning the stern through the wind. It is a way of changing tacks while heading downwind. Compared with coming about, a gybe is almost instantaneous. One moment the sails are off to port, then, as the stern passes through the wind, they are sent flying to starboard. There is no smooth or gentle transition unless you make it so. A gybe that goes unchecked puts unnecessary strain on the rigging, makes weapons of the swinging boom and sheet, and causes loss of control. All things to be avoided.

A controlled gybe requires timing, planning and careful sheet handling. Lower the centreboard slightly for extra stability, and upon the command 'Prepare to gybe', start sheeting in the main all the way while holding your course. When the boom is almost midships, cry 'Gybe ho!' and turn the helm slowly to bring the stern through the wind. The crew ducks, shifts over to the new windward side, and the main gently flops over, its swing restricted by the sheet. As the main comes over, slacken its sheet as fast as possible to trim for the new tack. Since the jib will not be drawing during most of the gybe, it can be resheeted at any time.

To initiate a gybe, the helm need only be turned enough to nudge the stern through the wind, a course change of only a few degrees, not 90 degrees as when coming about. Once the main is over it must be eased out quickly, particularly in a fresh breeze, or it will act like a giant weathervane trying to turn the boat into the wind. This sudden rounding up is *broaching*. The bow digs in, the stern slews around, the boat heels wildly, and you're out of control. Even in a perfectly performed gybe, the boat will want to round up a little and needs to be held back by the helm.

Some gybes are more free spirited than others. Large cargo sloops like the *Clearwater*, which worked the tight upper reaches of the Hudson River, flung themselves into *North River gybes* to stay within the narrow channels. The helm was put over, the mainsheet given a tug to get the sail going, and the boom would careen over to the other side. These boats were heavily rigged, and the main's massive sail area slowed the swing across – cushioning the shock. The same method can be used in very light winds on almost any boat. You grab all the parts of the mainsheet in your hand, pull the boom across, and let go once it begins to fill.

If your desired course forces you to sail by the lee, or it is too hard to hold her directly before the wind, you might find it easier and less nerve-racking to *zigzag* towards your destination in a series of very broad reaches. Sailing with the wind broad off the quarter is safer and faster than a dead run. It may even be fast enough to compensate for the extra distance sailed. This is called *tacking downwind*, but you are really gybing.

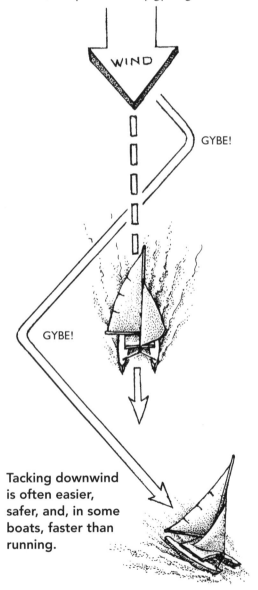

Tacking downwind is often easier, safer, and, in some boats, faster than running.

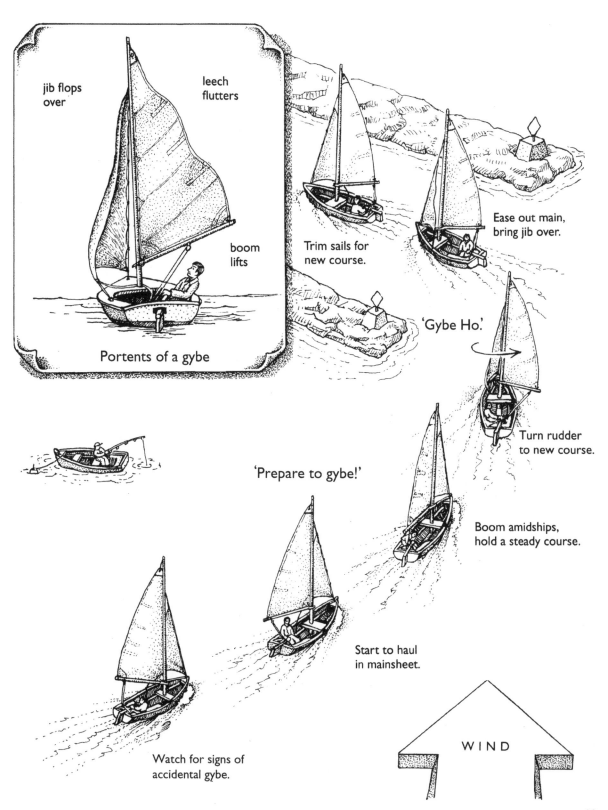

jib flops over

leech flutters

boom lifts

Portents of a gybe

Trim sails for new course.

Ease out main, bring jib over.

'Gybe Ho.'

Turn rudder to new course.

'Prepare to gybe!'

Boom amidships, hold a steady course.

Start to haul in mainsheet.

Watch for signs of accidental gybe.

WIND

Slowing Down

I'm sure that all of what you've read so far has been a lot to take in, and you probably won't be able to remember half of it the first time you go out. Everything will seem to be happening at once, and often at an overwhelming pace. Which is why there are going to be times when you'll want to slow down, have some time to catch your breath, and think things through.

The problem is that, unlike a car or motorboat, a sailing boat needs to be moving in order for you to maintain control. But sometimes you just don't want it to be moving quite so fast.

In response to this, one of the first things kids are taught in junior sail-training classes is the *safety position*: turning the boat so the wind is from the side, and letting go of the sheets so the sail is all the way out and the boom is away from your head. Kids are told to do it when things get out of hand or they get scared. All of sudden everything, at least temporarily, stops.

When the situation isn't quite as dire, here are four other ways to put on the brakes and slow the boat down, but still be able to manoeuvre.

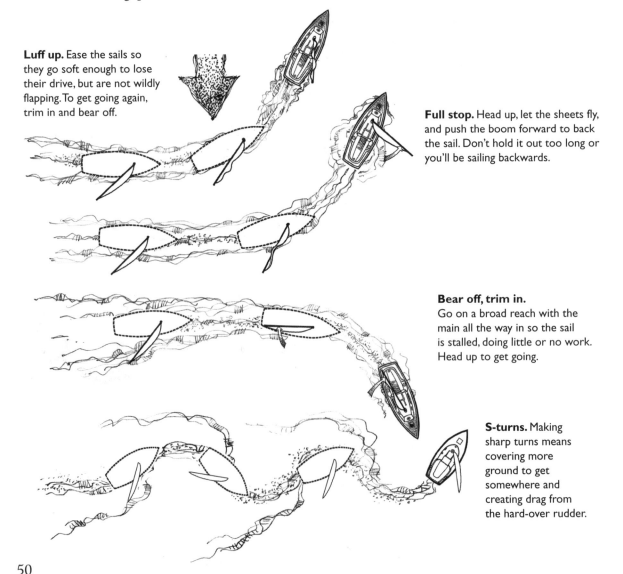

Luff up. Ease the sails so they go soft enough to lose their drive, but are not wildly flapping. To get going again, trim in and bear off.

Full stop. Head up, let the sheets fly, and push the boom forward to back the sail. Don't hold it out too long or you'll be sailing backwards.

Bear off, trim in. Go on a broad reach with the main all the way in so the sail is stalled, doing little or no work. Head up to get going.

S-turns. Making sharp turns means covering more ground to get somewhere and creating drag from the hard-over rudder.

Heaving-To

The Flying Dutchman was condemned to sail until Judgement Day, forever beating into the wind. He couldn't even stop for lunch. But you, you lucky soul, can stop anytime you like, even if you're miles at sea. By *heaving-to* you can take time to study a chart, pump the bilge, make a sandwich, or sit and wait for the Dutchman.

As we saw on the previous page, you could slow down or stop by letting the sails luff, which is fine for a minute or two in light winds. But in stronger winds luffing sails can flog themselves to destruction. The proper way to heave-to is to make the sails work against each other in order to hold the boat in place, bow towards the wind. This is an old square-rigger trick. They'd heave-to off Port Angeles with the sails on the foremast aback to counterbalance the other sails, waiting for the Seattle harbour pilot to come aboard. In a modern boat, the same can be done using the jib and main.

The most common technique is to trim the main for a close reach, lash the rudder to turn the boat to windward, and sheet the jib flat to weather. The main and rudder try to bring the bow to windward, while the backed jib tries to force it to leeward. The bow points up and falls off in a series of long sweeps, while the boat slowly drifts forwards and to leeward.

If your boat has a mizzen, it may lie easier if you sheet the mizzen flat with all other sails furled. Each boat is different. Experiment with rudder positions, angles of the centreboard, and sail combinations.

Another way to stop is by *lying ahull* (drifting with the sails down), which is often done when there is too much wind to carry sail. If you can, leave the sails up. This keeps the boat under control and dampens any rolling motion from the waves.

No matter how you heave-to, always maintain a good lookout and be sure you have plenty of *sea room* (distance from shore) for your drift.

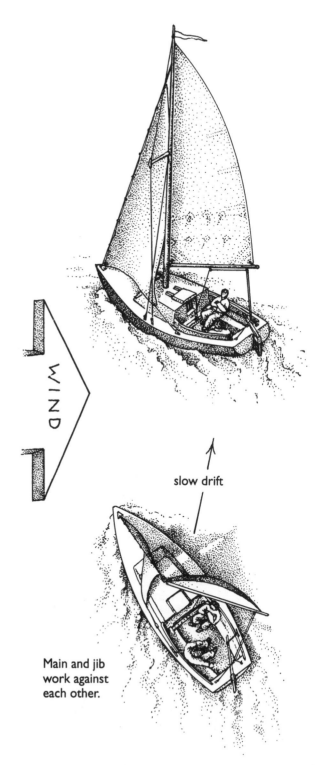

WIND

slow drift

Main and jib work against each other.

Heavy Weather

It's called heavy weather because when the wind pipes up it feels like there's some weight behind it. And there is.

Your best defence is to be prepared. Keep the boat and its gear in good shape. Have all the necessary equipment on board and properly stowed. Keep yourself warm, dry and comfortable. Most important, sharpen your skills so when the worst hits you'll be ready. Avoid bad weather if you can; be prepared for it if you can't.

Fisherman's Reef

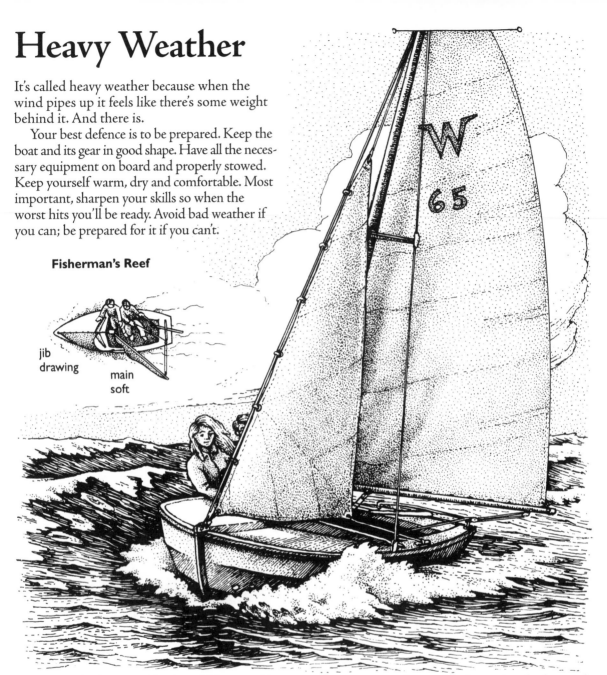

jib
drawing

main
soft

Starting back in 1958 Frank and Margaret Dye made long passages in their 16-foot Ian Proctor-designed Wayfarer. They were England's couple next door, except this couple sailed their little boat to Scotland, Norway, Iceland, Greece, Florida and the Persian Gulf. They proved that it's skill, not a large or fancy boat, that will get you through the worst of it.

The first and most important defensive skill you'll need to know is how to spill excess wind from your sails. When a gust hits, luff up or hold

your course and ease the sheets. In a bad gust, do both. Do not make the sheets fast to their cleats; instead hold them with a single turn around the cleat to take the strain, yet be ready to let fly. If the gust is sustained, use a *fisherman's reef*: keep the jib properly trimmed for your course while slacking the main. The leading portion of the main will luff and lose its shape. The heeling effect is reduced, with drive coming from the jib and a small part of the main.

52

When it breezes up, the hardest course to sail is downwind. There is always the possibility of an accidental gybe or broach. To make running safer, tend more to a broad reach than dead downwind, never sail by the lee, and rig a *preventer* (page 92). In a strong blow, lower the main and run under jib alone.

To change tacks while running in strong winds, come about instead of gybing. Although tacking may seem circuitous, it is safer and keeps the boat under control at all times. Head up to a reach, then to close-hauled, and then come about. If you try to tack directly from a broad reach, the boat will lose momentum and you'll either miss the tack, or worse, get caught in irons.

When there is too much wind you will have to *reef* (reduce sail area). A boat can translate only so much wind into boat speed. For most small boats, with all sails up, the wind's force reaches its maximum at about 18 mph. Above that, the wind has too much power. The boat heels more but goes no faster. At this point sail area must be reduced to match the wind. Reefing should reduce the sail area enough to eliminate excessive heeling, but not so much as to slow down the boat. Learn how to reef on page 108.

When is it time to reef? When you are heeling more than 30 degrees and forced to stay hiked out all the time, when the lee deck is constantly awash, when steering becomes difficult with the boat constantly

REEFING

wanting to round up into the wind, or when the boat is pounding too hard. Usually the best time to reef is when you first wonder if you should.

Above Force 6, daysailers become unsafe and larger boats uncomfortable. Consider not going out or, if caught out, seeking shelter. Always be aware of your proximity to land. Look for a haven that gives full protection from the wind and the waves. If you are being blown towards a lee shore, head out and get sea room. If the wind is blowing from the land, head in for protection.

Boats are tougher than people. In a blow, take care of yourself. The violent motion and being wet or cold can lead to fatigue, fear and seasickness, which in turn leads to mistakes. Donning foul-weather gear, being well rested, and feeling confident in your abilities should get you through the fatigue and fear. Seasickness may not be that easy to deal with. The best remedy is medicine taken well beforehand. Help this by not going below decks or forward. Movement is exaggerated at the bow and stern, so stay in the cockpit near midships. Almost everyone suffers at one time or another. Admiral Lord Nelson was seasick all through his career, and Charles Darwin, writing about the mixed joys of sea travel, said,'. . . if it was not for seasickness, the whole world would be sailors.' Do what you can to avoid it.

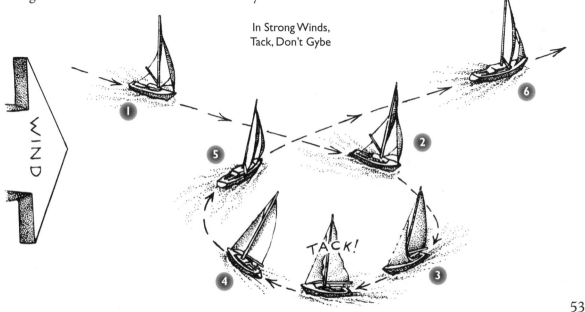

In Strong Winds, Tack, Don't Gybe

WIND

TACK!

Capsized!

Boats are supposed to stay upright, and ones with ballasted keels will do just that. Unfortunately, the average centreboard daysailer is not so forgiving and can capsize. But, unlike keelboats, it will be easy to right and won't sink. Going over in a 15-foot boat should amount to little more than a soaked ego. It happens to the best of us. As long as the boat has adequate flotation, and most do, you'll be safe.

How can you capsize? An accidental gybe is sometimes good for a flip. Being overwhelmed by too much wind can do it, too. It happens.

The first rule of a capsize is never to leave the boat. It will float, give you something to hold onto, and in a hard chance be easier to spot by rescuers. Once over, check that everyone is OK and nothing is floating off. The boat will most likely settle with the mast level to the water. To right the boat, release all sheets and extend the centreboard. Swim the bow around to face the wind. Climb onto the upturned hull, grab the deck, stand on the centreboard, and lean back to bring her up. If your boat has *turned turtle* (inverted 180 degrees), climb on the hull, hold onto the centreboard, and lean back. When up, keep the sails from filling. One crewmember climbs back in over the stern, keeps weight amidships, bails enough to improve stability, and helps the others aboard.

Sails offer a lot of resistance and can prevent a boat from righting. You may have to release the halyards (tie the loose ends where they can be reached later) and lower the sails. When *swamped* (full of water), some boats float with the opening of their centreboard case below water level. Plug this, or water will come in as you bail it out.

Practise capsizing early in your education, and on a warm, calm day. Trying to sort it all out after an accident on a blustery grey afternoon is not at all conducive to learning.

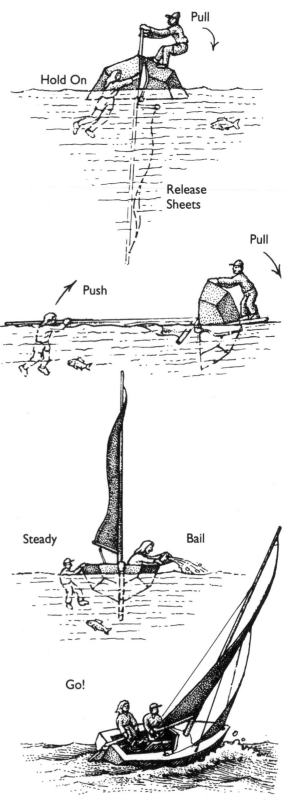

Practise

You're going to actually have to get out and sail to learn how it's really done. No words or drawings can give you the feeling of what it's like to have a boom slam across when you gybe, tack without going into irons, or trim a sail to make the boat come alive and the tiller tingle between your fingers.

Of course, you could do what most folks do and let time take care of your education. You'll eventually learn that way. It could take years and you might even become good at it. But why wait? Practise now, and get to know your boat and your capabilities. Otherwise your learning experiences might come through panic-driven emergencies. Your choice.

Start by getting a feel for your boat's balance and speed. To sail fast you want to minimise rudder drag with an almost neutral or slightly weather helm. Try lashing the tiller or wheel amidships, and trimming the sails and shifting crew weight until the boat is moving fast and straight, from close-hauled to a broad reach. Remember how she heels, the sheet and traveller settings, and your speed. Now you're getting the most out of her. To learn helmsmanship and control, try these:

FIGURE EIGHTS

Anchor two floats, such as PFDs or milk containers, about four boat lengths apart. It's all about tacking, gybing, keeping speed up and maintaining control. Do it twice one way, twice the other. Easy? OK, now put the floats two boat lengths apart.

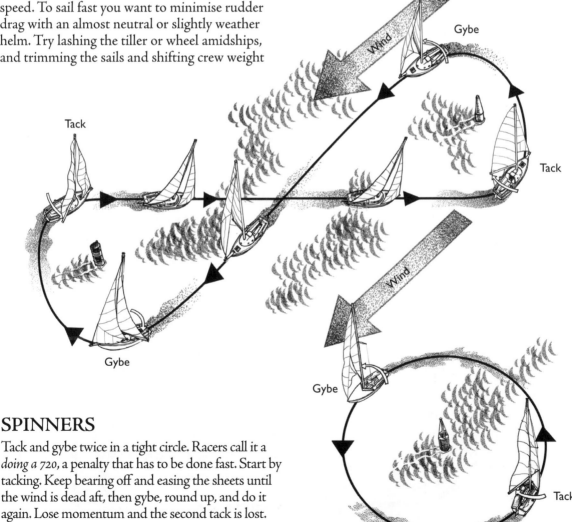

SPINNERS

Tack and gybe twice in a tight circle. Racers call it a *doing a 720*, a penalty that has to be done fast. Start by tacking. Keep bearing off and easing the sheets until the wind is dead aft, then gybe, round up, and do it again. Lose momentum and the second tack is lost.

Returning to a Mooring ...

The key to retrieving a mooring is knowing how far your boat coasts after power is taken from the sails. Try this in open water: while on a reach, turn into the wind and let the sheets fly. Heavier keelboats like a Soling will keep way on for long distances. Broad-beamed lightweights like an Optimist dinghy may shoot for only a boat length or two. And a catamaran may stop almost immediately. Know what your boat will do before entering the harbour.

Approach from downwind of the mooring on a reach or close reach. Adjust your speed by alternately trimming and easing the mainsheet. Come in slowly with the jib barely luffing, being careful not to lose steerageway. When within coasting distance, round up and free the sheets to let the sails luff. Aim the bow to one side of the pickup buoy. Grab or hook the pendant, and make it fast to the mooring cleat. As soon as possible, lower the jib and then the main. If you miss, try again. Start as though in irons. Back up, bear off, and come around another time.

With a strong breeze or high waves, you may not shoot as far. Stay alert for wind shifts or gusts. Watch out for other boats. Pass downwind of moored vessels so there is no chance of drifting down on them. Keep up your speed to maintain steerageway, and lower the centreboard to improve steering. If you need to slow down after making your final turn, push the main boom out to weather, where it will act as an air brake. Rounding up abruptly will also take way off. *Genoas* (large, overlapping jibs) are difficult to handle in quick manoeuvres and may obstruct the helmsman's view. If your boat sails well under main alone, drop the genoa.

On a river or tidal estuary, current becomes a factor. When it runs with the wind, you will lose headway faster. When the current runs against the wind, you must determine which has more effect on your boat. To judge, see if moored boats are sitting to the wind or the current. If the current is dominant, approach the mooring with the wind astern. Sail in under jib only, trimming it to adjust your speed.

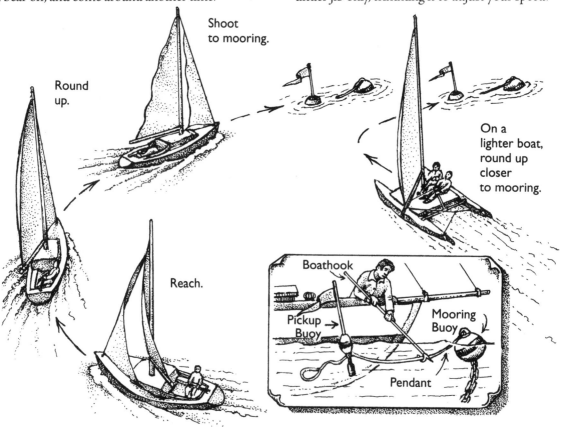

Shoot to mooring.

Round up.

On a lighter boat, round up closer to mooring.

Reach.

Boathook

Pickup Buoy

Mooring Buoy

Pendant

. . . or a Dock

Unlike picking up a mooring, approaching a dock under sail offers little room for error and rarely a second chance. Figure out what you are going to do before you do it. Take your time. Heave-to, or reach back and forth, before making your move. Check the wind's direction. Does it shift inside the dock basin, and is it gusting? Check for currents, and watch for boat traffic. Lower the centreboard for stability and better steering. Get docklines out, make them fast to bow and stern cleats, and lead them so they run *fair* (not over or around anything). Have them coiled and ready to be thrown, and rig *fenders* to cushion the landing (not your hands or feet).

1. Come in close-hauled, slowing the boat when near the dock by letting the jib luff completely and regulating speed with the main. Approach at a 45-degree angle with minimum headway, turning parallel to the dock just before the bow touches. Quickly make docklines fast

to prevent the boat from being blown away. This leeward berth is the best place to leave a boat, since the wind pushes it away from the dock, thereby preventing damage and scrapes.

2. Land on the windward side of a dock only in light winds, and then only as a last resort. Boats on this side are pressed against the dock and susceptible to damage. Smaller vessels can approach on a reach, turn to windward a few boat lengths off, lower all sail, and drift broadside down to the dock (making sure to have two or more fenders out). Larger boats should anchor to windward and then slowly ease back towards the dock. Set the anchor well off to give you more manoeuvring room later when leaving.

3. Round up as if coming to a mooring. Coast up to the dock with sails luffing. Gently lie alongside. Tie the bow dockline first, then the others. When secure, lower sails as soon as possible to prevent the boom or sheets from getting hung up on dock fittings or pilings.

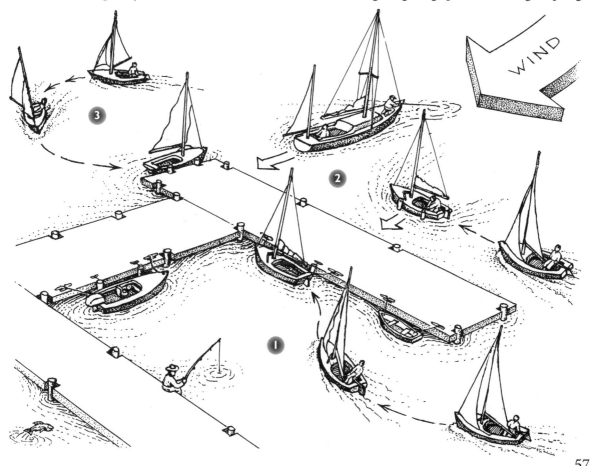

Beach Sailing

With permanent moorings and dock spaces becoming increasingly scarce, more sailors are trailering their boats – sailing from, and returning to, a launch ramp or beach. While beach sailing is no more difficult than using a dock, beaches do tend to be more exposed to the elements. Leave from and return to a beach only in light winds. If you see whitecaps, look for another spot.

To sail off a lee shore, sit the boat at the water's edge on the tack that will get you away from the beach and into deep water most quickly. The helmsman gets in, and the crew pulls the boat into water deep enough to partially lower the centreboard and rudder. The crew keeps the boat pointing into the wind as the helmsman sheets in the sails.

The crew then gives the boat a push and climbs in. The helmsman bears off to get the boat moving, while the crew lowers the centreboard as the water gets deeper. Be careful not to pinch her or have the sails trimmed so flat that they stall. Both will cause leeway, putting you back on the beach. An alternative is to paddle offshore, anchor, raise sail, and get underway as if from a mooring.

When returning to a lee shore, round up into the wind about eight boat lengths off the beach. Lower the main and raise the centreboard. Sail in under jib alone, or *bare poles* (no sail up) in winds above 10 mph, lifting the rudder out of the way before you hit the beach. Pick a sandy spot for your landing. Rocks or a concrete ramp can damage the hull.

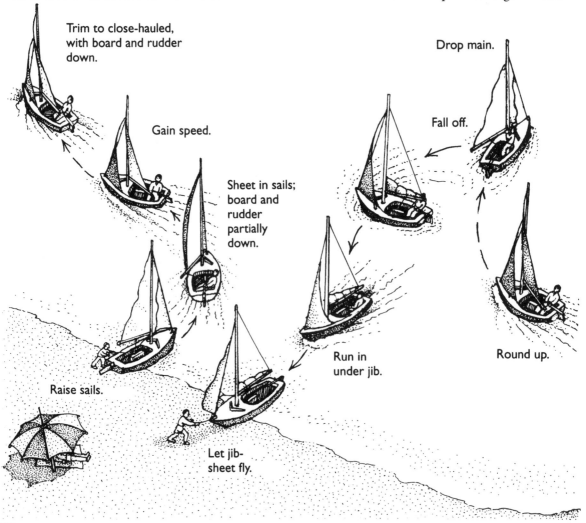

Trim to close-hauled, with board and rudder down.

Gain speed.

Sheet in sails; board and rudder partially down.

Raise sails.

Let jib-sheet fly.

Run in under jib.

Drop main.

Fall off.

Round up.

Winds along the beach are the easiest and safest. To leave, sit with all sails luffing, shove off, jump in, trim sails, and lower the centreboard as the water gets deeper. To return, come in slowly with sails luffing, raising the centreboard and lifting the rudder as you get close to shore.

When winds are off the beach you will leave on a downwind run. Your only worry here is to prevent an accidental gybe. On returning, come in on a close reach, round up, and shoot in to the beach.

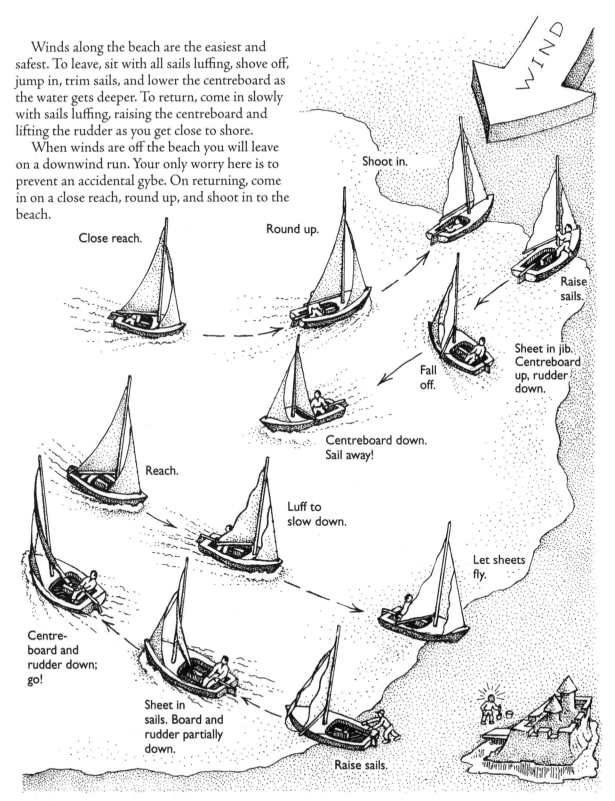

Shoot in.

Raise sails.

Sheet in jib. Centreboard up, rudder down.

Round up.

Close reach.

Fall off.

Centreboard down. Sail away!

Reach.

Luff to slow down.

Let sheets fly.

Centre-board and rudder down; go!

Sheet in sails. Board and rudder partially down.

Raise sails.

Dock Work

Wind and water are restless and forceful. Docks are fixed and immovable. And boats are trapped in between.

Docks are convenient things, much more so than moorings. You can step right aboard, take on gear, or have access to fresh water and electricity. They are also rough, often with protruding bolts, or coated with tar and slime. When tying to a dock, arrange your lines to keep the boat close enough to be handy, but far enough off to prevent damage.

Before tying up, consider these factors. The tide: What is its range, is it rising or falling, and is there enough water at low tide? The wind: What is the prevailing wind, which winds are you protected from, and which are you vulnerable to? The current: What is its strength and direction, and will it change? The dock: Is it safe and easy to approach or leave, is there room to manoeuvre, do nearby boats pose any problems, and what condition is it in?

Docklines should be made of nylon for elasticity, and at least ⅜-inch diameter for strength and ease of handling. Pass docklines under, never over, lifelines. Too few cleats? Use winches, but do not use lifeline stanchions. Neatly coil unused line so it stays out of harm's way.

The most commonly used knots for docking are the bowline, clove hitch, two half hitches, and hitching to a cleat (pages 146–150). If the eye on a dockline is too small to fit over a piling, thread the standing part through the eye to make a noose (page 151).

To tie up alongside for any length of time you'll need at least four lines. A *bow* and *stern* line, each about a boat length long, making an approximate 45-degree angle with the dock. A forward and after *spring line*, each about 1½ boat lengths, set almost parallel to the boat to act as 'springs' against fore-and-aft surges. In severe conditions you may also need bow and stern *breast lines*, each about ½ boat length, leading out at right angles to reduce sideways movement. Upon arrival, secure the bow and stern lines first. This may do for short stops. For longer stays, the forward and after spring lines need to be rigged. Do not pin the boat tightly against the dock. Leave room for fenders to hang freely, and sufficient slack in the lines to allow for the tide.

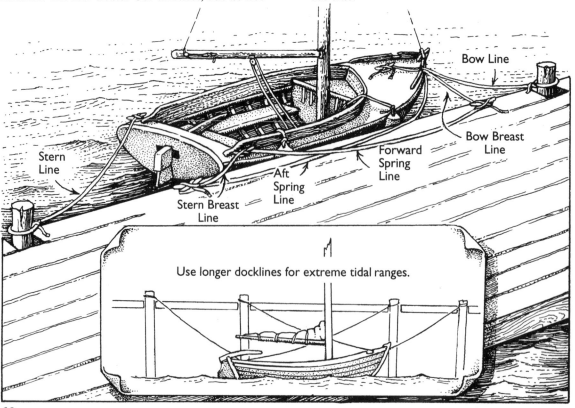

Bow Line

Bow Breast Line

Forward Spring Line

Aft Spring Line

Stern Breast Line

Stern Line

Use longer docklines for extreme tidal ranges.

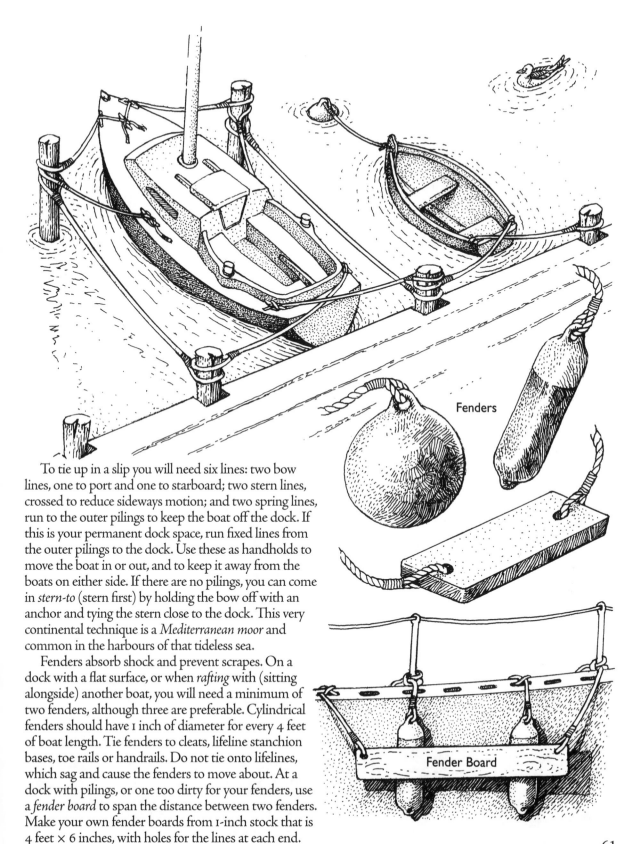

Fenders

Fender Board

To tie up in a slip you will need six lines: two bow lines, one to port and one to starboard; two stern lines, crossed to reduce sideways motion; and two spring lines, run to the outer pilings to keep the boat off the dock. If this is your permanent dock space, run fixed lines from the outer pilings to the dock. Use these as handholds to move the boat in or out, and to keep it away from the boats on either side. If there are no pilings, you can come in *stern-to* (stern first) by holding the bow off with an anchor and tying the stern close to the dock. This very continental technique is a *Mediterranean moor* and common in the harbours of that tideless sea.

Fenders absorb shock and prevent scrapes. On a dock with a flat surface, or when *rafting* with (sitting alongside) another boat, you will need a minimum of two fenders, although three are preferable. Cylindrical fenders should have 1 inch of diameter for every 4 feet of boat length. Tie fenders to cleats, lifeline stanchion bases, toe rails or handrails. Do not tie onto lifelines, which sag and cause the fenders to move about. At a dock with pilings, or one too dirty for your fenders, use a *fender board* to span the distance between two fenders. Make your own fender boards from 1-inch stock that is 4 feet × 6 inches, with holes for the lines at each end.

Leaving Her

While some may call what follows work, others see it as a way of extending the day's sail or an enjoyable involvement with their vessel. Think of setting her to rights and looking smart (all *Bristol fashion*, as they say in the British Navy) as another sailorly skill – an ancient tradition of pride and preparedness. Leaving her in good shape is the essence of practical seamanship.

The first step in securing the boat is to *douse* (lower) all sail. Before letting go a halyard, make sure that it will run smoothly and that the free end is tied to something so it won't fly out of reach. Pull sails down by their luffs. Clawing away at the leech or belly of a sail will accomplish little more than stretching the fabric.

Douse the jib first. Get as far forward as you can to gain a good purchase on its luff. On larger boats wedge yourself between the headstay and the *pulpit* (bow rail), and haul away in safety. To prevent the jib from being blown overboard, pull back on one of the sheets while lowering. If the sail is damp, lower it partway to flap gently in a light (and only a light) breeze, or let it sit on deck for a while before stowing. When dry, fold into narrow panels parallel to the foot, roll up loosely, and stow in its sailbag.

Lower the main next. Take up on the topping lift and then *bowse down* (haul downward) on the mainsheet, or place a boom crutch under the boom, to make sure the boom doesn't fall when the halyard is let go. If the sail won't come down on its own, pull it down by the luff. As the sail lowers try to keep it from being blown overboard. Nineteenth-century working craft on the Chesapeake used *lazyjacks* to hold sails in place while being reefed or lowered. They are still a good idea and can be rigged for any modern boat.

On some boats the mainsail is taken off the boom, battens removed, and then bagged like a jib. Other boats *furl* the sail into a neat package, lash it to the boom, and then cover it. The choice is yours.

To furl the main, pull the bulk of the sail aft to form a bundle of loose folds along one side (preferably to leeward) of the boom. Grasp a 2- to 3-foot-wide section along the foot and pull it away from the boom, making a hammock-like pocket into which the rest of the sail can be stuffed. Start at the mast and work aft, using the foot to enclose the sail by rolling it over to form a narrow sausage on top of the boom. Hold the sail in place with *gaskets* (long strips of canvas, also known as *stops*) every 4 or 5 feet. Cross the gaskets over the sail, down around the boom, back over the sail, and then tie with a slipped *reef knot* (page 149). An alternative to furling

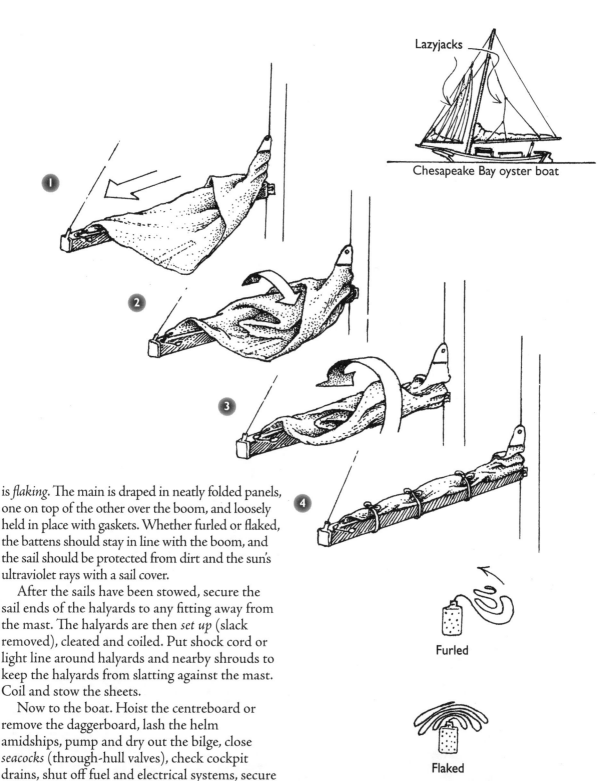

Lazyjacks

Chesapeake Bay oyster boat

Furled

Flaked

is *flaking*. The main is draped in neatly folded panels, one on top of the other over the boom, and loosely held in place with gaskets. Whether furled or flaked, the battens should stay in line with the boom, and the sail should be protected from dirt and the sun's ultraviolet rays with a sail cover.

After the sails have been stowed, secure the sail ends of the halyards to any fitting away from the mast. The halyards are then *set up* (slack removed), cleated and coiled. Put shock cord or light line around halyards and nearby shrouds to keep the halyards from slatting against the mast. Coil and stow the sheets.

Now to the boat. Hoist the centreboard or remove the daggerboard, lash the helm amidships, pump and dry out the bilge, close *seacocks* (through-hull valves), check cockpit drains, shut off fuel and electrical systems, secure hatches, wash down with fresh water, put cockpit cover in place, and finally – look back on a pleasant sail and a job well done.

THE BOAT

'To touch that bow is to rest one's hands on the cosmic nose of things.'
Jack London, *The Cruise of the Snark*

A boat is only a vessel, a container to keep water out. Yet it is at the very heart of sailing, and to many an end in itself. No other object made by man has a spirit so compelling as a sailing boat's. The most splendid work of art is dead, static, compared with it. Wonderful as sailing boats are to look at, they are even more satisfying to sail. And labour spent on them reaps rewards far beyond the effort invested. To a sailor, a life spent messing around in boats is a life that is very well spent indeed.

Who would dare think a sailor daft because he or she whiles away an afternoon gazing at his or her vessel? Even a Bedouin from the Sahara could understand it. But don't ask that sailor what he sees. It has been said that a mother going on about her child is slanderous compared with a sailor talking about his boat. And who can blame him? There may be some who claim a boat is but a tool, a means to an end, even if that end is only pleasure. But they too occasionally look back when walking up the dock and see something more. Be there a soul so dead? If there is, it does not belong to a sailor.

Form

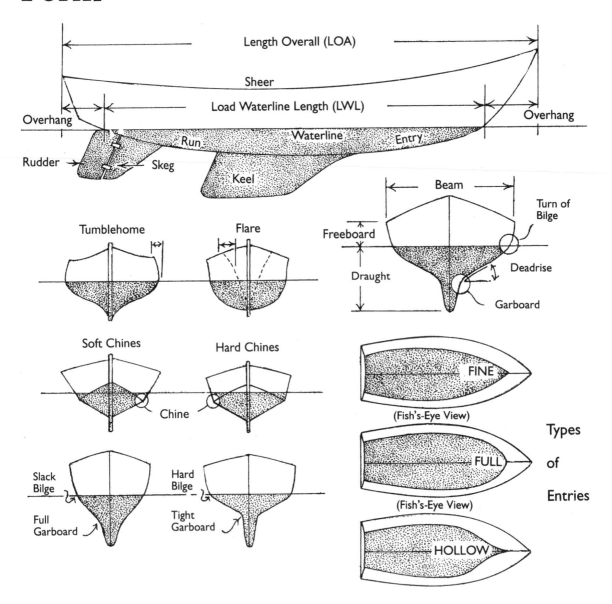

The hull of a boat is a complex form needing specialised terms to describe it. Most are self-explanatory, but a few may need clarification. For instance, *sheer* is the line created where the hull joins the deck, but the structural part of the boat it describes is the *gunwale* (rhymes with 'tunnel'). The *load waterline length* is the length of the waterline when the boat is floating with its load (crew and gear) aboard. If the boat is longer on deck than at the waterline, it has *overhangs*. Below the waterline, the forward part of the boat is the *entry* and the aft part is the *run*. In cross section, the upward angle of the bottom is the *deadrise*. The area where the bottom (or *bilge*) meets the side is the *turn of bilge*. If the bottom and side meet at a sharp angle, the edge they form is called a *chine*. The part of the bottom that meets the keel is the *garboard* (named for the lowest plank on a wooden boat). And if the sides curve inward they are said to have *tumblehome*.

Comparing Boats

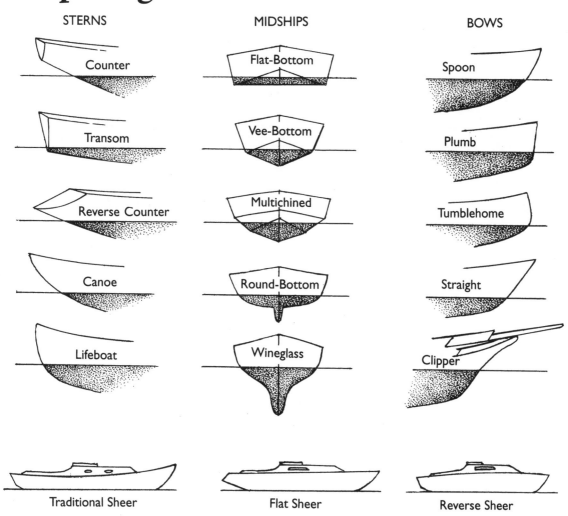

STERNS	MIDSHIPS	BOWS
Counter	Flat-Bottom	Spoon
Transom	Vee-Bottom	Plumb
Reverse Counter	Multichined	Tumblehome
Canoe	Round-Bottom	Straight
Lifeboat	Wineglass	Clipper

Traditional Sheer   Flat Sheer   Reverse Sheer

DISPLACEMENT/LENGTH RATIO

This describes how much *displacement* (weight and volume) the designer has packed into a given waterline length. Higher numbers indicate a boat that is chunky for its length. Its bulk will provide room and comfort, but a lot of sail area will be needed to force its mass through the water. Lower numbers indicate a boat that is slender for its length. Not as roomy or comfortable, but, being easier to push through the water, it will get more speed from less sail area.

Using the ratio you can compare dissimilar boats, for example, a traditional cruiser such as a Westsail 32 versus the more modern Beneteau 323. They are the same length overall, but the Westsail has a D/L of 425 while the Beneteau's is 152. The Westsail's much higher number shows it to be deeper, broader, heavier, roomier, and probably slower – a 'big' 32-footer with a high D/L to prove it.

Take the boat's displacement measured in long tons (2,240 pounds). Divide this by 0.01 times the waterline length (in feet) cubed.

$$D/L = \frac{displacement}{(0.01 \times LWL)^3}$$

Ultralight	50–100
Light	100–200
Moderate	200–300
Heavy	300–400
Massive	400–500

Lines

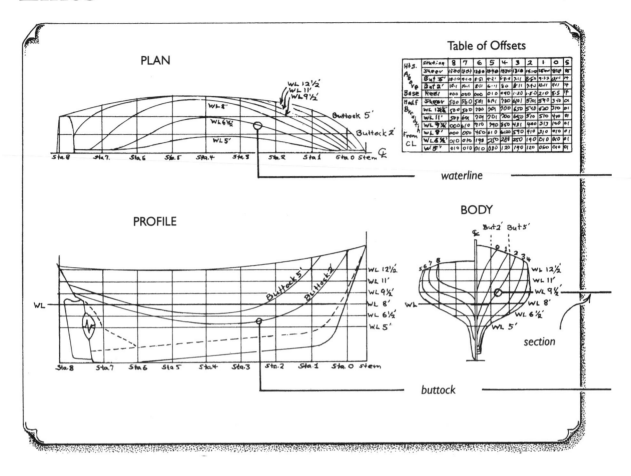

The table of offsets, plan, profile, body views are all part of the image.

Early boats were not formally designed; rather, they grew in the hands of their builders. There was no way to record a hull's shape so its features could be preserved or compared against another, nor were there ways of accurately describing a hull's form so other builders could produce a *sister ship* (an exact copy).

The first attempts to remedy this came in the 17th century with scale models. The builder took a block of clear pine and whittled, planed and sanded it down to a shape that looked 'right'. Since (if it is built properly) a boat is symmetrical along its centreline, the builder only bothered carving one side, thereby making what is known as a *half-hull model*. The dimensions and shape of the model would then be taken off (by cutting it up into sections) and expanded to full size for use in building the boat. Designing with models

may seem quaintly primitive, but it was done by some of the world's greatest designers. Nathanael Herreshoff, The Wizard of Bristol, used models almost exclusively from 1864 to 1935. But he was the exception. By the mid-1800s most naval architects were laying down lines on paper. Today's designers would use no other method. *Lines drawings* make it easier for them to do the many mathematical calculations and provide a common language that can be understood by everyone.

At first it is difficult to imagine how lines on a two-dimensional sheet of paper can clearly portray a boat's shape. Even the best designers sometimes find it hard, and often have models made to check what they have drawn. That's why the lines drawing shown on this page is connected to the half-hull models on the opposite page. By going

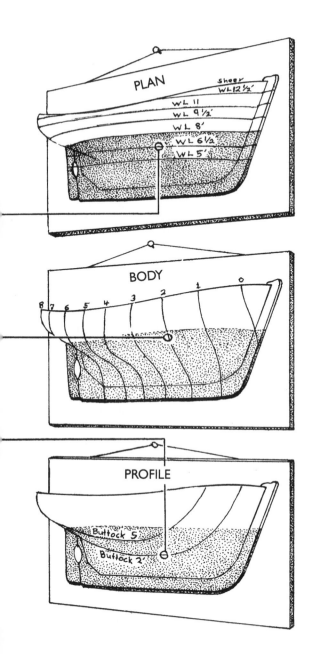

PLAN

sheer
WL 12½'
WL 11
WL 9½'
WL 8'
WL 6½'
WL 5'

BODY

8 7 6 5 4 3 2 1 0

PROFILE

Buttock 5
Buttock 2'

back and forth you'll see how each of the views describes the hull's form.

The lines are for a 40-foot schooner. Since she is a three-dimensional object, three projections are needed to show her shape. The *profile* projection is a view from the side. The *plan* projection is a fish's-eye view, looking up at the bottom from underneath. The *body* projection is a split-image view, showing the front half of the boat to the right of the centreline and the back half to the left.

Each of these projections shows off specific sets of lines. It is as if the boat had been passed through an egg slicer. The profile projection shows vertical slices along the length of the boat to give *buttock lines*. The plan shows horizontal slices to give *waterlines*. The body shows vertical slices across the boat to give *sections*. By combining the buttocks, waterlines and sections, you can envision the completed form.

Developing a set of lines is time-consuming work. Each buttock, waterline and section must be drawn as a smooth flowing curve with no harsh bumps, and meet other lines in the same place in all three views. On some plans a fourth set of lines, the *diagonals*, is added to ensure the accuracy of the other three. Getting the lines to look right and complement each other is called *fairing*, a process that has been made a lot easier with computers.

To construct a boat from a set of lines, the builder needs to take what is drawn and scale it up to full size. He does this by using the *table of offsets* compiled by the designer from the lines, which provides scaled measurements to different points on the hull. By placing these measurements on a grid laid out on a floor, the builder can generate patterns from which he can build the boat. This procedure is called *lofting* and must be done with a precision equal to that of the original set of lines.

Stability

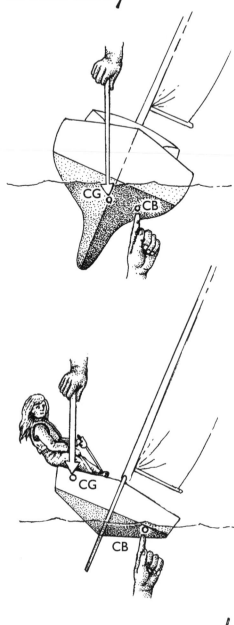

A sailing boat must have enough stability to resist the wind's pressure and prevent capsizing. Stability derives from two forces: gravity, which pushes down; and buoyancy, which pushes up. By centring these forces in the right places, you can keep yourself upright and moving at a good speed.

The *centre of gravity* (CG) is the focus of a boat's weight. If you could attach a string to that point, the boat would hang suspended, perfectly level. All downward forces concentrate at the centre of gravity.

The forces pushing upwards to keep the boat afloat are concentrated at the *centre of buoyancy* (CB). As a boat heels, its underwater shape changes and the centre of buoyancy shifts with it. The more a boat's leeward side is immersed, the more buoyancy there will be on that side to resist heeling.

To counteract the wind, a boat's centre of gravity must move to windward to pull that side of the boat back down, or its centre of buoyancy must move to leeward to push that side of the boat back up, or both can work together.

Keelboats have low centres of gravity. The typical cruising boat has a third or more of its weight in its keel. This *ballast* counter-balances the wind's pressure and works as a massive weight on the end of a lever (the keel) to keep the boat from going over. Most keelboats have enough stability to right themselves from a capsize.

Lightweight centreboard boats also get their stability from a weight on the end of a lever, but in this case ballast is supplied by the crew. When it breezes up the crew move to windward by hiking out. An agile crew can hold up a light boat in surprisingly strong winds, but cannot provide the same ultimate stability as ballast fixed low in a keel.

Wide boats get sail-carrying ability by moving their centres of buoyancy far to leeward when heeled. Cape Cod catboats are very *beamy* (wide) for their length and depend on this to support their one large sail. An extreme example of beam used for stability is a multihull, which can be more than half as wide as it is long. Different hull shapes (in cross section) also affect the movement of the centre of buoyancy. Flat-bottomed boats, and ones with hard chines, shift their centres of buoyancy further to leeward when heeled (making them *stiff*) than do rounded-hull forms (which are *tender*).

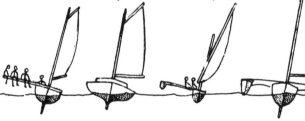

Heeling

Boats don't react well to excessive heeling. A certain amount is inevitable, and in some boats even desirable. But beyond that, heeling becomes detrimental to performance and speed, as well as to your comfort.

How much is excessive? It varies. In general, board boats like a Laser or Sunfish should be sailed as flat as possible, heeling no more than 10 degrees. Most centreboard daysailers should heel no more than about 15 degrees, and ballasted keelboats about 20 degrees. A good clue that you're pushing her too hard is when the lee rail begins to dip under. Many boats will become difficult to handle way before that, giving you plenty of notice that it's time to reef. Heeling way over under a press of sail may make it feel like you're going faster, but there is a point of diminishing returns beyond which heeling slows you down.

When heeled too far, a boat's underwater shape becomes distorted, causing speed-robbing drag and making her hard to steer. Its normal shape, which is symmetrical along the centreline, becomes increasingly asymmetrical as she heels. This uneven bulge becomes difficult to drag through the water and creates forces that try to turn the boat to windward. To counteract this *weather helm* (tendency to turn to windward), you have to use more rudder, which slows you down. Rudder angles of up to 3 degrees offer little resistance, and even provide some lift to windward. But greater angles create drag, until at 40 degrees the rudder becomes a brake. Excessively heeled boats also lose speed by presenting less sail to the wind. When heeled at 45 degrees, your effective sail area is diminished by 30%. Heeling increases leeway too. Keels or centreboards resist sideways forces best if they are vertical. When heeled they begin to lose their grip on the water, thereby increasing the chances of leeway.

There is a story of a schooner returning from the Grand Banks that closed with the famous *Bluenose*. Both had everything flying except the captain's shirt. Water boiled along their lee decks, and it took three men to hold the wheels. The unnamed schooner inched ahead as they raced to the Halifax fish market. Then a dry crack was heard from the *Bluenose* as the jumbo, her second-largest sail, exploded. No longer pinned down, she lifted to her proper sailing lines and stood up to the wind. Instead of falling behind, as the other captain had expected, *Bluenose* began to surge ahead, forever leaving in her wake the anonymous schooner that almost beat the *Bluenose*. When it comes to heeling, less often means more.

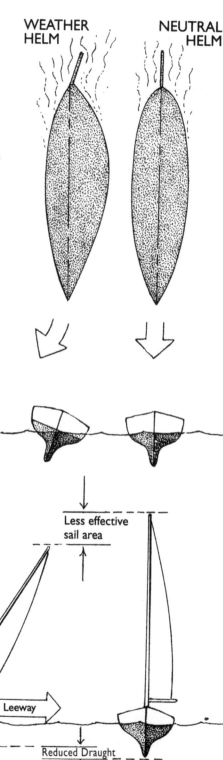

WEATHER HELM

NEUTRAL HELM

Less effective sail area

Leeway

Reduced Draught

Resistance

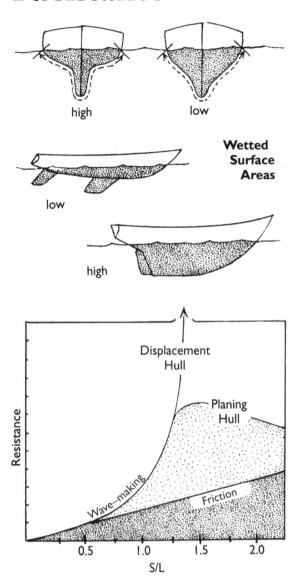

high   low

Wetted Surface Areas

low

high

Displacement Hull

Planing Hull

Wave-making

Friction

Resistance

0.5   1.0   1.5   2.0

S/L

Flying Dutchman

LOA 19'10"   LWL 18'

At 835 times the density of air, water is a decidedly sluggish medium. Its viscosity (stickiness) causes resistance from friction and waves to form around a moving boat, which when combined account for almost all of a boat's drag.

It is hard to believe that something as slippery as water could offer any frictional resistance, but it is the primary source of drag on sailing boats at lower speeds. When an Etchells racing boat (with its 22-foot LWL) is travelling at 4 knots, 75% of the resistance is from friction. You can see it for yourself as a fine line of bubbles being dragged along next to the hull. The turbulence that causes this is friction, which is proportional to the amount of hull in contact with the water (*wetted surface area*) and the hull's smoothness. The greater and rougher the wetted surface, the greater the frictional resistance. High wetted surface area means slow going in light airs, which is why a small, light boat may be faster than a larger one in these conditions. While you can't alter the amount of hull your boat presents to the water, you can keep it smooth. Since sailing boats spend most of their lives at low speeds, it is well worth the effort to keep their bottoms clean.

As speed increases so does resistance, and at a wildly escalating rate. The Etchells has only 15 pounds of resistance at 3 knots, but at 5 knots there are 70 pounds, and at 7 knots an incredible 450 pounds! This dramatic increase comes from energy lost to wavemaking. A moving boat pushes water ahead, to the side, and downwards, letting it fill in behind as the boat passes. The waves it creates make up half the resistance for our Etchells at 5 knots, and 75% at 6.3 knots. The amount of wavemaking resistance is directly related to a boat's form.

The deeper and longer the waves a boat produces, the more power is lost to them. Wave depth is a product of the boat's weight. Heavy vessels (with high D/Ls), like a tugboat, make deep waves. Wavelength is a product of speed.

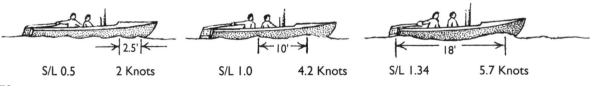

S/L 0.5   2 Knots   S/L 1.0   4.2 Knots   S/L 1.34   5.7 Knots

2.5'   10'   18'

The longer the wave (measured from crest to crest), the faster both it and the boat making it are moving. A boat's speed is therefore a function of its waterline (wavemaking) length. This is expressed as the *speed/length ratio* (S/L), where the speed of a vessel (in knots) is divided by the square root of its waterline length (in feet).

At low speeds, say 3 knots, the Etchells is operating at an S/L of 0.64. It will be dragging numerous short waves along with it, each about 5 feet long. As the boat speeds up, the number of waves decreases and their lengths increase. At 6.3 knots, or an S/L of 1.34, there is only one wave, with a crest at the bow and the other just aft of the transom. The S/L of 1.34 is the highest speed that can be obtained for a given wavelength. Therefore the Etchells, and the wave it makes, will not readily go faster than 6.3 knots.

To go beyond an S/L of 1.34 takes monumental amounts of power for negligible advances in speed. This barrier of wave resistance is called the *hull speed*, a wall of water that *displacement boats* (boats that displace water as they move through it) cannot push through. The only way to get past this barrier is with plenty of sail area applied to a light boat that is wide and flat in the stern. When pushed by a gust, this type of boat leaves its stern wave behind, climbs onto its bow wave, and shoots forward. It is now partially supported by dynamic forces, rather than buoyancy only, as it skims the surface with a new, longer, and shallower wave system. This is *planing*.

A Flying Dutchman with an LWL of 18 feet might only be able to reach 5.7 knots at an S/L of 1.34 if it were a displacement boat, but since it has a planing hull, it can break past that and get up to an S/L of 3, or almost 13 knots. Once planing starts (at around an S/L of 1.5), wavemaking resistance rapidly diminishes. But there is no free ride, for even when planing the sticky fingers of friction set a final limit on just how fast we can go.

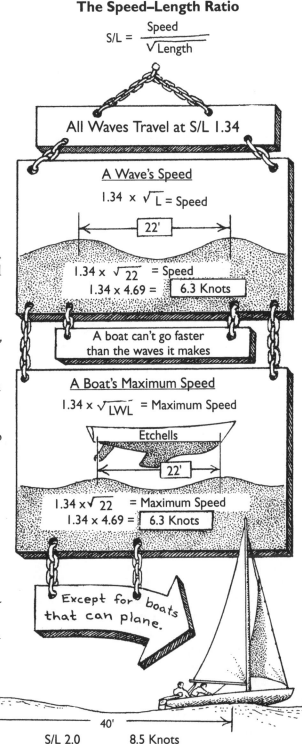

The Speed–Length Ratio

$$S/L = \frac{Speed}{\sqrt{Length}}$$

All Waves Travel at S/L 1.34

A Wave's Speed

$1.34 \times \sqrt{L} = Speed$

22'

$1.34 \times \sqrt{22} = Speed$

$1.34 \times 4.69 = $ | 6.3 Knots

A boat can't go faster than the waves it makes

A Boat's Maximum Speed

$1.34 \times \sqrt{LWL} = Maximum\ Speed$

Etchells

22'

$1.34 \times \sqrt{22} = Maximum\ Speed$

$1.34 \times 4.69 = $ | 6.3 Knots

Except for boats that can plane.

23'

S/L 1.5   6.4 Knots

40'

S/L 2.0   8.5 Knots

Preventing Leeway

As your boat moves forward, it simultaneously slips sideways. The results of this crabwise slide through the water are slower speeds and not being able to sail directly towards your destination. Obviously, we'd be a lot better off without leeway.

When going to windward, even the most efficient craft can convert only one-third of its sail's drive into forward motion when close-hauled. The remaining two-thirds are trying to heel the boat over or push it sideways. This is why sailing boats need to minimise forward drag while at the same time maximising resistance to lateral motion. There are a number of ways this can be done.

Man's first attempt at reducing leeway was probably to hold a paddle on the downwind side of a canoe or dugout, using water pressure and muscle to hold it in place. One or more paddles could be used, with their positions varied to help steer the craft.

Leeboards are like permanently mounted paddles. There is one on each side, with the leeward one swung down to grip the water. They are a Dutch invention and often look awkward to our eyes. Yet leeboards are easy to use, and do not take up room inside the boat. Their one drawback is that, hanging off the sides as they do, they are vulnerable to damage.

Early sailing rafts also adapted the paddle idea. Their 400-year-old descendants, the jangadas, are still sailing off the beaches of northeastern Brazil. A paddle-like board is inserted between the logs so it can be adjusted for depth and position, or pulled out of the way when beaching. This is the predecessor of the *daggerboard* found on so many modern small boats. Daggerboards are simple, strong and effective, but have the disadvantage of not kicking up to prevent damage when grounding.

The *centreboard* differs from the daggerboard in that it pivots and can be hoisted by a line. The idea

Dugout Sailing Canoe

Brazilian Jangada

was first patented by the Swain brothers of New Jersey in 1811 as a replacement for the leeboards that were typical on many local sloops. A centreboard is little more than a leeboard that has been moved inside the boat. It is a little more complicated than the daggerboard, but can be weighted for extra stability and swings up when it hits something.

Most boats and ships have a backbone called a *keel*. Until recently this shallow extension under the hull was primarily structural, with the vessel depending on the depth of its hull to prevent leeway.

The idea of a deep keel projecting down from the hull came about in the mid-1800s from an increased interest in yacht racing. Today it is the most common way to prevent leeway on larger boats. A keel is an integral part of the boat, so it is strong and can hold a substantial amount of stabilising ballast. As a trade-off, its fixed depth prevents sailing in *shoal* (shallow) waters and makes the boat difficult to trailer.

Keels come in a variety of configurations: *full keels* for ocean voyaging; *fin keels* for reduced wetted surface, speed and windward performance; *keel/centreboards* to get the advantages of both; *twin keels* for reduced draught and to stand upright when beached; and *winged keels* like the one *Australia II* used to win the America's Cup from the United States in 1983.

Whatever is used to combat leeway must have its area, along with the area of the hull and rudder, correctly distributed so the boat will be in balance with the force of the sails. To do this designers find the *centre of lateral resistance* (CLR), the vertical line on a boat's underwater profile that marks its pivot point. This is the fulcrum on which the boat rotates when it turns, and around which the sail's *centre of effort* (CE) must be properly aligned (see Balance, pages 98 and 99).

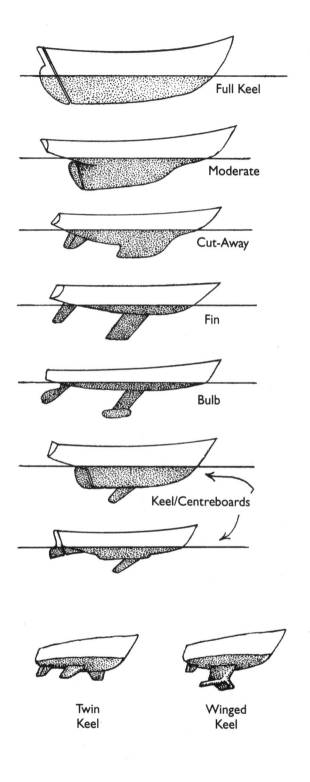

Full Keel

Moderate

Cut-Away

Fin

Bulb

Keel/Centreboards

Twin
Keel

Winged
Keel

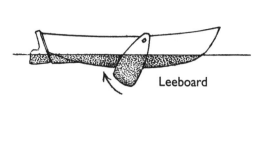

Leeboard

Daggerboard

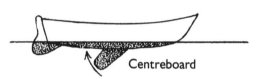

Centreboard

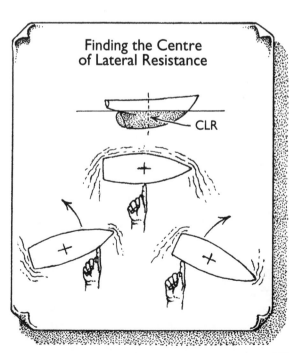

Finding the Centre
of Lateral Resistance

CLR

Wooden Boats

Long before Noah built the ark from gopher wood, and for thousands of years after, there was almost nothing but wooden boats. Then, starting around 1950 and in less than a generation, they became an endangered species. What nearly killed off the wooden boat in favour of fibreglass was not the material or the boats it produced, as much as the expense of building and maintaining them. Boatbuilding in wood is very labour-intensive, requiring care, a great deal of time, and highly specialised skills. Maintaining them also takes a commitment of time and effort.

But wood is strong for its weight, naturally buoyant, a good heat and sound insulator, and pleasant to work and live with. A well-built wooden boat can outlive its owner, but to do this it must be carefully looked after, a task made easier by modern adhesives and sealants.

There are many types of wooden construction, but probably the best known is *plank on frame*. A skeleton of frames, radiating out from a central keel, supports the planking that forms the skin. If the planking is smooth, with the edges of the boards butted to each other and caulking between, it is known as *carvel planking*. In *lapstrake planking* the boards are thinner and overlap each other with no caulking between them, letting the natural swelling of the wood create a watertight fit. Lapstrake planking is lighter and more flexible than carvel, but harder to keep tight and not suitable for larger vessels.

Framed construction can also be covered with plywood. This reduces the number of seams, requires less framing, and is lightweight and less expensive. But because plywood can be bent in only one direction at a time, it is limited to chined hulls.

An altogether different approach is *strip planking*, where square strips are edge-nailed and glued to each other rather than to frames. Because of the strength of adhesives such as epoxy, a strip-planked hull is stronger than a comparable framed one. Construction costs are lower, and the possibility of leaking almost eliminated.

In the 1930s a few boats were built by laminating many thin layers of wood veneer together over a temporary framework to produce a moulded wood hull. Since the glues at that time needed both heat and pressure to adhere, the process was known as *hot moulding*. After World War II, epoxy glues allowed laminating to be done at room temperatures, and the process became known as *cold moulding*. Moulded hulls are monolithic, stiff, waterproof, and almost impervious to rot. Since no framing is needed, there is more usable internal space (sometimes as much as 10% more). A popular cold-moulding method is the *WEST* (Wood Epoxy Saturation Technique) system, where all the wood on the boat is saturated and sealed in epoxy.

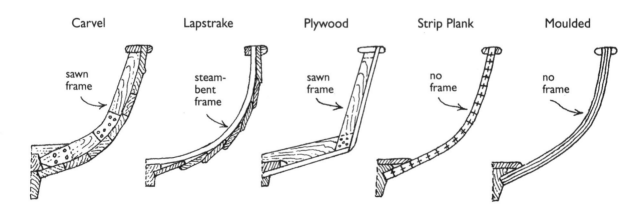

Carvel — sawn frame
Lapstrake — steam-bent frame
Plywood — sawn frame
Strip Plank — no frame
Moulded — no frame

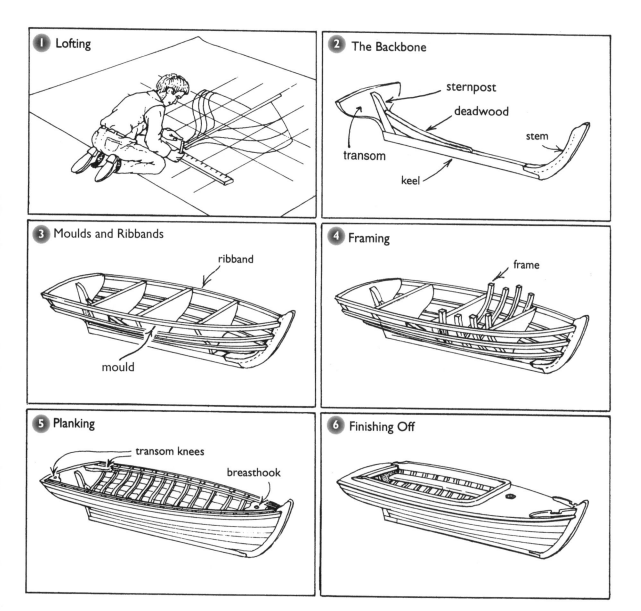

1 Lofting

2 The Backbone

sternpost

deadwood

stem

transom

keel

3 Moulds and Ribbands

ribband

mould

4 Framing

frame

5 Planking

transom knees

breasthook

6 Finishing Off

BUILDING IN WOOD

Building a carvel-planked vessel has not changed much over the years. The builder starts by lofting, or making full-size templates from dimensions found on the table of offsets (1). With this information he then erects the boat's backbone. The *keel* is laid out with the *stem* joined forward, and the *sternpost, deadwood* and *transom* aft (2). Then *moulds*, a series of temporary frames shaped to the correct cross sections, are joined to the keel. To hold them in place and ensure that they will produce a fair hull, *ribbands*, thin strips of wood running fore and aft, are nailed

to the moulds (3). Within the form made from the moulds and ribbands, the *frames* are worked into place (4). Frames can be sawn to shape, built up from many pieces, or bent to fit after being steamed to make them flexible. As the frames go in, the moulds are removed. When all the frames have been installed, the planking starts (5). As the *planks* go on, the ribbands are removed. This completes the hull, but not the work. Finishing off a boat – laying decks, erecting cabins, painting and rigging – can take longer than building the hull (6).

Fibreglass Boats

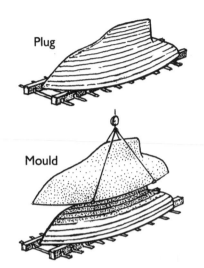

Plug

Mould

Mould

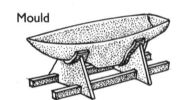

'Pop!'

Hull

Mould

Fibreglass

A typical wood 20-footer might be made from more than 3,000 parts – all trying to flex, separate or rot away from each other. With fibreglass the same 20-footer needs only five parts, and its hull is of one piece, so it won't leak. When fibreglass became available in 1948, boatbuilders saw a material that did not corrode or rot, was strong, made high-volume building a reality, and would seemingly last for ever.

Fibreglass, or *FRP* (fibre-reinforced plastic), is molten glass that has been drawn into thin fibres, made into a fabric, and then encapsulated in a plastic resin (typically polyester). The glass provides most of the strength, while the plastic resin holds the fibres in place. Fibreglass is heavier than most woods (three times heavier than mahogany), but since less is used, fibreglass boats are usually lighter. It is also strong. And even though fibreglass is comparatively expensive, it is still one of the most economical of all boatbuilding materials. Little skilled labour is necessary, the man-hours needed to build a boat are one-quarter what wood requires, and production runs can be high. The end result is that costs per boat are drastically lower than for any other method of construction.

The building of a fibreglass boat begins with the *plug*, a full-size mock-up of the part to be built, such as the hull, deck or other component. From the plug a female (concave) *mould* is made, usually from fibreglass. Since many parts will come from the mould, it is carefully built so its shape never varies and is polished to an ultrahigh finish.

Before the *lay-up* is begun the mould is prepared with a *releasing agent* to keep the fibreglass laminates from sticking to it. First to be applied is the *gelcoat*, the eventual outer surface of the finished product. It is sprayed on in a thin layer to provide a glossy and waterproof finish. This is very important, as fibreglass is not impervious to water. As a backing for the gelcoat, a smooth layer of tightly woven fibreglass cloth is laid up next. Then alternating layers of *mat* and *roving* are applied until the desired thickness has been achieved. Mat is a random weave of short, chopped strands that absorbs a lot of resin to provide bulk. Roving is a coarsely woven fabric that provides strength

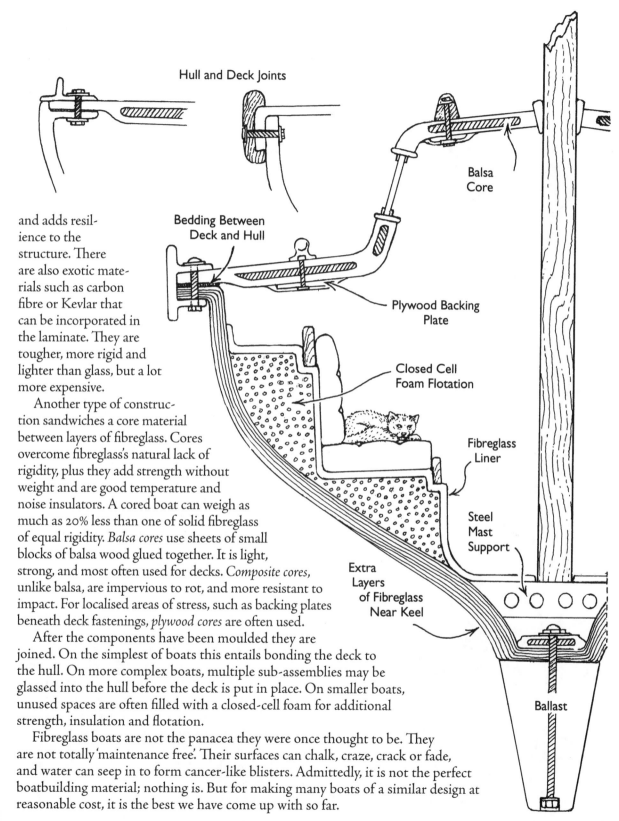

Hull and Deck Joints

Balsa Core

Bedding Between Deck and Hull

Plywood Backing Plate

Closed Cell Foam Flotation

Fibreglass Liner

Steel Mast Support

Extra Layers of Fibreglass Near Keel

Ballast

and adds resilience to the structure. There are also exotic materials such as carbon fibre or Kevlar that can be incorporated in the laminate. They are tougher, more rigid and lighter than glass, but a lot more expensive.

Another type of construction sandwiches a core material between layers of fibreglass. Cores overcome fibreglass's natural lack of rigidity, plus they add strength without weight and are good temperature and noise insulators. A cored boat can weigh as much as 20% less than one of solid fibreglass of equal rigidity. *Balsa cores* use sheets of small blocks of balsa wood glued together. It is light, strong, and most often used for decks. *Composite cores*, unlike balsa, are impervious to rot, and more resistant to impact. For localised areas of stress, such as backing plates beneath deck fastenings, *plywood cores* are often used.

After the components have been moulded they are joined. On the simplest of boats this entails bonding the deck to the hull. On more complex boats, multiple sub-assemblies may be glassed into the hull before the deck is put in place. On smaller boats, unused spaces are often filled with a closed-cell foam for additional strength, insulation and flotation.

Fibreglass boats are not the panacea they were once thought to be. They are not totally 'maintenance free'. Their surfaces can chalk, craze, crack or fade, and water can seep in to form cancer-like blisters. Admittedly, it is not the perfect boatbuilding material; nothing is. But for making many boats of a similar design at reasonable cost, it is the best we have come up with so far.

Metal Boats

The first metal boats were of wrought iron. Though not as strong for its weight as wood, it was malleable, easy to work, and resisted corrosion. To improve iron's strength, carbon was added to create the alloy steel.

For its weight, steel is stronger than almost anything else. It is resilient, able to stretch by 30% before failing, and resists abrasion. Steel is tough, fireproof, and, except for production fibreglass boats, the least expensive of all materials to build in.

Iron or steel plates were originally joined by rivets, with the plate edges hammered down to make a watertight seal. This method originated in the mid-1800s and was superseded in the 1930s by arc welding, which made steel boats both stronger and lighter. A weld in steel has the same qualities as the material it joins, making a welded steel vessel a solid one-piece unit. Steel's main problems are its weight and loss of material through rust and galvanic corrosion. In order to compensate for the slow loss of material, plates must be of a minimum thickness to last. This in turn limits how small a boat can be built. Around 22 feet seems to be the lower range. But from 40 feet up, steel has a decided advantage in strength and lower costs, and will weigh about as much as a wooden boat. Like other sheet materials, steel can be bent only in one direction at a time, so chined hull forms are most common. Complex curves and round-bilged boats can be built, but require expensive hydraulic bending machines and a lot of labour.

Since 1940, new alloys of aluminium have made it what some think to be the finest of all boatbuilding materials. It will not rust, is light (one-third the weight of steel), almost indestructible, and, if not painted, is maintenance free. Aluminium's primary drawback is that it corrodes in the presence of other metals. It is also very expensive. Aluminium's cost per pound is high, and welding it requires specialised skills.

Buoyancy

It's been over two thousand years since Archimedes shouted 'Eureka!', proclaiming his discovery of the laws of buoyancy. Yet most of us are still at a loss as to why a non-wood boat floats. Drop a sheet of metal or fibreglass in water and it sinks; shape it into a boat and it floats. How can that be?

Part of the answer lies in the old Greek's bathtub experiment, which showed that if you put something in water it will be buoyed up by a force equal to the weight of the water it pushes aside (displaces).

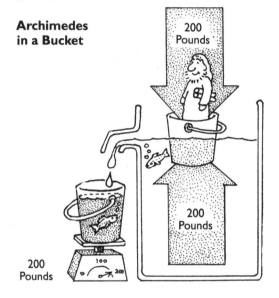

Archimedes in a Bucket

200 Pounds

200 Pounds

200 Pounds

Therefore, a boat will settle into the water until it has *displaced* (taken up the same space as) a volume of water whose weight equals that of the boat. Seawater weighs 64 pounds for every cubic foot of space it takes up (fresh water about 62 pounds). So as long as there is enough hull to push aside a cubic foot of water for every 64 (or 62) pounds of boat weight, it will float.

Steel, aluminium and fibreglass are all a lot heavier than water's 64 (or 62) pounds per cubic foot, but they are also strong for their weight. They can be used to enclose a space whose total density (the amount of weight packed into a given volume) is less than the construction material and of water – so it will float. If you take a steel boat apart and drop the parts in the water, they

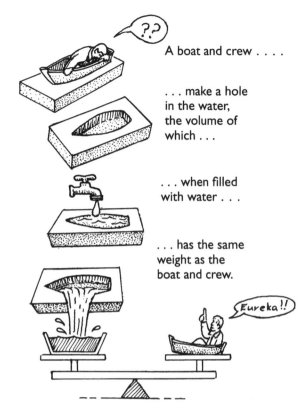

A boat and crew . . . .

. . . make a hole in the water, the volume of which . . .

. . . when filled with water . . .

. . . has the same weight as the boat and crew.

Eureka!!

will sink. But if you assemble them into a hollow object whose total density is less than water, it will float.

The relationship between a boat's weight and the amount of water it displaces is so important that naval architects (whose primary job is to design things that float) speak of a boat's displacement (page 67), rather than its weight. To be sure a boat floats on the desired waterline, the designer calculates the weight of everything that goes into it – fastenings, plumbing, rig and crew – to make sure there is enough underwater volume to support it all.

You can get a good idea of a boat's weight by estimating its underwater volume. Look at a boat while it is on land. If there is a lot of it below the waterline – if it requires a lot of underwater volume to stay afloat – it is heavy for its length. Then find a boat of the same length with very little underwater volume. This boat will be comparatively light.

Light Displacement   Heavy Displacement

Boats

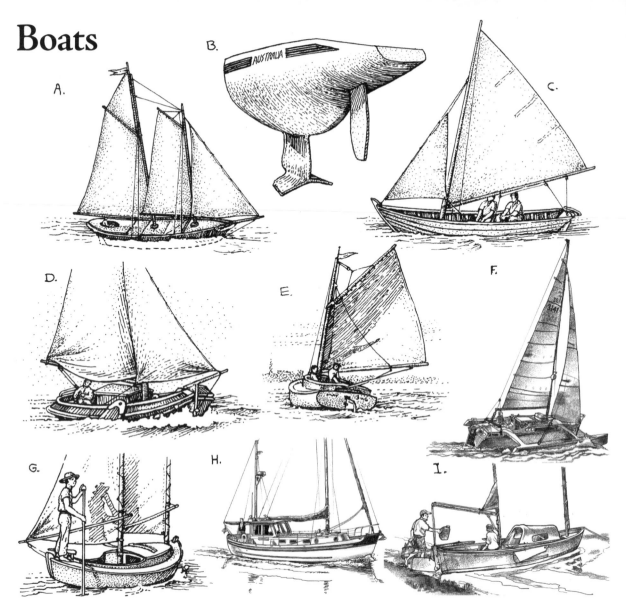

A   *America:* Her builder claimed that no boat could beat her, and in 1851 this 101-foot schooner proved herself by winning what would become known as the America's Cup.

B   *Australia II:* The first 12-metre boat with a winged keel. '12 metres' refers to a formula that incorporates many measurements that must combine to equal 12.

C   Beachcomber dory: A 21-foot racing offshoot of the hardworking dories used for fishing on the Grand Banks. Safe for children, yet fast enough for spirited racing.

D   Boier yacht: One of many traditional Dutch types that over the last few centuries have proved best for high winds, short steep waves and shallow waters.

E   Catboat: Broad beam, shallow draught, and a tough, purposeful look are its trademarks. First used for fishing, now does everything from cruising to racing.

F   Corsair F27: The folding outriggers and floats bring the beam down to 8 feet 6 inches for legal trailering. Very fast, in excess of 20 mph, yet seaworthy enough for ocean passages.

G   Sharpie: Flat bottomed, fairly narrow, fast and surprisingly seaworthy, this sharpie once worked as a mail-delivery boat in 1886.

H   Banjer 37: With its large engine, this 'motorsailer' works well as a motorboat that can also sail. Best for long-distance, downwind cruising in comfort.

I   Sea Pearl 21: A shallow open boat that makes an ideal beach cruiser with a canvas tent for overnights. She is long and narrow and uses water ballast to help stay upright.

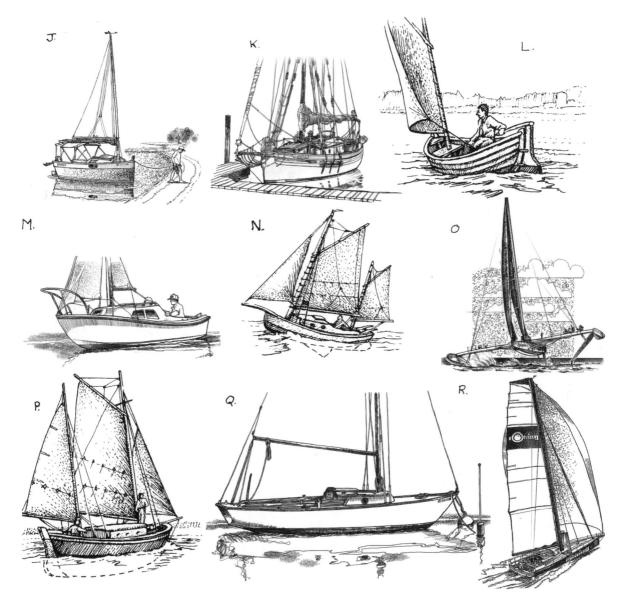

J   Peep Hen 14: Slab-sided, flat-bottomed and fat, yet charming in her simplicity. A shoal-water mini cruiser for sneaking into quiet backwater anchorages.

K   Bristol Channel Cutter: Lyle Hess's tribute to the tough 19th-century fishing and pilot boats that plied the waters off Wales and Ireland. She's full-keeled, heavy, and ready to cross an ocean or two.

L   Peapod: These double-enders are almost the same forward and aft. Originally used by Maine coast lighthouse keepers, they now make delightful family daysailers.

M   West Wight Potter 14: Originally built of plywood on the Isle of Wight, England, for 'pottering about' in the island's challenging conditions. Now in fibreglass, but still hard-chined and beamy for stability.

N   *Sea Bird*: In 1911 this simple V-bottomed yawl became a legend when three amateur sailors crossed the Atlantic in her to prove that anyone could do it.

O   *L'Hydroptere*: A boat that flies. She lifts out of the water on foils, and in 2009 was the first sailing boat to go faster than 50 knots (57.5 mph).

P   Tahiti ketch: A John Hanna cruising design for a roomy 30-footer. She was slow, but well-balanced and rugged, and took a lot of dreamers to Tahiti and beyond.

Q   Typhoon: Typical of most of Carl Alberg's designs, this 18-footer with its full keel is a wholesome, seaworthy daysailer or weekender.

R   Open 60: A single-handed ocean racer that can sustain 30 mph or more planing down giant waves in the Roaring Forties. They are ultralight, have large sail plans, and are self-righting.

RIGGING

'Men in a ship are always looking up, and men ashore generally looking down.'
John Masefield, *The Bird of Dawning*

It's rigging that reveals the sailing boat to be the anachronism it is – a machine lost in time, and forever timeless. Spars may be of aerospace carbon fibres, their shapes derived in a wind tunnel and supported by strands of exotic alloys. Yet a boat's rig is still dependent on some of the most ancient of mechanical devices. Where else is it still necessary to understand the principles of levers, mechanical advantage, and block and tackle? Here is a modern device that relies on equipment more appropriate to the building of a pyramid than the moving of a yacht.

Even if you accept the rig for what it is, it still fools you. While it may look like a passive structure intended to achieve absolute rigidity, it is very much the opposite. Rigging should be thought of like the internal workings of a bird's wings. All those wires are tendons, lines are muscles, and spars are hollow bones. They are controls to shape and move the working surfaces, which are made of cloth rather than feathers. By pulling, twisting and pushing you can affect the sail's shape and how it presents itself to the wind, thereby transforming mere rope and wire into something alive.

Standing Rigging

The primary purpose of standing rigging is to support the mast, or masts. The two main categories are *shrouds*, which provide athwartship bracing, and *stays* for fore-and-aft support. Stays are also used to hang sails (collectively known as *staysails*) such as jibs. Standing rigging is further subdivided into a variety of specialised types, the most common of which are shown on the rig below.

Stays and shrouds are attached to the mast by metal strips called *tangs*, and joined to the hull by *chainplates*. The rig is usually tensioned by turnbuckles, although many daysailers use *adjusters* with movable pins to make the daily chore of rigging and unrigging easier. On some racing boats backstay tension can be changed underway, using hydraulic or mechanical adjusters to affect mast *rake* (angle) and bend. There are also *running backstays*, which are used when no permanent backstay can be fitted or when extra bracing is needed.

A boat's rig is often named for its forestay. Larger boats typically have *masthead* rigs, with the forestay attached to the top (*head*) of the mast (the forestay is then properly called a headstay). Smaller craft, or those wanting more control over fore-and-aft mast bend, use *fractional* rigs with the forestay attached only partway up the mast. Many fractional-rigged boats, such as Lightnings and Stars, use *jumper stays* above the forestay to stiffen the mast against the pull of the sail and backstay.

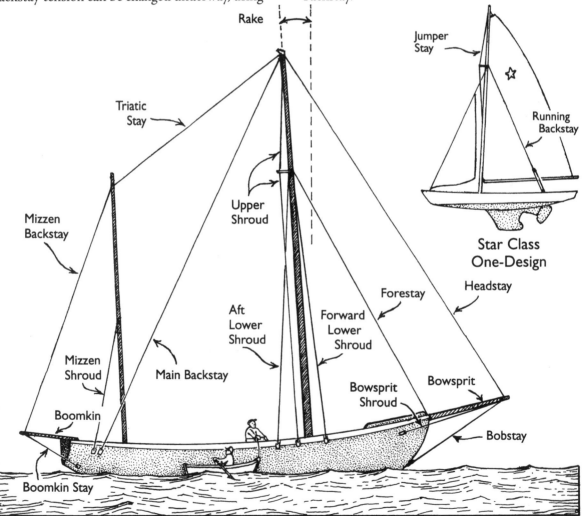

Star Class
One-Design

Tuning the Rig

Rigging needs to be *tuned* to achieve proper support for the mast, tension for the stays, and balanced positioning of the sails. High-performance boats often have masts that can bend to alter the mainsail's shape for different wind conditions. With most boats, though, the mast should remain as straight as possible.

Begin with all rigging loose. If there are jumper stays, set them up so the top of the mast bends slightly forward. This will straighten when you take up on the backstay. Next work with fore- and backstays to achieve proper mast rake (refer to the designer's sail plan or a similar boat). To measure rake, hang a weight from the main halyard as a plumb bob. When correct, take up on the turnbuckles to provide enough headstay tension to keep the jib's luff from sagging when on the wind. Recheck rake after tightening.

Next, set up the upper shrouds to centre the masthead athwartships. Check this by leading the main halyard to the upper-shroud chainplates. If halyard length is the same on both sides, the mast is centred. Set up the turnbuckles so the upper shrouds are taut, then recheck alignment. Adjust the angle of the *spreaders* so they bisect the shrouds with equal angles above and below. Lower shrouds need not be as taut as the uppers, with slightly more tension on the aft ones than on the forward.

The rigging should not be bar taut. If one side needs taking up, unscrew the opposite turnbuckle the same number of turns. Tightening the turnbuckles each time an adjustment is made will eventually put severe strains on the hull and rig. For casual sailing, favour a little play in the rigging rather than rigid tension.

To see if what you have done is correct, go out and sail to windward on both tacks. When looking up the mast from the back or sides, it should be straight. The windward shrouds should be very taut (but not like solid rods) and the leeward ones fairly slack (but not flopping around). The headstay should have very little sag.

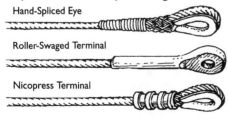

Hand-Spliced Eye

Roller-Swaged Terminal

Nicopress Terminal

Three Most Common Terminals

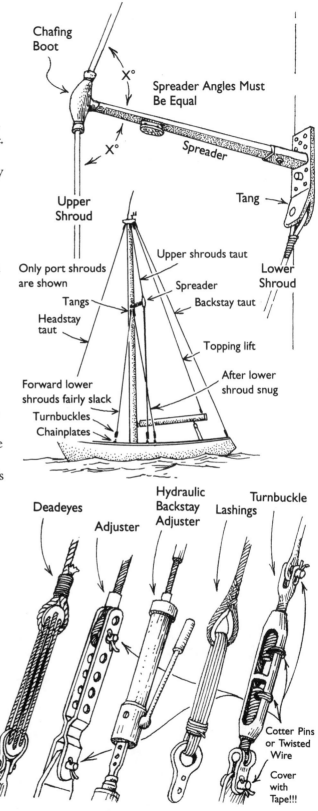

Chafing Boot

Spreader Angles Must Be Equal

X°

X°

Spreader

Tang

Upper Shroud

Lower Shroud

Upper shrouds taut

Only port shrouds are shown

Spreader

Backstay taut

Tangs

Headstay taut

Topping lift

After lower shroud snug

Forward lower shrouds fairly slack

Turnbuckles

Chainplates

Deadeyes

Adjuster

Hydraulic Backstay Adjuster

Lashings

Turnbuckle

Cotter Pins or Twisted Wire

Cover with Tape!!!

Running Rigging

Running rigging hoists sails and controls their movement. The halyards and sheets are essential, and all boats must have them. Other pieces of running rigging – including *boom vang kicking straps*, *cunninghams* (page 90) and *preventers* (page 92) – enhance sail control and, while not necessary, improve performance.

Halyards raise and lower sails, and provide tension to keep a sail's leading edge straight. This is particularly important for the jib, which has no mast to support its luff. Tension is sometimes applied directly to the halyard from winches or tackle. In other installations the sail is raised, the halyard made fast, and tension applied with a downhaul.

To maintain tension, halyards should not stretch. The least elastic halyards are of stainless steel wire. But it is difficult to handle, its strands split to make

flesh-cutting 'meat hooks', and it needs a *reel winch* to contain the gathered wire. Sailors less obsessed with stretch and more interested in ease of handling use Dacron line. It is easier on the hands and, with braided pre-stretched construction (particularly with a Kevlar core), has little stretch. A compromise is to use a rope *tail* spliced to wire. To hoist, haul on the rope tail until the wire reaches the winch, wrap the wire around the winch at least four times, crank taut, and make the line fast to a cleat.

Rope halyards need to have their ends kept from flying out of reach. An expedient solution is to lead the line through the base of the cleat and make a figure-eight knot (page 146) in the end. Stow halyards by making the sail end fast to a deck fitting and hauling tight. Keep both parts away from the mast to prevent slapping.

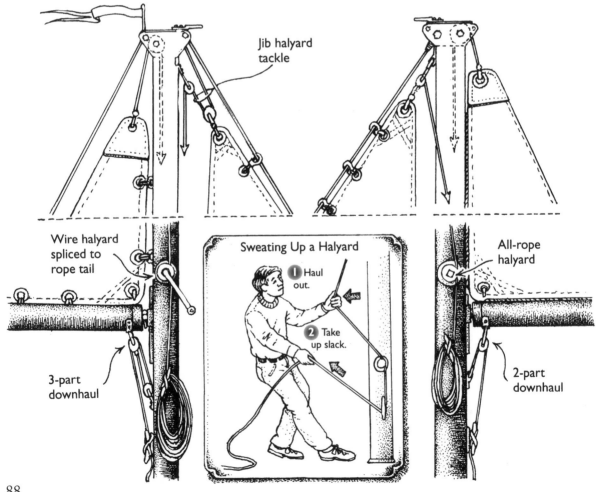

Jib halyard tackle

Wire halyard spliced to rope tail

3-part downhaul

Sweating Up a Halyard

1 Haul out.

2 Take up slack.

All-rope halyard

2-part downhaul

SHEETS

If you grab a sheet while sailing, it will become obvious that a great deal of power is transferred through these lines. To cope with the strain, and to make them comfortable to grip, sheets should be no less than ⅜ inch in diameter for boats up to 25 feet, and ½ inch for boats to 40 feet. Dacron is suitable for all sheets, while lightweight polypropylene can be used for light-air sails.

The mainsheet controls boom swing and lift. When a boom lifts, it lets the sail twist, with its head falling off to leeward. To control lift (and twist), a downward pull can be added by attaching the mainsheet near the centre of the boom. Lift can also be controlled by a *traveller*, which is a sheet attachment point that moves athwartships. A traveller can be a *block* (pulley) mounted on a *car* that moves on a track, a simple rope *bridle*, or a metal-rod *horse*.

Jibs have two-part sheets: one leading off to port, the other to starboard. Shackles are often used to attach the sheets, but these can be dangerous at the end of a wildly flogging sail. *Bowlines* (page 147) work just as well and are a lot safer. The sheets are led through a block or *fairlead* (rope guide) on deck, back to the cockpit, and then to a winch, a cleat, or both. Jibsheet blocks or fairleads must be carefully located, since they affect how the sail sets (page 105).

Jibs can be rigged to use only one sheet if they are fitted with a boom. While the jib does not take up its best shape with a boom, and some efficiency is lost, there is a great gain in convenience in that the jib is *self-tending*, and the boat can be tacked just by moving the helm.

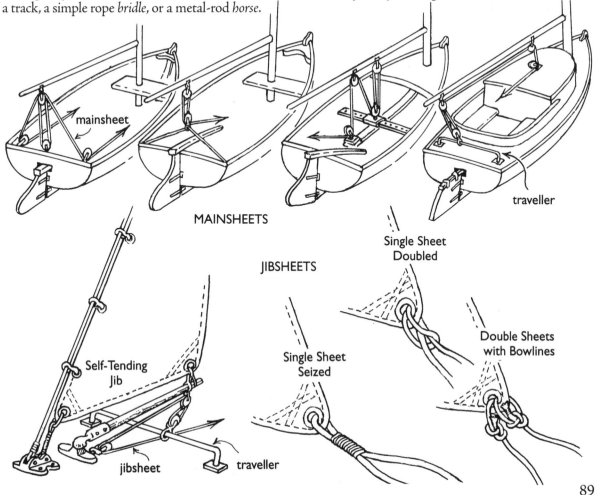

mainsheet

MAINSHEETS

traveller

JIBSHEETS

Single Sheet
Doubled

Self-Tending
Jib

Single Sheet
Seized

Double Sheets
with Bowlines

jibsheet   traveller

Sail Controls

UPWIND ADJUSTMENTS

To control a sail you must be able to adjust its shape as an airfoil, which will determine how much of the wind's force is converted into useful drive or wasted as heeling. For windward sailing, the jib's shape is controlled by its halyard and sheets. The mainsail's shape is controlled by its cunningham or downhaul, mainsheet and traveller, boom vang kicking strap and outhaul. (For more information on sail shape, see page 104.)

Downhauls stretch the luff (page 35), and by doing so draw the mainsail's point of maximum *draught* (fullness) forward. But on some boats the boom is fixed in place and there is no downhaul. As an alternative, back in the 1940s Briggs Cunningham came up with the idea of installing a *cringle* (reinforced eye) about 8 inches up from the tack and running a line through it. By pulling on the line, luff tension could be regulated as with a downhaul. Cunninghams, as they became known, crease the sail (where downhauls will not), but this is much less detrimental to performance than having poor sail shape. Some jibs are fitted with cunninghams, but most often their luff tension is controlled by the halyard.

The traveller and sheet must be thought of as working together. The two help control mainsail twist by keeping the boom's end from lifting. Some twist is good, and in fact necessary, but too much can induce weather helm or ruin the slot between the main and jib.

A boom vang kicking strap also controls sail twist, taking over for the sheet and traveller as the boom is eased out. Most vangs are a *three-part tackle* (page 93) with one end fixed to the base of the mast and the other to the boom, making no less than a 45-degree angle with the deck. On performance boats with bendy masts, the vang, which pulls the boom forward as well as down, bows the mast and the sail's luff forward, thereby flattening the sail. These boats often use powerful hydraulic or spring-loaded vangs.

The clew *outhaul*, which you used when bending on the main, tensions the sail's foot. Taking up on it flattens, while easing off (until small wrinkles appear along the foot) increases, the sail's draught in the lower third of the sail.

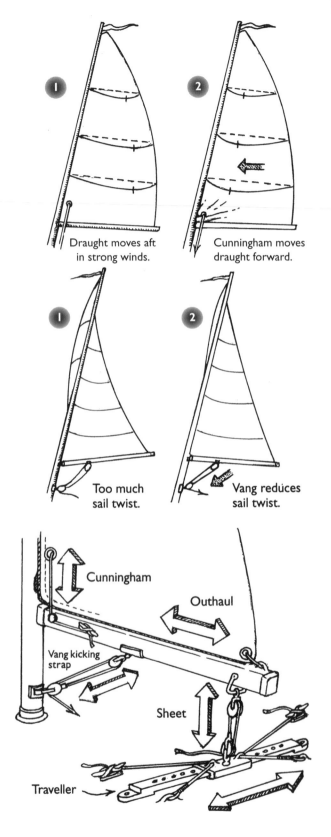

1 Draught moves aft in strong winds.

2 Cunningham moves draught forward.

1 Too much sail twist.

2 Vang reduces sail twist.

Cunningham

Outhaul

Vang kicking strap

Sheet

Traveller

When sailing close-hauled in light winds you will get more drive out of a sail if it is *full* (rounded) in cross section. As the wind picks up, proportionally flatter shapes are more effective. By using its controls you can adjust the sail's shape to match the wind.

Light Wind   Moderate Wind   Heavy Wind

	LIGHT WIND (under 8 knots)	**MODERATE WIND** (9–13 knots)	**HEAVY WIND** (over 14 Knots)
Jibsheet:	Eased (full curve)	In Slightly	In (flattened curve)
Jibsheet Lead:	Forward (firm leech/loose foot)	Middle	Aft (soft leech/tight foot)
Jib Luff Tension:	Light Tension (no wrinkles)	Increased Tension	Full Tension
Mainsheet:	Eased	In Slightly	In
Traveller:	To Weather	On Centreline	To Leeward
Vang:	Off	Some Tension	Pulled Down Hard
Main Luff Tension (downhaul/Cunningham):	Off	Pulled Down Slightly	Pulled Down Hard
Outhaul:	Eased	Tight	Tight

DOWNWIND ADJUSTMENTS

As the wind draws aft, sails need to have a full, rounded shape to catch as much wind as possible. Jibsheet leads are moved to their forward positions, luff tensions for main and jib are reduced, the main's outhaul is eased, and its *leech line* is pulled taut. The leech line is a thin line run through the *tabling* (hem) of the leech that acts like the drawstring on a bag. Tightening the line draws in the leech to deepen the sail's belly.

In light winds the topping lift can induce some extra draft by lifting the end of the boom slightly. A proper topping lift is of low-stretch Dacron line made fast to the end of the boom, led to a block near the masthead, and down the mast to a cleat. Rigged this way, the boom can be controlled when *broad off* (eased all the way out), or while the sail is being raised or lowered.

While fullness is desired, excess twist is not. A sail with its head sagging off to leeward produces yawing and rolling forces that can make the boat hard to steer. The standard boom vang kicking strap helps, but a better solution is a vang that can be moved to any part of the boom and then led to a deck fitting directly below. This vang's pull is almost straight down, reducing twist and holding the boom back in case of an accidental gybe. They are inconvenient, though, needing to be adjusted each time the main is trimmed, and disconnected and moved each time you tack or gybe.

In rough going, or when there is only a standard boom vang, a preventer should be rigged. Lead a line from the end of the boom and secure it to a fitting forward, then take up on the sheet. This will firmly lock the boom in place. Jibs set on a boom can also be rigged with a preventer to keep them winged out. Loose-footed jibs need a *spinnaker pole* to do the same, in which case it is properly called a *whisker pole*. These need to be rigged with a topping lift and *foreguy* to hold them in place.

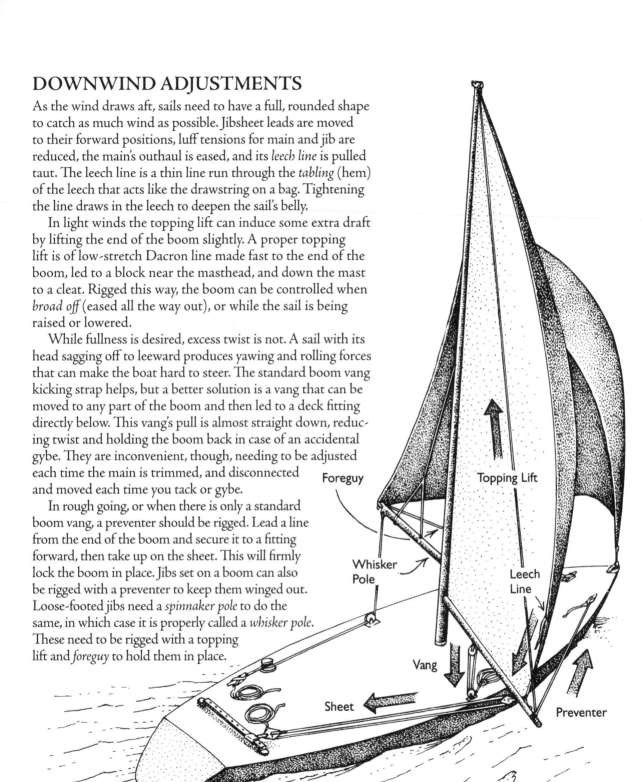

Foreguy

Topping Lift

Whisker Pole

Leech Line

Vang

Sheet

Preventer

Tackle

A *tackle*, or *purchase*, is made up of blocks with line *rove* (passed) through them to give a mechanical advantage when you pull on the *fall* (hauling part). The more lines within a tackle, the more power, but at a price of slower hauling and ever-increasing friction. To calculate the advantage, count the number of lines that are rove through the block attached to what you want to move. Notice that the same tackle can provide different advantages depending on how it is used.

Many sailors make up a *handy billy*, a four-part (four lines) general-purpose tackle, for their rope lockers. This can be used as a vang or preventer, to help with the anchor, for repairs, or to hoist you up the mast.

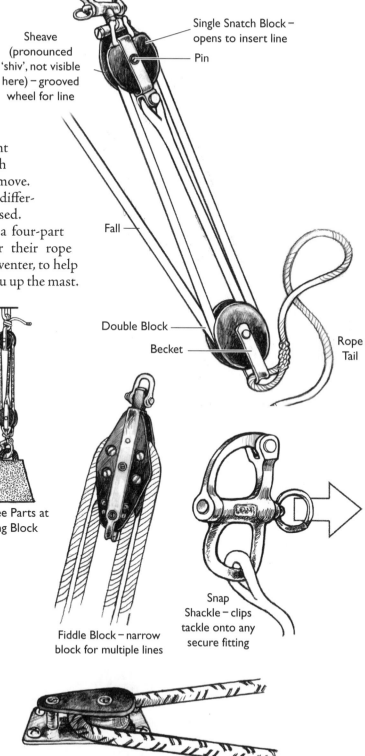

Sheave (pronounced 'shiv', not visible here) – grooved wheel for line

Single Snatch Block – opens to insert line

Pin

Fall

Double Block

Becket

Rope Tail

4:1 Four Parts at Moving Block

3:1 Three Parts at Moving Block

Fiddle Block – narrow block for multiple lines

Snap Shackle – clips tackle onto any secure fitting

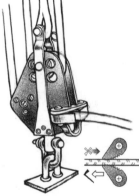

Cam Block – secures line at block

Cheek Block – fixed to deck, boom or mast

Winches

Winches get their mechanical advantage from the difference between the radius of the drum and the length of the handle. This is improved upon in some models with internal gearing.

To use a winch, wrap the line clockwise once around the drum and pull in as much as you can. When you feel resistance, take two or three more turns (for a better grip) around the drum, insert the handle, and start cranking with one hand while *tailing* (keeping tension) with the other. Watch the incoming line so it does not ride over existing turns and jam. If there is a lot of strain, one person should crank while another tails.

Once the line is in, keep tension on the tail, belay it to a cleat, and remove and stow the handle. In an emergency, or when a cleat isn't free, secure the line with a towboat hitch (page 166).

When releasing line under strain, *snub* it by keeping a turn around the cleat to maintain friction on the drum. The line can then be *checked* – by letting a little out and then holding, *eased* – by letting out continuously but very slowly, or *letting go* – by taking the last turn off the cleat and throwing the coils off the winch in an anticlockwise direction.

If the winch binds up with a *riding turn*, caused by incorrectly lead line, undo the jam by pulling the line off anticlockwise. If the line is under pressure, as with a jibsheet, clap on a tackle to relieve the strain.

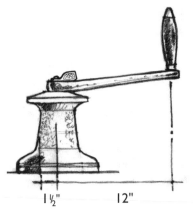

1½"   12"

1-to-8
Mechanical Advantage from a Winch

Tail

Sheet to Jib or
Other Sail

Winch
Jammed
with a Riding
Turn

Jammed!

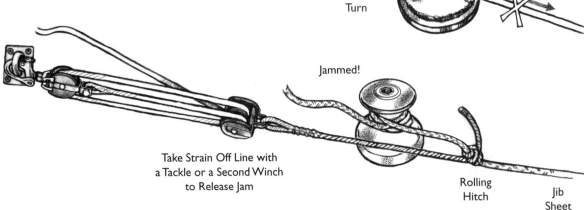

Take Strain Off Line with
a Tackle or a Second Winch
to Release Jam

Rolling
Hitch

Jib
Sheet

Stepping the Mast

A *mast step* is a notch in the keel that the mast's *heel*, its bottom, rests in, which is why the process of putting a mast in place is called *stepping*.

On larger boats, masts are always stepped in this traditional manner, and said to be *keel stepped*. The mast is hoisted by a crane, its end gently guided through a hole in the deck and then secured to the boat's backbone. A job best left to riggers at the boatyard.

On smaller boats the mast is often *deck stepped*, with its heel fitting into a metal receiving structure, a *tabernacle*, on the deck. Masts are rigged this way to allow for more room below in already cramped cabins, and so they can be easily raised and lowered when trailering. The tabernacle will have a hinge or a pivot. If it is *aft hinged*, the most common situation, the unraised mast hangs off towards the stern. If it's *forward hinged*, the mast goes out over the bow. The idea is that you can just push it up, like raising the flag on *Iwo Jima*, and lock it in place.

But it's not that simple as you're working on an uneven, slippery deck, trying to grunt a heavy pole up from a bad angle. That's why it is often easier and safer to have the yard's crane do it. If you can't, gather some friends: one or two to get the mast up and steady it, and another to pull on the forestay. If it's only you, here's a way to get the mast up, and back down, safely. Either way, before starting, make sure to *dress* the mast by bundling any rigging that will not be used so it isn't swinging around and getting in the way.

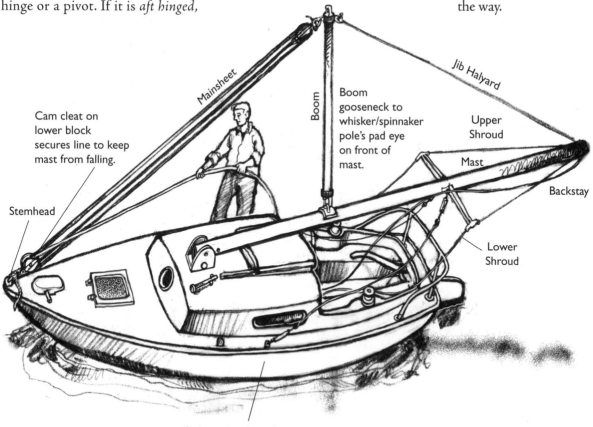

Cam cleat on lower block secures line to keep mast from falling.

Stemhead

Mainsheet

Boom

Boom gooseneck to whisker/spinnaker pole's pad eye on front of mast.

Jib Halyard

Upper Shroud

Mast

Backstay

Lower Shroud

Only secure shrouds to chainplates that are even with or aft of the tabernacle. Set up loosely.

Rigs

A Sprit: With its low centre of effort, short spars that stow easily, no standing rigging, and only two lines, this rig is perfect for craft up to 16 feet.

B Wishbone: Two curved booms encircle the sail, allowing it to take an airfoil shape over its full height. The angle of the booms acts like a vang to prevent sail twist.

C Windsurfer: First patented in 1969, this wishbone rig can be tilted towards the wind so the sail's thrust helps lift as well as drive the boat.

D Junk: The Chinese had great success with the rig, and H. G. Hasler revitalised it on his 25-foot *Jester* by entering the first single-handed transatlantic race in 1960.

E Gunter: A long, high-peaked gaff, shown here loose footed with no boom. It is a seaworthy rig that took this little 18-foot Drascombe Lugger across two oceans.

F Sloop: Since its introduction in the 1920s, the marconi sloop has proved to be one of the best rigs for going to windward, and practical in boats up to 40 feet.

G Cutter: A sloop with its mast stepped further aft, thereby allowing two foresails to be set. This provides more sail combinations to balance the centre of effort.

H Gaff cutter: A rough-water rig used by ship's pilots in England and France. Shown here is *Jolie Brise*, winner of the first Fastnet Race in 1925.

I Yawl: Originated as a way to add sail area without being penalised by racing handicaps. The small mizzen balances the sail plan while providing some drive.

J   Ketch: Has proved to be one of the most versatile of all cruising rigs. A ketch differs from a yawl in that the mizzen is larger and its mast further forward.

K   Cat ketch: A traditional rig from the 19th century, it is self-tacking and needs no extra light-air sails. This one is a Chuck Paine-designed 24-foot cruiser.

L   Schooner: America's indigenous rig dating back to 1713. This one is gaff rigged with topsails – a popular combination for working and racing until the 1930s.

M   Staysail schooner: Easier to handle and more weatherly than traditional schooners. The 236-foot *Club Méditerranée* is the largest single-handed boat ever built.

N   Cat schooner: The 'cat' prefix means the mast is too far forward to set a jib. This 18-footer by William Garden has an overlapping gaff foresail and a marconi main.

O   Bahamas smack: A low, powerful rig, with a deep roach in its foot and a wide, curved headboard. It pulls like a mule in the boisterous trade winds of those islands.

P   Sprit & club: Found only on Chesapeake Bay, these log canoes are used for racing. The rig is hard to handle and inefficient, but allows a lot of sail to be piled on.

Q   Sandbagger: The rig was so oversized that movable sandbags were shifted on each tack to balance it. This 26-foot gaff sloop carried over 1,400 square feet of sail.

R   Wing sail: The 2010 America's Cup winner, *BMW Oracle*, had a 233-foot tall, 7,000-square-foot wing made in two vertical sections that moved separately and were controlled by computers.

Balance

Forces acting on the rig and hull must be kept in balance so the boat will be safe, fast and easy to steer. As we have seen, the hull has a centre of lateral resistance (CLR) that is the focus of all leeway-preventing forces, acting like an imaginary pivot point around which the boat rotates. Working against this is the sail plan's *centre of effort* (CE), which is the focus of the wind's pressure on the sails. The relationship of these two centres determines a boat's balance.

Proper balance when sailing to windward in a moderate breeze (Force 4) means there should be a slight weather helm (no more than 3 or 4 degrees). This is achieved by keeping the CE just aft of the CLR. If the CE is too far aft, you get excessive weather helm, making the boat hard to handle. Moving the CE forward of the CLR produces a *lee helm*, with the boat constantly wanting to bear away. Balance is the key.

You may notice that a designer's plans show the CE as being quite a bit forward of the CLR. This separation is the lead (pronounced 'leed') used to compensate for a boat's natural tendency to turn to windward when heeled. All a sailor needs to know is where these centres fall when underway and how their balance (or imbalance) feels through the tiller.

Your goal is to adjust the rig and boat to give the right amount of weather helm. With this, the boat will head up in a gust, fall off in a lull, come into the wind if left on its own, and impart a gentle pressure to the tiller so it feels alive in your hands.

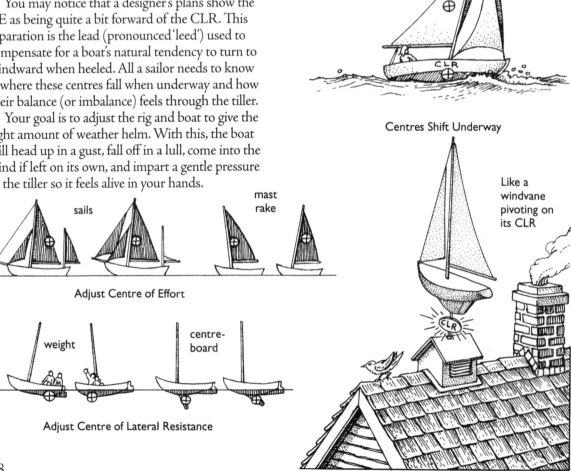

Sail Plan

Balanced!

Centres Shift Underway

Like a windvane pivoting on its CLR

Adjust Centre of Effort

Adjust Centre of Lateral Resistance

STEERING WITHOUT A RUDDER

There are vessels that steer with the balance between the rig and the hull, rather than with a rudder. For example, ancient balsa rafts on the west coast of South America used a system of two daggerboards – one forward, the other aft – to adjust their CLR and thus steer.

On the Great South Bay of Long Island, winters produce ice that varies from frozen solid to cold mush. Back in the late 1800s the scooter, a boat with sledlike runners on its bottom, evolved. Since it was impossible to use a rudder under these conditions, the scooter was steered with its jib and by moving the crew.

In 1911, Frederic A. Fenger toured the Caribbean in the 17-foot, two-masted sailing canoe *Yakaboo*. He thought a rudder to be unnecessarily complicated and steered by trimming the three sails, shifting his weight, and using an ingenious centreboard that could be moved forward and aft using a small tackle.

Today the most common example of steering by balance is the windsurfer. The mast is mounted on a universal joint so it can be raked forward or aft. Leaning the mast forward brings the CE ahead of the CLR, so the board turns downwind; leaning the mast aft turns the board into the wind. The CLR also shifts position as the rider moves back and forth.

Most small boats can be steered without a rudder. To bear off: Trim in the jib, ease the main, and move the crew aft. To head up: Trim the main, ease the jib, and move the crew forward. Crew weight can also heel the boat so its asymmetrical underwater shape makes it turn towards the higher side. If you want to turn to starboard, heel the boat to port.

Balsa Raft

Windsurfer

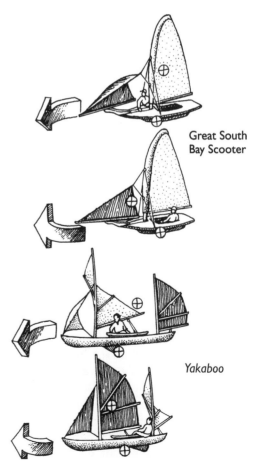

Great South Bay Scooter

Yakaboo

SELF-STEERING

If you go out only for an occasional sail or to race, it may be hard to understand why anyone would care whether or not a boat can steer itself. Only after you've had to sit at the helm for far too long – denied the opportunity to navigate, reef, eat, get out of the weather, or just relax – will you understand the 'tyranny of the tiller'. When you sail alone, you're a prisoner of the helm.

As sailors began crossing oceans, the need for self-steering became obvious. World voyagers Eric and Susan Hiscock made good use of their boat's natural ability to hold a course. Their 30-foot *Wanderer III*, like most boats with reasonable *directional stability* (tendency to stay on course), could be made to self-steer when close-hauled. The jib was trimmed in, the main eased, and the helm lashed slightly to windward or allowed to swing free. Each boat is different, and experimentation a must, but when close-hauled, a steady and accurate course can be kept in relation to the apparent wind.

It is the rare boat, though, that will steer itself when off the wind, so sheet-to-tiller systems were developed. By attaching the sails' sheets to the tiller through a series of blocks, sail power can be applied to the tiller for course corrections. One of the most common set-ups for downwind runs is with twin jibs poled out on each side. If the boat strays off course the windward sail pulls harder on its sheet, tugging on the tiller to bring the boat back.

The problem with natural or sheet-to-tiller self-steering is that the sails are trimmed for balance and not speed. *Windvanes* were first experimented with in the 1930s to remedy this. You set your course, trim sails for efficiency, engage the windvane, and let it, not the sails, do the steering. This system uses a small vane mounted near the stern. As it swings in response to the apparent wind, its motions are transmitted to a small auxiliary rudder that controls the vessel. Windvane steering came into popularity in 1960 when all five entrants in the first Singlehanded Transatlantic Race had some sort of vane aboard. In that race the 25-foot *Jester* crossed in 48 days, of which its lone crewmember spent only one hour at the helm. From then on, vanes became de rigueur for long-distance cruisers.

Windvanes are slaves to the wind, and will alter course as capriciously as the breeze they follow. They are often not sensitive enough to react in light airs, and are useless when the boat is under power. Electronic *autopilots* have none of these problems. The boat is put on course, sails are trimmed, a button on the pilot is pushed, and the autopilot's internal compass holds a course more accurately than a windvane or most helmsmen. The drawbacks are that it is constantly using up the boat's limited supply of electrical energy and cannot be repaired at sea. Although single-handed racers now use autopilots almost exclusively, they always keep a backup unit stowed below. Just in case.

Caution: A boat may be able to steer itself, but it cannot watch where it is going. Self-steering doesn't relieve you of the responsibility of keeping a proper lookout.

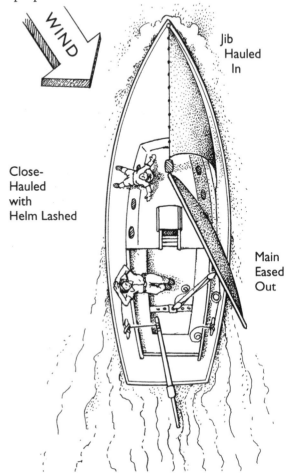

WIND

Jib Hauled In

Close-Hauled with Helm Lashed

Main Eased Out

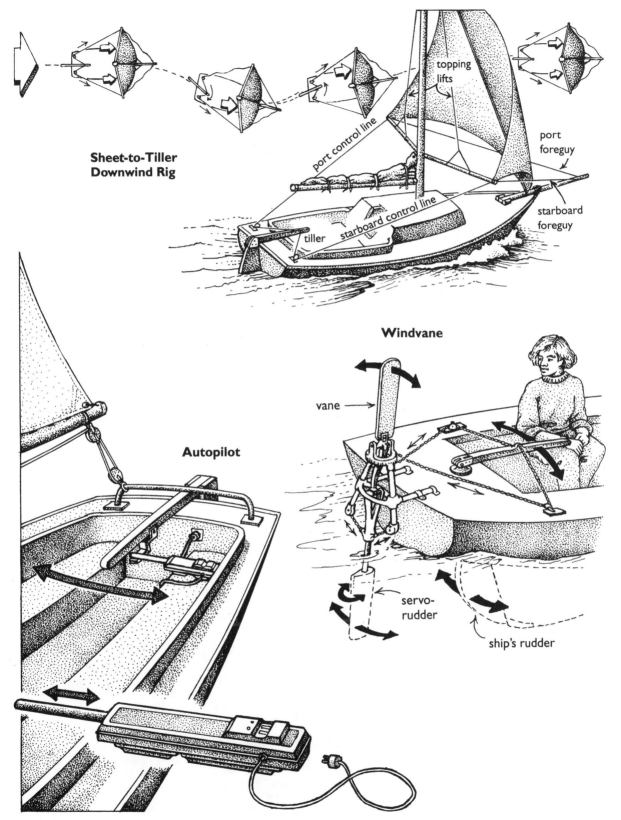

Sheet-to-Tiller Downwind Rig

topping lifts

port control line

port foreguy

starboard control line

starboard foreguy

tiller

Windvane

vane

Autopilot

servo-rudder

ship's rudder

SAILS

'I was so lost in the sight that I forgot the presence of the man who came out with me, until he said . . . half to himself, still looking at the marble sails—"How quietly they do their work!"'
Richard Henry Dana, *Two Years Before the Mast*

Many of us never get past the basics, thereby missing a world of possibilities. Modern boats are so good that sailors can all but ignore the fine points of sail shape and trim, yet still manage to get where they want to go. So why bother with the subtleties? A fair question. But then again, why do sailors suddenly become so interested in their sails, attempting to squeeze an extra tenth of a knot out of them, each time another boat hoves into view? Who knows?

What is certain is that these same sailors will always be let down when they try. Like piano students who never progress beyond 'Chopsticks', to them is lost the satisfaction of mastering a Chopin étude, or ever realising a boat's full potential.

Many never make the effort, believing that sails are too ethereal or too hard to make sense of. But there is really not very much to a sail. All it does is provide a thin division between higher and lower pressures, and direct the flow of air. So very simple, yet so full of possibilities that can bring improved performance, comfort, safety and enjoyment if you'll just take the time.

Sail Shape

A sail's airfoil shape is described by its cross section. The imaginary reference line from the luff to the leech is the *chord*, and a perpendicular from the chord to the sail is the *draught*, or *depth*. The location of maximum draught along the chord is the *draught position*, expressed as a percentage of the chord's length aft of the luff. The ratio of the maximum draught to the chord is the sail's *camber*, an indication of its fullness.

Since there is no universal all-purpose sail shape, sailmakers put in what they believe to be (sailmaking is not yet a foolproof science) the proper camber and draught position for close-hauled sailing at a theoretical 'average' wind strength of 10 to 12 mph. Typically the camber of a mainsail might be 1:10, and the draught position about 40% of the chord aft of the luff. In all other winds the sail's shape will need to be altered (pages 90–92).

It might help to think of a sail's shape in terms of an aeroplane's wing. A relatively slow biplane's wing is well rounded on top with considerable draught located almost midway back. A moderate-speed prop fighter has less draught and it is further forward. And the wing of a fast jet is almost flat, with a small amount of draught located very far forward.

To better see what shape your sails are taking, use black tape to make temporary *draught stripes* on the sail, or have your sailmaker put on permanent ones.

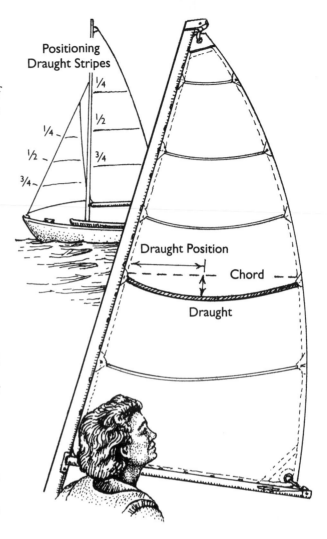

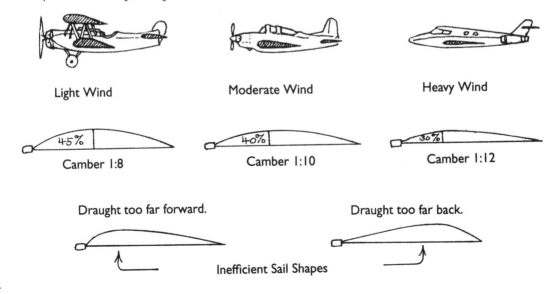

Light Wind — Camber 1:8 — 45%

Moderate Wind — Camber 1:10 — 40%

Heavy Wind — Camber 1:12 — 30%

Draught too far forward.

Draught too far back.

Inefficient Sail Shapes

Telltales

For a sail to do its job when on the wind, air must pass over it smoothly and evenly. Any turbulence or separation of flow on either side means a loss of efficiency. To make the wind's route along the sail visible we use telltales. Watching how they *stream* (point) will help you steer by the wind when close-hauled, and determine sail trim when you bear off.

Install telltales on a jib by melting a tiny hole in the sail with a hot awl. Then pass a piece of dark yarn through, knot it on both sides to hold it in place, and cut each end to 6 inches. The windward telltale will be easy to see; the leeward one will show up as a shadow on the sail. Telltales on the mainsail are tied to batten pockets in the leech.

When the jib's windward and leeward telltales are flowing back at the same near-level angle, or with the windward telltale angled very slightly upwards, the sail is splitting the wind and achieving its potential as an airfoil. If the leeward telltale flutters the sail is *stalled*, with wind pushing mostly on the windward side. When the windward telltale gets restless, that side of the sail is starved for wind and you are pointing too high. A simple rule is to trim the sail towards, or to turn the boat away from, the fluttering telltale.

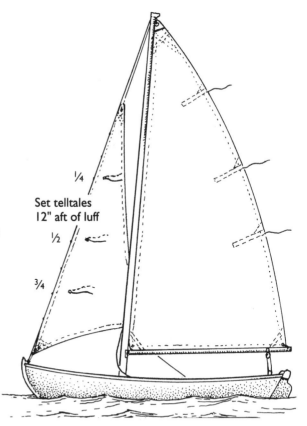

Set telltales
12" aft of luff

¼

½

¾

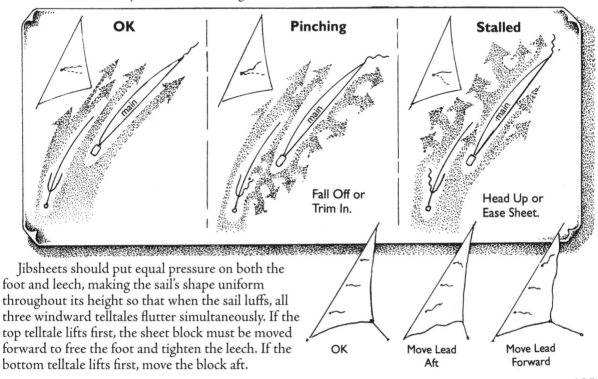

OK

Pinching

Fall Off or Trim In.

Stalled

Head Up or Ease Sheet.

OK

Move Lead Aft

Move Lead Forward

Jibsheets should put equal pressure on both the foot and leech, making the sail's shape uniform throughout its height so that when the sail luffs, all three windward telltales flutter simultaneously. If the top telltale lifts first, the sheet block must be moved forward to free the foot and tighten the leech. If the bottom telltale lifts first, move the block aft.

Fault Finder

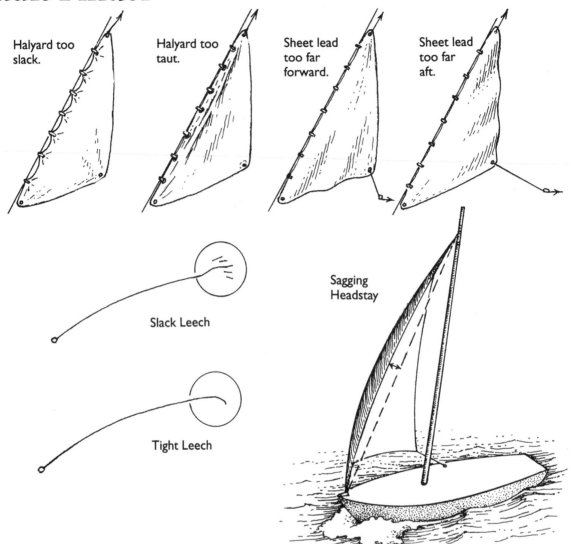

Halyard too slack.

Halyard too taut.

Sheet lead too far forward.

Sheet lead too far aft.

Slack Leech

Tight Leech

Sagging Headstay

Not all sails are created equal. The give, take and stretch of the fabric, and the variables a sailmaker must contend with when cutting the sail, make sure of that. Like a suit off the rack or one that has been well used, the sails on your boat may need some help to look their best. Most of the time you can solve the problems on your own. Sometimes, though, the answers will lie solely in the hands of a sailmaker.

To properly assess your sails, observe them on both tacks with all leech lines slack. If you can, get off your boat and look at the sails from slightly ahead and to leeward. Take your time, or even better, take photos to use for reference.

Leeches are a common problem area, as they are the longest unsupported parts of a sail. *Tight leeches*, ones that cup to windward, are detrimental, for they stop the exiting flow of air. This will be most pronounced in light winds, with the cupping usually blown out as the wind increases. A tight leech on a jib can backwind the main by directing the wind into its luff. This is often caused by the jibsheet lead being too far forward, or cinching the leech line too taut. Try trimming in the main, easing the jib, or flattening the main. If none of these helps, it's a job for the sailmaker.

Slack leeches, ones that *motorboat* (the last few inches flap noisily about), are less damaging to

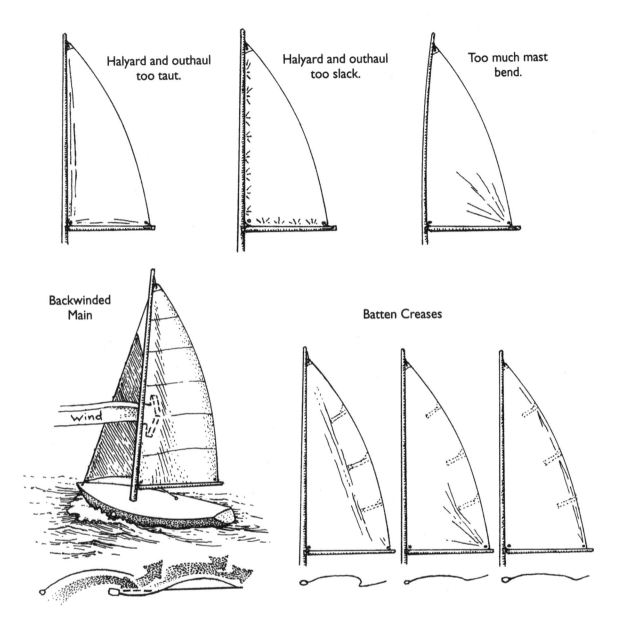

Halyard and outhaul too taut.

Halyard and outhaul too slack.

Too much mast bend.

Backwinded Main

Wind

Batten Creases

performance than they are annoying. The problem comes from stretched fabric in the leech. Careful tensioning of the leech line may help. For a mainsail, try increasing sheet tension. If the cloth is too old and stretched, or the roach too large, the only answer will be to take it to a sailmaker.

Wrinkles or creases are not necessarily bad. All sails should have some when luffing, which disappear once the sail fills. Marconi sails should have a slight crease along the luff and another along the foot. Gaff sails should have creases running from tack to peak. If a crease runs from clew to throat, take up on the peak halyard (page 109).

Creases that stay with the sail once it is drawing should be eliminated. Those running from clew to luff are a sign of too much mast bend, which can be reduced by easing off the backstay, mainsheet or vang. Another mainsail problem is a fold along the forward ends of the battens, or from the clew to the forward end of the lower batten. These can often be relieved by tightening halyard and outhaul tension. If not, it may be a sign that the battens are trying to support too great a roach.

The goal is to have sails with smooth airfoil surfaces that are properly shaped and offer the least amount of resistance to the wind.

Reefing

Sail area must be adjusted to match the strength of the wind. All you need is enough to keep the boat going at its best speed. Any more than that is wasted.

When should you reduce sail? Usually when you first begin to think about it. Shortening sail early will make your life easier and sailing more comfortable. If you're already pounding into the waves, or heeling too far over with a less than obedient weather helm, you've waited too long.

Headsail area is most often reduced by changing to a smaller jib or rolling the sail up along its luff (page 110). Mains are made smaller by reefing. This can be done by rolling up the sail around the boom or into the mast, or by the more traditional method of tying down a section along the foot. Since the introduction of stronger sail fabrics, traditional reefing has been improved upon and incorporated into most boats as *jiffy reefing*, where the foot is tied down only at the clew and tack.

To jiffy reef: Keep the boom inboard and the main luffing by heading on a close reach with the mainsheet eased and the jib just pulling (or you can heave-to). **1.** Take up on the topping lift to support the boom, then lower the halyard until the *luff cringle* is at the gooseneck. Secure the cringle. **2.** Set up the halyard. Then, using the pendant, pull the *leech cringle* to the boom and make it fast. **3.** Ease the topping lift and trim the sheet. If you like, you can now tie in the reef points, or reeve a *lacing line*, to bundle the doused portion of the sail.

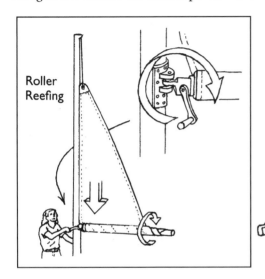

Roller Reefing

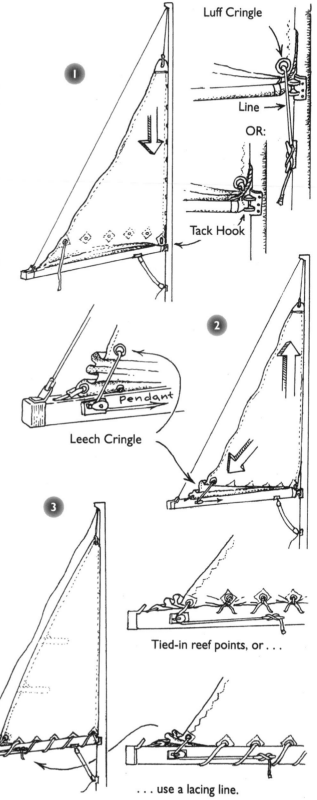

Luff Cringle

Line →

OR:

Tack Hook

Leech Cringle

Pendant

Tied-in reef points, or . . .

. . . use a lacing line.

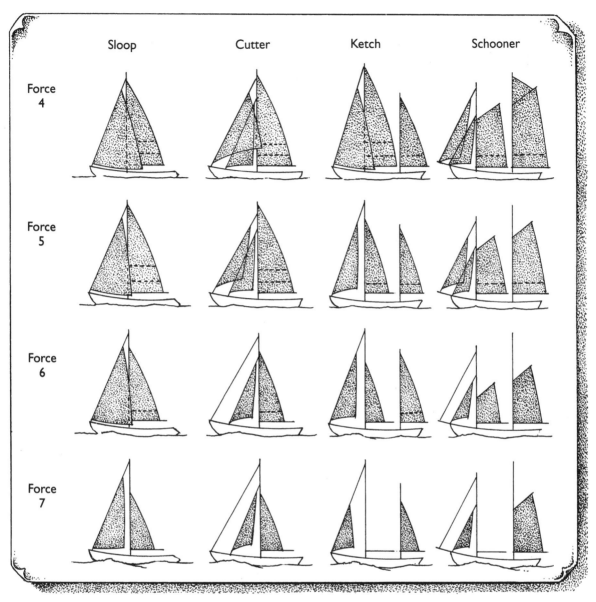

	Sloop	Cutter	Ketch	Schooner
Force 4				
Force 5				
Force 6				
Force 7				

To *shake out* a reef, take up on the topping lift, ease the halyard, undo the reef points or lacing line, free the leech and luff cringles, take up on the halyard, ease the topping lift, retrim, and sail away.

On most modern sloops with relatively large jibs and small mains, your initial sail reduction will be changing down to a smaller jib, followed by a reef in the main. Sloops with relatively large mains will reef first, then change jibs. The object is to avoid shifting

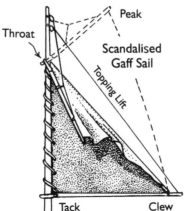

Peak
Throat
Scandalised Gaff Sail
Topping Lift
Tack   Clew

the centre of effort. With multi-masted boats, you have even more balancing options to choose from.

You can quickly reduce sail area in a gaff-rigged boat by *scandalising* the main, slacking off the peak halyard so the peak drops behind the sail. The large rectangular sail now becomes a much smaller triangle. Before doing this, make sure your topping lifts are set up to support the boom; otherwise the sail will be mercilessly stretched out of shape.

109

The Genoa

A sloop's *working sails* – a mainsail and a working jib that fills most of the *foretriangle* (the area between the forestay, deck and mast) – are its primary source of power. To get the most from your boat, though, you will need at least one other sail – a *genoa*.

The genoa, or *genny*, is a jib whose clew reaches *abaft* (aft of) the mast. Its size is designated as a percentage of the foretriangle. The smallest is a *lapper* at 110% (10% greater than the foretriangle); the largest is a *drifter* at 165% (65% greater). The genoa came into prominence after bringing about a dramatic win in the 1927 6-metre regatta in Genoa (hence the name), Italy. This win was the result of adding extra sail area to the jib that was not taxed by the rating rules. But the genoa is more than just a rule-beater. In light breezes there is no substitute for its expansive area, and overlapping sails can provide tremendous drive by enhancing the slot between the jib and main. On the other hand, they also block the helmsman's view forward, and their handling may require an extra crewmember.

A genoa's sheets are always led outside the shrouds. When tacking, the boat is turned more slowly and the leeward sheet released a little earlier to give the genoa more time to get its bulk around the mast and over to the other side. In light winds a crewmember may be needed to walk it around. When close-hauled the genoa should be trimmed to just miss touching the spreaders and shrouds, never rubbing against either.

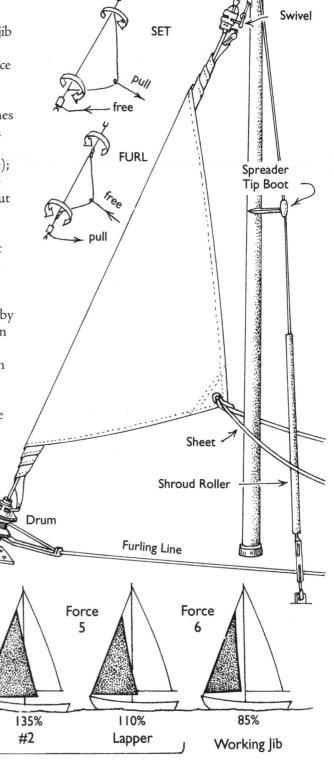

Roller Furling

SET

pull

free

FURL

free

pull

Swivel

Spreader Tip Boot

Sheet

Shroud Roller

Drum

Furling Line

Force 2 — 160% Drifter

Force 3 — 150% #1

Force 4 — 135% #2

Force 5 — 110% Lapper

Force 6 — 85% Working Jib

Genoas

The Spinnaker

An immutable law of the wind states that on a downwind course your apparent wind decreases as the boat's speed increases. There's no getting around it. If you want downwind speed, you have to add sail area to make up for the diminishing wind. Clipper captains knew this and piled on *studding sails* set from extended yards. Fishing schooners added giant *gollywobblers*. And we use *spinnakers* – baggy, lightweight sails designed for points of sail from a beam reach to a dead run.

The unusual name might have come from *spinmaker*, a sail set below the bowsprit on ships of the line, or from 1866 and the racing yacht *Sphinx* (colloquially pronounced 'spinks'), which flew a 'spinks' acre' of sail. This was eventually corrupted to spinnaker (also called a *chute*, for the parachute it resembles).

Not all boats need, nor do all sailors want, to use a spinnaker. It is a racing sail, requiring specialised gear and careful handling. It can be a beast with a mind of its own in strong winds, or a thing of joy and beauty in gentle breezes and a smooth sea. What makes the spinnaker so temperamental is its size (often greater than the jib and main combined) and the fact that it has no supporting spar or stay. The sail is connected to the boat only at its three corners, and depends on correct trim to stay up and spread to the wind. Even its terminology can be tricky, with some parts assuming different names according to the tack you are on.

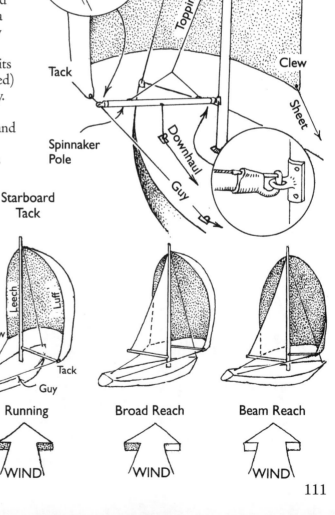

Swivel

Bowline or Snaphook

Forestay

Topping Lift

Clew

Tack

Sheet

Spinnaker Pole

Downhaul

Guy

Port Tack

Head

Shoulder

Luff — Leech

Leech — Leech

Clew

Tack

Guy

Sheet

Running

Foot

Clews

Sheets

Starboard Tack

Leech — Luff

Clew

Sheet

Tack

Guy

Running

Broad Reach

Beam Reach

WIND

WIND

WIND

WIND

HOISTING & DOUSING

The success of a spinnaker launch begins when it is carefully folded and stowed in a bag, bucket or box so there are no twists or snags when it is hoisted. Leave both clews and the head (label the corners) sticking out of the bag. Rig the sheets so they are outboard of all stays and shrouds, with their ends meeting just forward of the leeward shroud where the packed spinnaker is sitting on deck. Fasten the halyard and sheets to the sail using bowlines (page 147) or snap shackles.

Get the *spinnaker pole* ready by hooking the windward sheet (called the *guy*) through the pole's outboard end. Attach the topping lift and the downhaul (sometimes called a *foreguy*) if one is used. Clip the inboard end of the pole to the mast fitting, and hoist with the topping lift so the pole is horizontal.

When you're ready to hoist the sail, the helmsman puts the boat on a broad reach, and the crew hauls smartly at the halyard. Once up, the tack is pulled around to the pole with the guy, and the pole is squared to the wind as the sheet is eased out. Lower the jib, adjust the sheet, and sit back to watch her fly!

To douse, put up the jib and steer a broad reach. Make sure the halyard, sheet and guy are free to run. Haul the sheet in on the leeward side until you can grab the clew, then free the guy and let it run through the end of the pole. Gather in the sail on the leeward side of the boat so it is blanketed behind the main. Ease off the halyard as you pull the sail down, being careful not to get it tangled in the spreaders. Finally, bring the pole in by releasing it from the mast and then letting go the downhaul and topping lift.

Hoist Smartly!

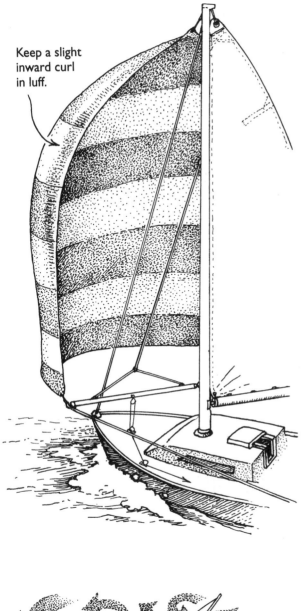

Keep a slight inward curl in luff.

TRIM

The spinnaker is controlled by its sheet, guy and topping lift. The sheet is the primary control, keeping the sail full and drawing. The guy controls the fore-and-aft position of the pole, which should be kept perpendicular to the wind. The topping lift (balanced by the downhaul) raises and lowers the pole, which should be held close to horizontal and adjusted so the sail's tack is at the same height as its clew.

Spinnakers are suspended by air, floating in the wind, seemingly alive and sensitive to even the slightest tweaking of their rigging. They demand constant attention. A well-trimmed spinnaker will ride high and ahead of the boat, with an evenly rounded shape. Watch the luff. Play the sheet so the luff has a very small curl in its shoulder. To find that point, ease the sheet until the luff curls, and then trim back a touch.

The spinnaker's size and power give it a great effect on steering. Sheeted in too tight, it may cause excessive weather helm, which in high winds can overwhelm the rudder, leading to a broach with a sudden rounding up into the wind. If the sheet is eased too far out or the pole brought too far aft, the sail develops a sideways force that can heel the boat to windward in a gust or cause rhythmic rolling.

Spinnaker handling is an art. Use what is here to get you started. After that, study and sail with those who know. Learn in calm winds and seas with a well-choreographed crew. Practise.

Wind Flow

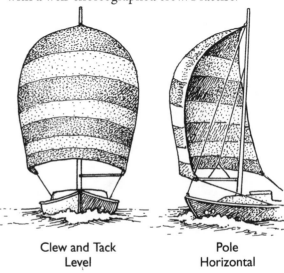

Clew and Tack Level

Pole Horizontal

113

GYBING

To gybe a spinnaker you shift the pole from one side to the other. Since the main must be brought around at the same time, it takes planning and teamwork. A small daysailer is a good place to start, learning the *double-ended pole gybe* before graduating to larger boats and more difficult techniques.

Put the boat on a downwind run. On the command 'Prepare to gybe', unhook the pole from the mast and clip the freed end to the sheet (which will become the new guy). The pole is now *double-ended*, with each end clipped to a sheet. At the same time the main is hauled all the way in. On the command 'Gybe ho!' the boat is steered over onto the new tack, and the pole is released from the original guy (which will now become the new sheet) and once more secured to the mast. Meanwhile, the spinnaker sheets must be played to keep the chute flying, and the main must be allowed to run out under control on the opposite side of the boat. As you can imagine, it takes practice.

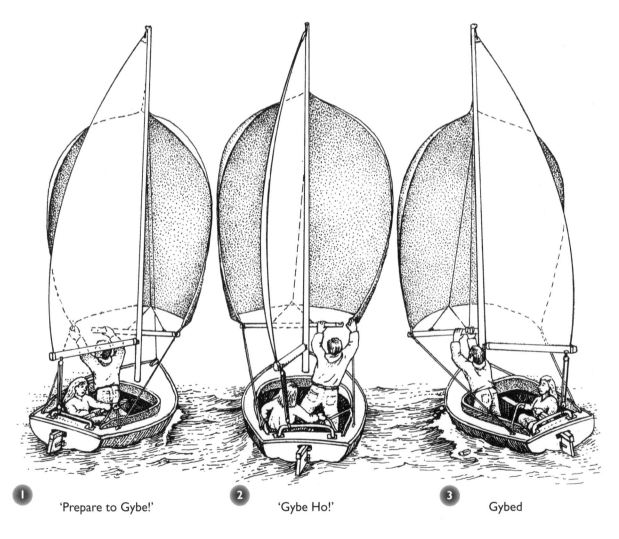

1 'Prepare to Gybe!'   **2** 'Gybe Ho!'   **3** Gybed

Sail Care

NEW SAILS: Sails appreciate gentle treatment when new. Start them on a broad reach in light winds for an hour or two. Creases and leech flutter in a new sail will often disappear if given time to settle in.

HANDLING: Sharp folds or creases break down the fabric's filler and reduce the life of the sail. Don't stuff sails into their bags or step on them, and always furl with care. Never let sails flog unnecessarily. This breaks down fibres, wears away stitching, and causes battens to break or poke through their pockets.

ULTRAVIOLET LIGHT: Prolonged exposure to sunlight destroys sails. UV-damaged Dacron feels dry and brittle, like parchment, tearing easily. Keep sails bagged or under sail covers when not in use. A good sail cover for the main is waterproof as well as lightproof, with a tight collar around the mast and open along its bottom to allow air to circulate. Roller-furling genoas should have protective panels sewn to the leech and foot that cover the sail when furled.

CHAFE: Stitching is particularly susceptible on Dacron sails because it sits on top of the material, not embedded as with canvas. Mainsails can rub against the lee spreader and shrouds if not trimmed properly. Their leeches can be worn by the topping lift, and battens are always chafing away in their pockets. Genoas, when close-hauled, can rub against spreader tips, shrouds, lifelines and turnbuckles. Watch cotter pins in turnbuckles, exposed screw heads and broken wire strands. Chafing patches can be sewn on problem areas of the sail, but it is always better to remedy the cause.

You will need a palm, Dacron sail thread, beeswax, and a selection of needles (page 144). Darn the tear with a *herringbone stitch*. Double the thread, then run it across the wax a few times. Start an inch or two beyond the tear to anchor the stitches in good cloth. Put in about six stitches per inch without drawing them so tight that the fabric puckers. To finish, tie off with a half hitch and tuck the thread back under the stitches.

WASHING: Sails used in salt water should be hosed down frequently with fresh water. Salt retains moisture that can corrode metal fittings and cause mildew (which, while harmless to Dacron, is unsightly). Salt crystals are also an abrasive. Never wash your sails in a washing machine, put them in a dryer, or iron them. Spread the sail out on clean concrete, gently scrub using a mild soap and warm water, and rinse several times to wash away the soap. Hang to dry. Consult your sailmaker on how to remove tough stains. Don't experiment.

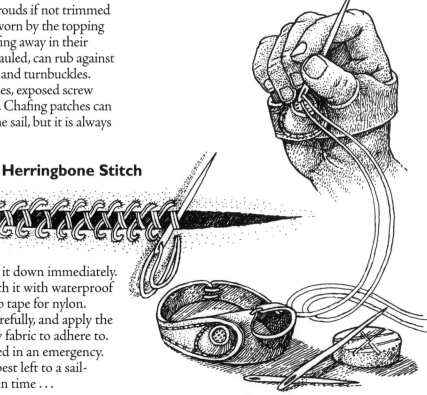

Herringbone Stitch

Knot
End

REPAIRS: When a sail rips, get it down immediately. If you have to use the sail, patch it with waterproof sail tape for Dacron, or ripstop tape for nylon. Match the edges of the tear carefully, and apply the tape so it has plenty of healthy fabric to adhere to. Duct or carpet tape can be used in an emergency. Repairing a tear by sewing is best left to a sailmaker, but very often a stitch in time . . .

UNDER POWER

'He was now convinced that the most valuable sail on board was the diesel.'
Ray Kauffman, *Hurricane's Wake*

Sailors don't like to admit it, but sailing boats are nearly helpless for more than a quarter of the time they are underway. Calms, currents and foul winds are the enemy, making worthy opponents if you take the time to engage them. Time, then, is the problem.

Sailing boats are lavish with time in a way that approaches decadence. A boat under sail might take you nowhere fast and get you back when it will. The sailors of the past knew that time and tide wait for no one and couldn't care less for our vanities. They learned patience, and in that way became masters of time.

Today the game of wind, water and sail can still be played to the full if yours is a small, handy vessel and you don't have to show up for work on Monday. The rest of us must stack the cards in our favour with fuel and metal. Others have no choice. There may be crowded or narrow channels to negotiate, bridges to pass through, or marinas to dock in. For some, it's security: When all else fails there is the 'iron wind'.

Once you choose to have an engine on board – and most of us do – you had better learn its ways. For, like sails, the engine repays in kind.

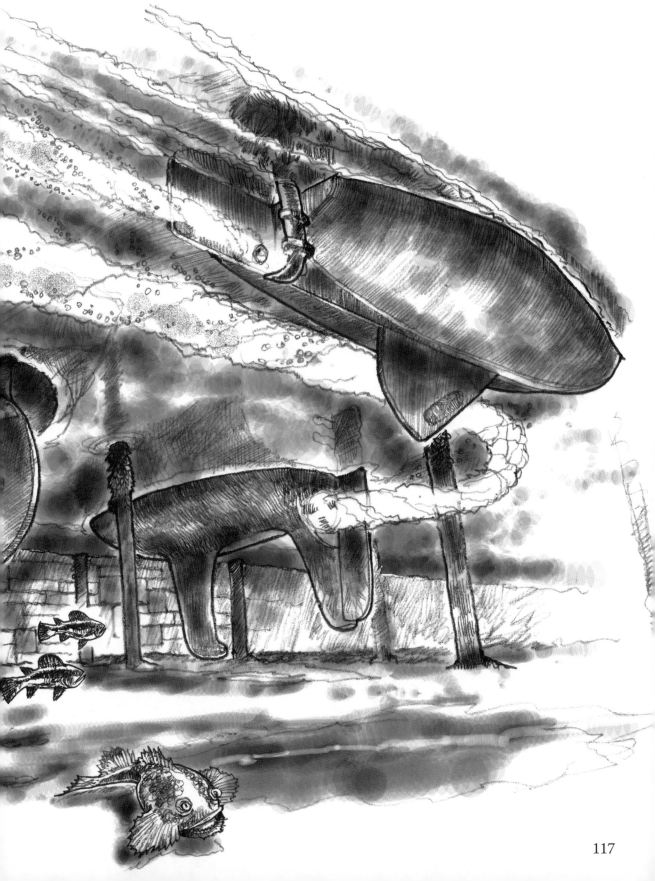

Inboards

You might think that if you could manage a boat under sail, driving it under power would be child's play. Well, it's not. In fact it's full of surprises.

The biggest surprise is that inboard engines can cause a boat to go sideways as well as forward and back. This secondary effect is called *side thrust*, a tendency for the boat's stern to *walk* in the direction of the propeller's spin. It is caused by unequal blade pressure from the prop rotating on an inclined shaft. Most props are right-handed, rotating clockwise as seen from behind when going forward. This makes a boat's stern walk to starboard, and the bow veer to port. When going astern, the prop's rotation reverses, and the stern will walk to port.

The more water flowing over a rudder, the more effective the rudder becomes. Therefore, a boat can be made more responsive to its helm by going faster through the water or by increasing the velocity of the prop's stream. Since the usual location for the propeller is just ahead of the rudder, both can occur when a boat is going forward, making her relatively easy to steer. When going astern, however, there is no propeller stream over the rudder, making the boat harder to turn.

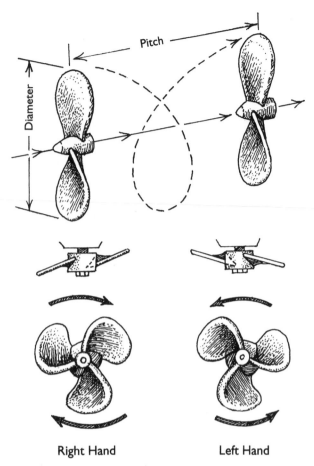

Right Hand **Left Hand**

Right-Hand Prop Forward

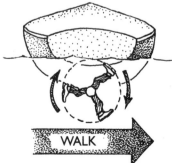

WALK

For a boat with a right-handed prop:

STOPPED
Power ahead: stern to starboard
Power in reverse: stern to port

AHEAD
Some starboard rudder to go straight
Tighter turns made to port

ASTERN
Side thrust most noticeable
Easier to turn to port
May not turn to starboard
Difficult to go in straight line
Rudder ineffective at slow speeds

Right-Hand Prop Reversed

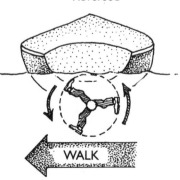

WALK

MANOEUVRING

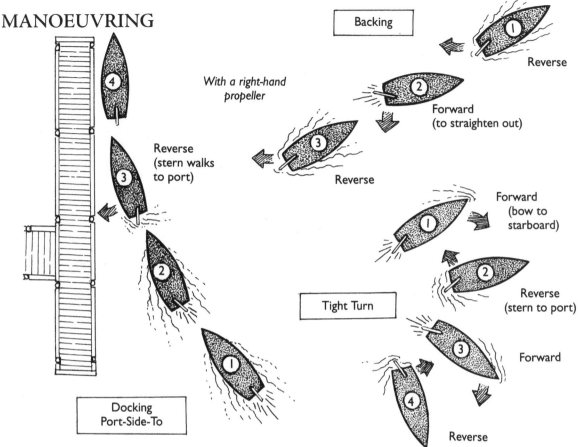

Backing

Reverse

Forward (to straighten out)

Reverse

With a right-hand propeller

Reverse (stern walks to port)

4

3

2

1

Forward (bow to starboard)

Reverse (stern to port)

Tight Turn

Forward

Reverse

Docking Port-Side-To

To dock with a right-handed prop, bring her port-side-to. Approach at a shallow angle, keeping just enough forward momentum to maintain steerage. As you get close, turn the boat almost parallel to the dock, then give the engine a short burst in reverse to stop her and walk the stern in.

Always come in slowly and under control. Don't depend on full engine power to stop her. Sailing boats have small props that take time to grip the water.

Turn to starboard when needing to make a tight turn with little way on in a confined area. Put the rudder hard to starboard and give a short burst forward. The bow will swing to starboard. Before the boat gains too much headway, give a short burst in reverse. This will stop your forward motion and swing the stern to port. With repeated bursts ahead and in reverse, while holding the rudder to starboard, the boat can be pivoted in a tight space.

Since the bow will want to fall off downwind, always turn with the wind, not against it. Turns

into the wind are slow, wide, or even impossible in strong winds.

To back up in a straight line, increase speed slowly to keep stern swing to a minimum and give the rudder a chance to overcome it. Hold the rudder slightly to starboard when backing. Even so, the stern will most likely want to veer toward port. Before you get too far to port, put the engine in forward, turn the rudder to port, and apply a strong short burst of power. This will bring the stern back in line without losing too much sternway, so you can continue backing. Repeat as necessary.

The boat can be run under power and sail at the same time. In bad weather this may be the only way to make progress to windward. The sails take some of the burden off the engine, and the motor keeps the boat from being held back by waves. When motoring in light winds, keep the sails up to reduce rolling and take advantage of the enhanced apparent wind.

Outboards

Outboard power makes sense on boats under 28 feet. Compared with inboard engines, outboard motors are light for their power, less expensive, easier to maintain, take up little or no room in the boat, and can be raised to eliminate drag while sailing.

Some outboards have been designed for use on sailing boats, but most aren't. Sailing boat outboards are geared down to use a propeller more suitable for moving a displacement hull through the water than a planing one over it. The best prop for sailing boat service has the largest diameter and least amount of pitch that will still keep the engine's rpm within a safe, usable range. An outboard used on a sailing boat should have a long shaft (20 inches), not the standard short shaft (15 inches). This helps the prop remain in the water even when the boat is dancing on the wave tops.

Outboards handle differently from inboards. Since the prop is vertical there is little if any side thrust, and what there is can usually be removed by adjusting the motor's trim. Their smaller, high-revving propellers have less bite, so they require more time to get the boat going and to stop it. The prop's grip is further diminished in reverse by the exhaust gases exiting through its hub, forcing it to spin in aerated water. With an outboard you can steer by rudder alone, or you can use the motor for sharper turns going forward and precise control when backing up.

Forward

Reverse

Docking with an Outboard

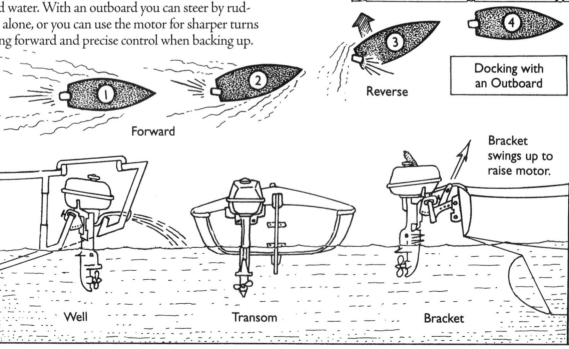

Well

Transom

Bracket

Bracket swings up to raise motor.

Oars

Before the iron wind, there was the 'ash breeze'. Up until the last century, oars pulled the largest ships in calms and smaller vessels whenever needed. In reduced size and made of precious metals, the oar was the symbol of power, held by those of authority in port cities. Oars still make sense. They are quiet, cheap, and always start when you need them. If you occasionally have to move your boat when there is no wind, oars might be the most practical way.

Small open craft can be rewarding to row if properly set up for it. Secure seating, low freeboard and moderate beam make for good rowing, but most important are oars of the right length. A 10-foot dinghy needs 6-foot oars, while a 16-foot skiff might do well with 8-foot oars, and a 20-foot boat with 9-foot oars.

When rowing, have good foot braces to push against – letting your back and legs do the work, not your arms alone. In smooth water use long, slow strokes; in a chop use short, quick strokes. If you can, lower the sailing rig to reduce windage. In deeper boats you may have to row fisherman style: standing up, facing forward and pushing rather than pulling. For much larger boats you may have to stand and row with one long oar (a *sweep*) and steer with the rudder. Fortunately, sailing boats need very little power to keep them moving at low speeds, and one person can keep a 24-footer going in a calm.

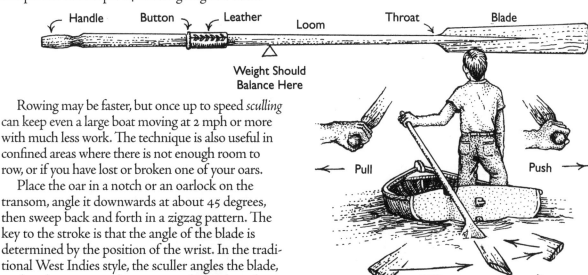

Handle   Button   Leather   Loom   Throat   Blade

Weight Should Balance Here

Pull ←   → Push

Rowing may be faster, but once up to speed *sculling* can keep even a large boat moving at 2 mph or more with much less work. The technique is also useful in confined areas where there is not enough room to row, or if you have lost or broken one of your oars.

Place the oar in a notch or an oarlock on the transom, angle it downwards at about 45 degrees, then sweep back and forth in a zigzag pattern. The key to the stroke is that the angle of the blade is determined by the position of the wrist. In the traditional West Indies style, the sculler angles the blade, pushes the oar away, then reverses the angle and pulls the oar back, all in a smooth, rhythmic motion.

121

RULES OF THE ROAD

'From an early age, the child is told "watch where you are going!" Good advice'.
Roger C. Taylor, *Elements of Seamanship*

It's surprising, but more often than you'd expect two people crossing an open field from opposite directions will bump into each other. It happens. And for thousands of years ships have been heading out to sea and doing very much the same thing. Coast Guard figures tell us that of all the accidents possible on the water, we prefer (by 51%) to ram into each other. This is not good.

To save us from ourselves, there are the International Regulations for Preventing Collisions at Sea (COLREGS), as well as the United States Inland Rules. They cover all watercraft and delineate, in no uncertain terms, your responsibilities. If you are to sail you *must* know these rules, for nothing 'shall exonerate any ... master or crew ... from the consequences of the neglect to comply with these rules'. Ignorance is no defence.

The rules are there to guide the wise and protect the foolish. Yet they do not release you from the obligation of practising good seamanship in doing whatever is necessary to ensure the safety of your vessel.

By all means keep a good lookout, for at sea eternal vigilance is the price of safety. Look and listen, and react according to the rules. When all else fails, have the good sense to behave as lawyers do: Forget about right or wrong, and give way.

Right of Way

UNDER POWER

A sailing boat is considered a powerboat whenever her engine is running, even though her sails may also be up.

When two boats converge, one, and only one, has the right of way. That boat is said to be the *stand-on* vessel and must maintain its course and speed so the other vessel can predict its movements. The other boat is the *give-way* vessel and must take early and positive action to keep clear. The only exception is when meeting head on. Here both boats are required to take evasive action, preferably by turning to starboard and passing port to port.

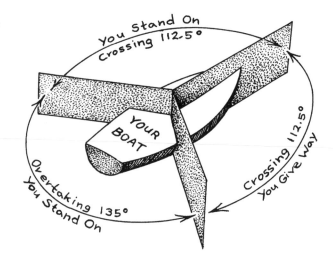

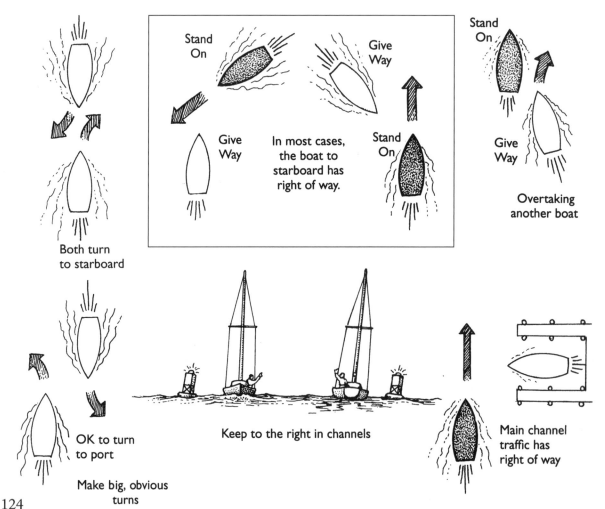

Both turn to starboard

Stand On / Give Way / Give Way / Stand On

In most cases, the boat to starboard has right of way.

Stand On / Give Way

Overtaking another boat

OK to turn to port

Make big, obvious turns

Keep to the right in channels

Main channel traffic has right of way

UNDER SAIL

Generally, sail has right of way over power. This will not be so if the sailing boat is overtaking a power vessel. A powered vessel may also have the right of way if its ability to manoeuvre is in some way limited. The order of privilege is vessels that are: disabled; difficult to manoeuvre (a dredge); constrained by excessive draught (tankers); and engaged in commercial fishing (trawlers). Next come sailing boats, and then power. The rule is that those with more manoeuvrability must give way to those with less.

Rights of way between boats under sail can be reduced to three basic rules.

1. Starboard tack has the right of way over port tack.

2. When on the same tack, the leeward boat has the right of way.

3. The overtaking boat must stay clear of the boat ahead.

Always heave-to on starboard tack to retain right of way.

Starboard tack has right of way.

Same Tack: Leeward boat has right of way.

Stand On

Give Way

Sail over Power

Stand On

Give Way

Give Way

Overtaking

Avoiding Collisions

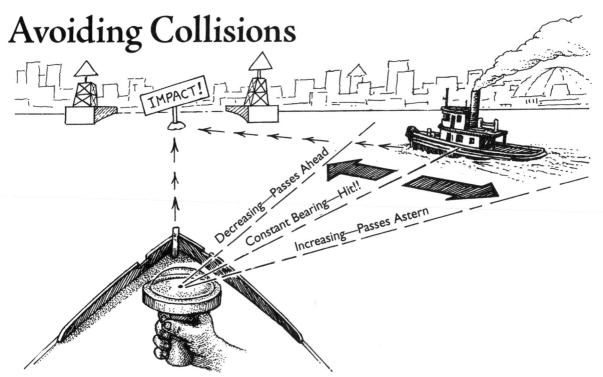

You should try to keep from hitting anything at all costs. Avoidance starts long before an incident occurs by maintaining a good lookout. Continually sweep a full 360 degrees; if there are blind spots, occasionally change course to take a look around them. And listen.

When converging with another boat, check for the likelihood of a collision by taking frequent compass bearings (page 197) of that vessel. If the bearings are constant, you are on a collision course. If the bearings decrease, she will pass in front of you; and if they increase, she will pass astern. When you can't take compass bearings, judge the other boat's position relative to the land behind it, or by sighting along a shroud or stanchion on your boat.

If yours is the give-way vessel, always take action early and in such a manner that your intentions are obvious to the stand-on boat. Make big course changes, slow down, or stop. The object is to remove any ambiguity from your actions.

Be careful of large ships. They are almost always going much faster than they seem to be. They probably can't see you, usually can't stop in time to keep from running you down, and might not know if they did. Stay away.

Finally, the rules require that you 'Use all available means . . . to determine if a risk of collision exists. If there is any doubt, such risk shall be deemed to exist'. As Descartes put it, '*Dubito ergo sum*' (I doubt, therefore I am). Carve it in your tiller.

But can HE see YOU?

Sound Signals

You must have a horn on board for signalling. Hand-held, pressurised-air horns are excellent. Where stowage is limited, use the 'mini' ones made for bicycles. Do not use horns or whistles that you blow into. They haven't enough clout to be heard at a useful range. A short blast is 1 second; prolonged, 4 to 6. Boats over 12 metres long must also carry a bell to be sounded when anchored or aground in reduced visibility (page 173).

One of the few places that the International and Inland Rules differ is regarding sound signals.

Under International Rules, a signal indicating a steering action to port or starboard requires no response from the other vessel. Under the Inland Rules, these signals require the other boat to respond with the same signal to show it accepts the intended action, or by giving the danger signal (five short blasts) to reject it.

Lines of demarcation separate the authority of International and Inland Rules. They are shown as a dashed magenta line on charts, usually between headlands or across harbour mouths.

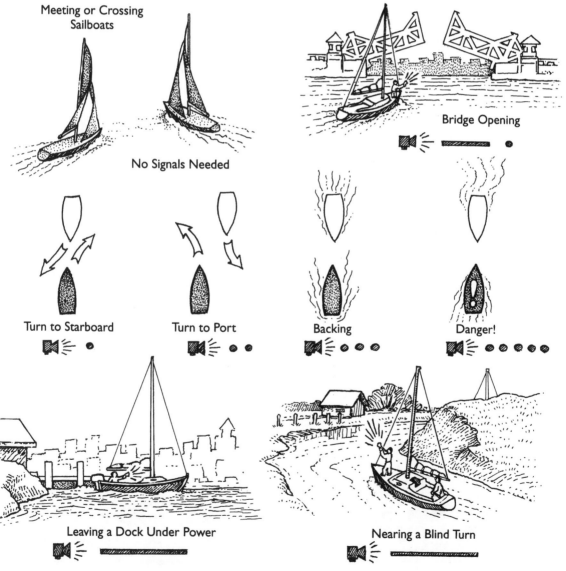

Meeting or Crossing Sailboats

No Signals Needed

Bridge Opening

Turn to Starboard

Turn to Port

Backing

Danger!

Leaving a Dock Under Power

Nearing a Blind Turn

Lights & Shapes

Navigation lights (or *running lights*) are required on all moving, and some stationary, boats between sunset and sunrise or in times of poor visibility. *Day shapes* are forms carried in the rigging to signify something that affects the boat's right of way and might not otherwise be obvious.

Navigation lights correspond with a boat's right-of-way sectors as seen on page 124. From the bow back 112.5 degrees on the starboard side, the running light shows green. There is a similar red light to port and a 135-degree white light astern.

If you are unsure who has the right of way when under power, during the day or night, look at the running lights of the approaching boat or your own. Port is red (remember: port wine is red), which means give way; starboard is green, which means stand on. What you see on the other boat is how you should react. What they see on yours is what they should do.

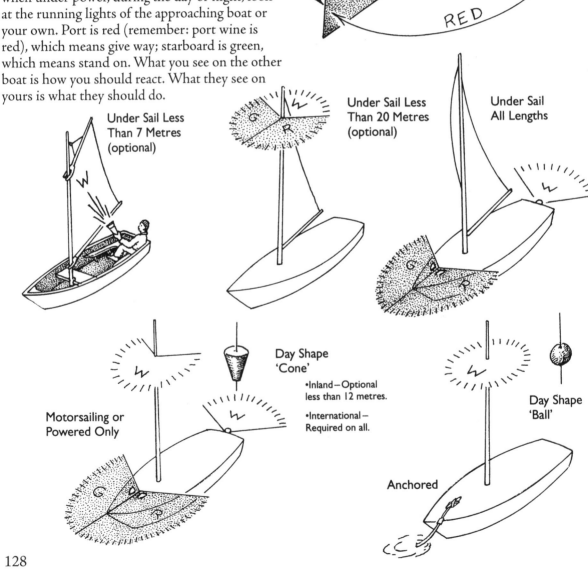

Under Sail Less Than 7 Metres (optional)

Under Sail Less Than 20 Metres (optional)

Under Sail All Lengths

Motorsailing or Powered Only

Day Shape 'Cone'
- Inland – Optional less than 12 metres.
- International – Required on all.

Anchored

Day Shape 'Ball'

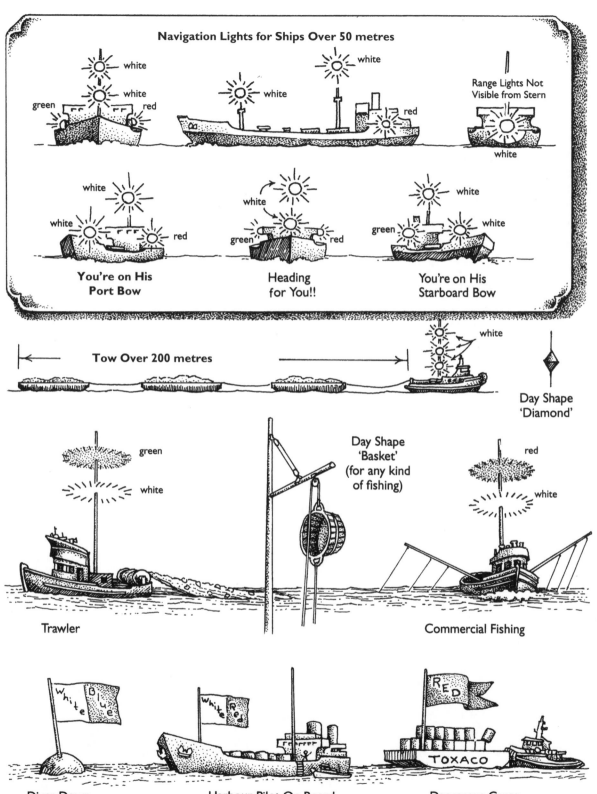

Navigation Lights for Ships Over 50 metres

white
white
green red

white

white
red

Range Lights Not Visible from Stern
white

white
white red

white
green red

green white
white

You're on His Port Bow

Heading for You!!

You're on His Starboard Bow

white

◄── **Tow Over 200 metres** ──►

Day Shape 'Diamond'

green
white

Day Shape 'Basket' (for any kind of fishing)

red
white

Trawler

Commercial Fishing

white blue

white red

RED

TOXACO

Diver Down

Harbour Pilot On Board

Dangerous Cargo

129

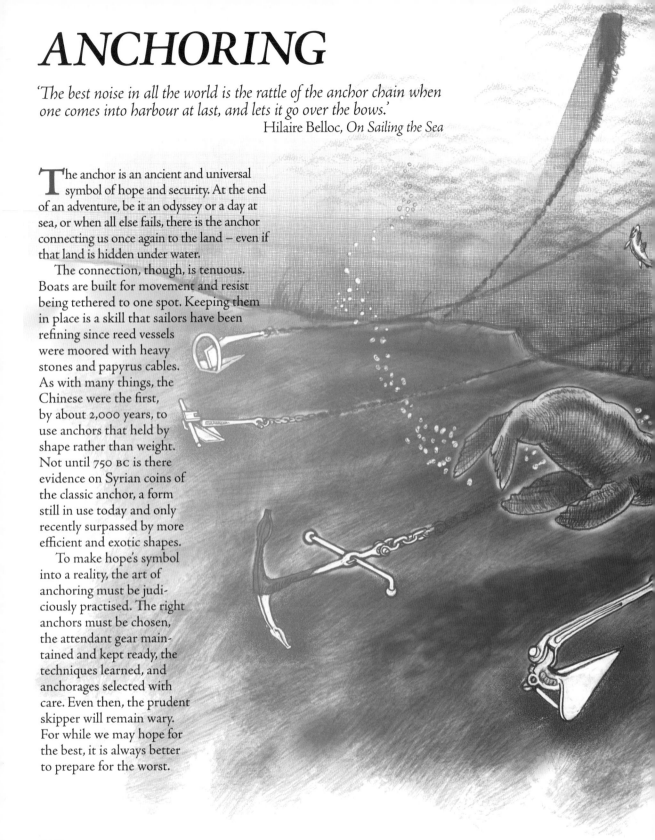

ANCHORING

'The best noise in all the world is the rattle of the anchor chain when one comes into harbour at last, and lets it go over the bows.'
Hilaire Belloc, *On Sailing the Sea*

The anchor is an ancient and universal symbol of hope and security. At the end of an adventure, be it an odyssey or a day at sea, or when all else fails, there is the anchor connecting us once again to the land – even if that land is hidden under water.

The connection, though, is tenuous. Boats are built for movement and resist being tethered to one spot. Keeping them in place is a skill that sailors have been refining since reed vessels were moored with heavy stones and papyrus cables. As with many things, the Chinese were the first, by about 2,000 years, to use anchors that held by shape rather than weight. Not until 750 BC is there evidence on Syrian coins of the classic anchor, a form still in use today and only recently surpassed by more efficient and exotic shapes.

To make hope's symbol into a reality, the art of anchoring must be judiciously practised. The right anchors must be chosen, the attendant gear maintained and kept ready, the techniques learned, and anchorages selected with care. Even then, the prudent skipper will remain wary. For while we may hope for the best, it is always better to prepare for the worst.

131

Ground Tackle

The anchor and all the gear attached to it are collectively known as *ground tackle*. Each component should provide an ample margin of strength to avoid that disastrous weak link. Start by choosing your anchors.

If you only daysail or race, returning within a few hours to the same mooring, you can get by with one anchor. Once you start roaming, you'll need two anchors, and serious cruisers will want at least three.

Your main anchor, the *bower*, is kept ready for immediate use at the bow and should be strong enough to hold you overnight in moderate conditions. Your second anchor, called a *kedge*, should be an easily handled lightweight providing backup to the bower. Last is the *sheet* anchor, your heaviest, for storms and conditions you hope to never see.

Choose the type of anchor according to the bottom conditions you are most likely to anchor in. Then look to the manufacturer's tables for the right anchor weight – always erring on the heavy side for safety. The most successful anchors have been:

Fisherman. The classic anchor. The pickaxe flukes make it one of the few that can grip rocky or coral bottoms, or penetrate thick grass. The anchor hooks into the bottom rather than burying, so it needs to be heavy to do the job. It is awkward to handle and difficult to stow.

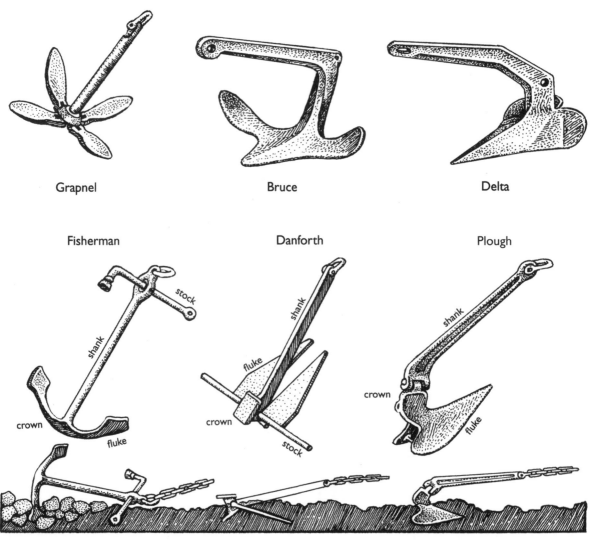

Grapnel   Bruce   Delta

Fisherman   Danforth   Plough

Danforth. Extremely lightweight for its holding power – which is phenomenal in thick mud, sand, clay and gravel, but poor in weeds and rocks. It may accidentally break out if wind or current reverses. It stows flat on deck and is a good all-round anchor for small craft.

Plough. Like the farmer's instrument it resembles, this anchor burrows its way in. It holds as well as the Danforth (although heavier) in the same conditions, and it has a better chance of staying dug in if the boat swings. Ploughs do not work well in rocks or thick weeds. They are difficult to stow and are most often seen in special roller chocks on the bows of boats over 24 feet.

Whichever anchor you choose, it will be shackled to chain, nylon line (called *rode* when used with an anchor), or a combination of the two. Chain is chafe-proof and its weight holds it to the bottom, giving a near horizontal pull. But that same weight restricts its use to larger boats. It is hard to handle without a *windlass* (winch) and is messy and comparatively expensive.

Nylon rode is light, easy to handle, can be spliced, cushions shocks by stretching, and does not bring up bottom grime, but it is susceptible to chafing. Since a rode's elasticity is of prime importance, use only *three-strand laid* (twisted), not *braided*, line; and avoid using line that is too thick. A good compromise is 6 to 12 feet of chain leading from the anchor, followed by nylon rode from the chain to the boat.

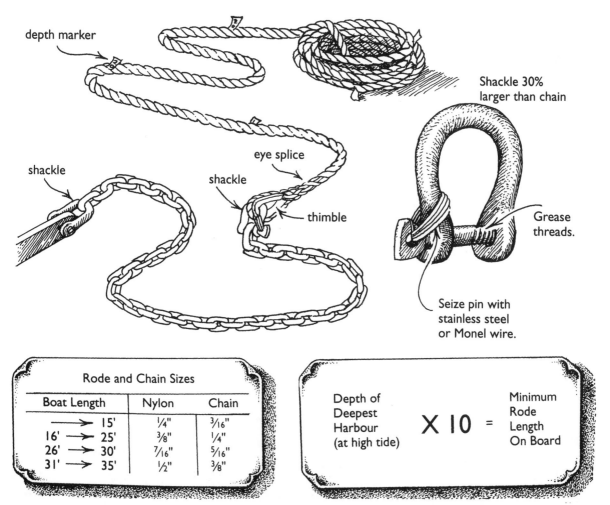

depth marker

Shackle 30% larger than chain

shackle

shackle

eye splice

thimble

Grease threads.

Seize pin with stainless steel or Monel wire.

Rode and Chain Sizes		
Boat Length	Nylon	Chain
→ 15'	1/4"	3/16"
16' → 25'	3/8"	1/4"
26' → 30'	7/16"	5/16"
31' → 35'	1/2"	3/8"

Depth of Deepest Harbour (at high tide) **X 10** = Minimum Rode Length On Board

Scope is the ratio of anchor line length to the distance of the bow above the bottom. Since anchors work best when the pull is nearly horizontal, proper scope is important. The right scope also helps to absorb shock loads by enhancing nylon's elasticity and giving chain a deeper *catenary* (sag). When computing scope, consider the state and range of the tide so you won't get caught short.

For ground tackle that combines a length of chain and nylon rode, a scope of 5:1 is the absolute minimum – you let out 5 feet for every foot of water depth plus bow height. A scope of 7:1 is satisfactory for average conditions with winds under 15 mph, and 10:1 for storms. With all-chain tackle, 3:1 is generally safe, with 7:1 for storm conditions. In all cases more scope helps. When your anchor begins to drag, the first thing to do is to *veer out* (let out) more scope. Only after that fails should you get the anchor up, clear its flukes of mud, rocks, shells or weed, and try to reset it.

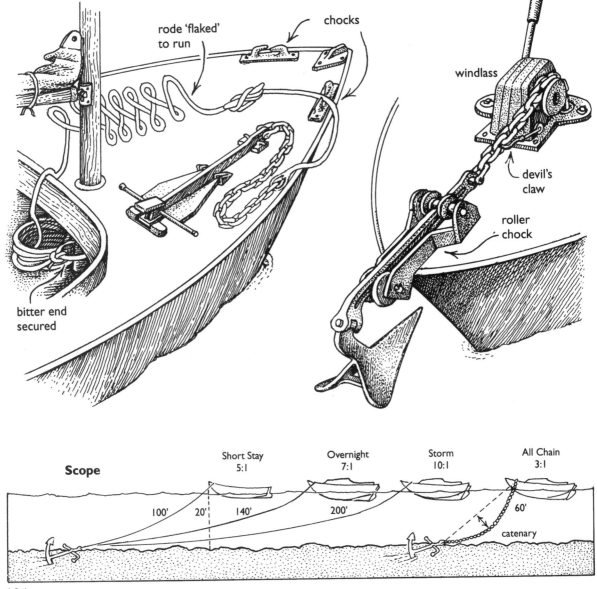

The Anchorage

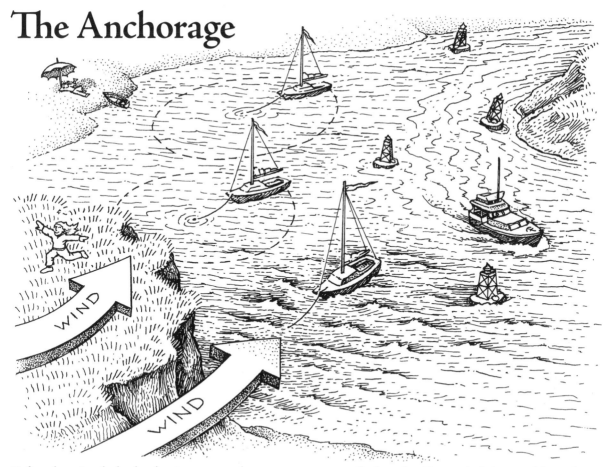

Before *dropping the hook*, take time to see what you are getting yourself into. Study the chart first, and note the bottom characteristics. Clay and mud make for good holding; soft mud (silt), gravel and loose sand do not. Hard sand and weeds may not let the flukes dig in, and rocks or grass may foul them. Inspect depth contours and the charted locations of underwater cables, moorings, wrecks or snags. Don't anchor in a channel. Charts also show land features that could either block winds or funnel them. If you are staying for a while, consider the rise and fall of the tide, and what sort of currents this will bring. Let out enough scope for the highest tide. And listen to a weather forecast to see if the wind will pick up or shift, leaving you anchored off a dangerous lee shore.

Be choosy about where you anchor. After arriving at the anchorage, sail around for a while. Study the force and direction of the winds, and watch for naturally created waves and those from passing boats. Pick a spot that is protected and shallow enough so you don't need a lot of rode for the right scope, but not so shallow or near a shoal that you'll

ground when the tide or wind changes. Note where other boats are anchored and how they are sitting. Leave plenty of room between the nearest boats, at least two rode lengths. In congested areas anchor near boats of your own size and type, and anchor in the same way, so you will all swing together. The rule of the anchorage is that the earliest arrivals have priority. When anchors foul, or boats swing too close or hit, the last one in should be the one to move.

Anchoring takes time and effort, and no one will be too anxious to re-anchor if the spot you've chosen isn't right. So spend the time before lowering away. And if, when all is set, you don't really feel right about the spot, or you have a feeling that things might get rough and you'll want a second anchor, make your changes now – instead of in a squall at two in the morning.

Once anchored, fix your position relative to objects on shore and the boats near you, checking periodically to see if your anchor is dragging. When in doubt, take turns keeping an *anchor watch*. This way everyone gets at least some rest during the night.

135

Anchoring Under Sail

Enter the anchorage with the foredeck clear, the rode free, and the anchor ready to be lowered. Sail in slowly under working jib and main, or main only if she'll tack like that. It's all very much like coming up to a mooring. Your genoa should be down and secured (or bagged) so you can see ahead, tack quickly if necessary, and not have it underfoot.

Pick a spot four or five boat lengths upwind from where you want to lie. Luff up with jib and mainsheet free. When the boat has stopped, just as the bow begins to fall off, lower (don't drop or throw) the anchor. After it hits bottom, take a turn around the cleat and pay out line as you drift back. By keeping light resistance on the rode, you can feel the anchor bounce along the bottom until it digs in and the line becomes taut. To set the anchor, give it a sharp tug, then slowly let out the right scope, snub it again, backwind the main to put pressure on the anchor, and make fast. As a precaution, leave extra rode ready to veer out if you need to increase scope in an emergency.

Keep your fingers clear of chocks, cleats and windlasses. Always have at least one turn around the cleat or bitt to keep the rode under control. But if the line starts to run, let it go rather than lose a finger.

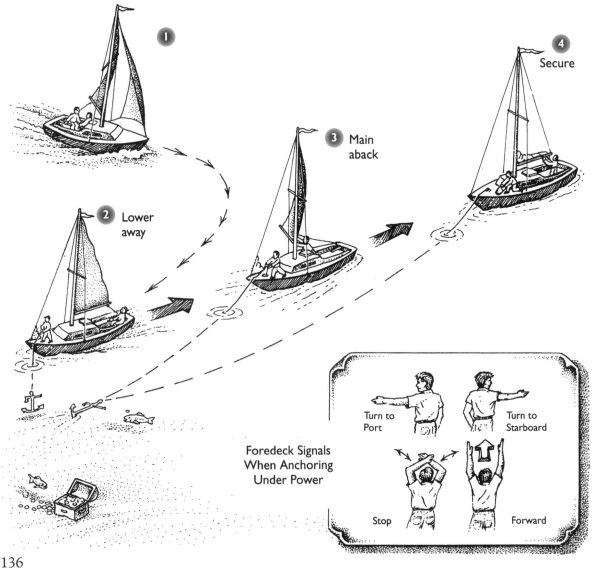

1

2 Lower away

3 Main aback

4 Secure

Foredeck Signals When Anchoring Under Power

Turn to Port

Turn to Starboard

Stop

Forward

A Second Anchor

'It is always well to moor your ship with two anchors.'
Publius Syrus, 50 BC

Putting out the kedge as a backup to your bower will reduce the boat's swing when wind or current changes, and give you a bit of insurance if the wind picks up. Sailors call this kind of security that lets them sleep peacefully through a stormy night as 'having an anchor to windward'.

If the wind is expected to continue from its present quarter, the best tactic is to lay out two anchors to divide the load. Set one off each bow with an angle between them of about 45 to 60 degrees. After the bower is set, the kedge can be sailed into place or rowed out and dropped from a dinghy.

When you expect a major wind or current shift, set the anchors 180 degrees from each other in a *Bahamian moor*. Island fishing smacks anchor this way in the cuts between small cays where the current follows the tide, often running against the prevailing trade winds. They also use it in crowded Nassau Harbor, reducing swing to little more than a boat length.

Some sailors like to set their second anchor off the stern. This eliminates all swinging and holds the boat in one spot, but can be dangerous if you are caught stern-to a rising wind.

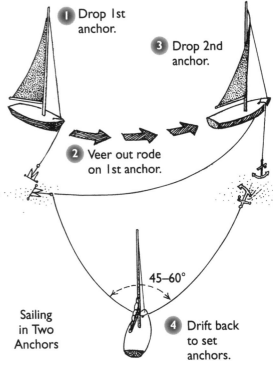

1. Drop 1st anchor.
3. Drop 2nd anchor.
2. Veer out rode on 1st anchor.
45–60°
4. Drift back to set anchors.

Sailing in Two Anchors

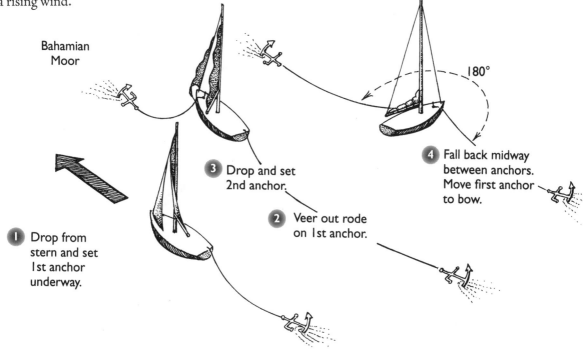

Bahamian Moor

1. Drop from stern and set 1st anchor underway.
2. Veer out rode on 1st anchor.
3. Drop and set 2nd anchor.
4. Fall back midway between anchors. Move first anchor to bow.
180°

Weighing Anchor

If a horizontal pull digs an anchor in, a vertical pull should break it out.

Prepare to get underway as you would from a mooring, with sails up and sheets free. Haul in on the rode until you are above the anchor, or slowly sail up to it on a luffing main. When the rode is *up and down* (vertical), the anchor is ready to be broken out. Choose your tack by bringing the rode to the opposite bow and preparing to back the jib to the same side. When her bow has swung over, *weigh* anchor (haul it free of the bottom) with a strong heave and begin pulling it in as fast as possible. Once up, hold the flukes away from your topsides, clean off any bottom muck, and stow for sailing. Pay off on the desired tack, staying in protected waters until the foredeck work is finished.

If the anchor will not break out easily, pull in as much rode as possible with everyone on board near the bow. Make the rode fast and then move quickly to the stern, using the boat's buoyancy to pry the anchor up. The waves from passing motorboats can also help lift the bow.

Stubborn anchors can be *sailed out* by tacking and gybing around a shortened rode to pull at the anchor from all sides until it comes loose. If still more force is needed, ease out plenty of rode. Then bear off under sail, building up speed and taking in rode as you go. Once abreast of the anchor, make the rode fast and come up hard against it. The sudden jerk will throw you onto the other tack while wrenching the anchor free.

In bottoms that might foul the anchor, rig a *trip line*, a strong, light line tied to the anchor's crown. The line is buoyed so it can be picked up and hauled on to overturn the anchor, thereby releasing it.

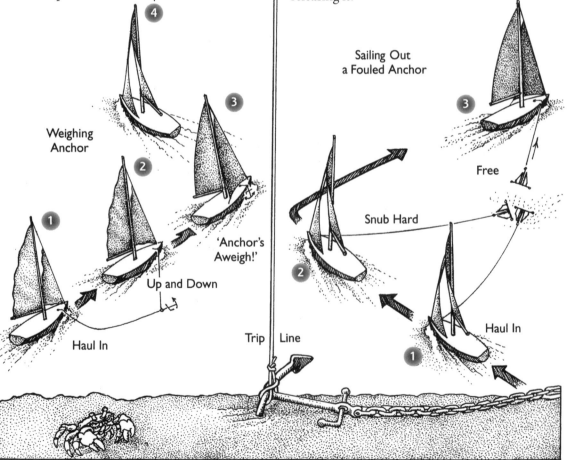

Weighing Anchor

'Anchor's Aweigh!'

Up and Down

Haul In

Sailing Out a Fouled Anchor

Free

Snub Hard

Haul In

Trip Line

Moorings

If an anchor is the symbol of hope, then a mooring is salvation. Moorings imply permanence. Once set, a mooring should be able to hold its ground regardless of the forces marshalled against it.

Moorings are often made from heavy weights such as a car engine or a cement block, but these are not dependable unless a great weight is used relative to the boat. A better option is the *mushroom anchor*, which uses its weight and shape to bury itself in the bottom, holding through suction. A 25-foot cruiser is safe with a 175-pound mushroom, while a lighter daysailer of the same length can get by with 125 pounds.

Modern anchors have given rise to other mooring options. In the storm-raked North Sea, oil rigs are held in place with multiple lightweight anchors. This mooring system is claimed to be stronger than a single mushroom and limits boat swing to an absolute minimum.

A mooring buoy lessens the downward pull of the chain, permitting the boat's bow to lift to oncoming waves. In many anchorages mooring buoys are required to be white with a horizontal blue band. All of the mooring's tackle, including the buoy, should be as strong as possible and overhauled at least once a year.

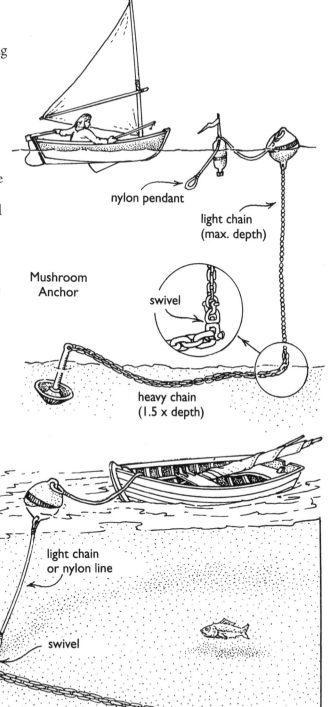

nylon pendant

light chain (max. depth)

Mushroom Anchor

swivel

heavy chain (1.5 x depth)

Multiple Lightweight Anchor Mooring

light chain or nylon line

swivel

heavy chain

MARLINSPIKE SEAMANSHIP

'Upon acquiring his first boat the embryo yachtsman discovers that its use is going to involve intimate, personal contact with rope and cordage, and to a far greater extent than he anticipated.'
Hervey Garrett Smith, *The Arts of the Sailor*

Ashore, the closest most of us come to ropework is tying our shoes or fumbling attempts with string around a parcel. In the Great Age of Velcro, rope, knots, and all the things done with them seem charmingly irrelevant. Then you step aboard a sailing boat and realise that the rules have changed.

It is surprising that rope handling has not been imprinted in our genes. Gorillas square-knot vines for their nests, and we, off on another branch of evolution, came to rope-making and knotting not long after learning to use sticks as weapons, and well before we learned the secret of fire. Remains of nets made with sheet bends dating back to 7800 BC have been found in Finland. It's in our blood. So it's unlikely that tying the occasional clove hitch will strain your abilities.

The comprehensive body of knowledge known as marlinspike seamanship (named for a unique tool of the trade) constitutes one of the highest and most pleasurable arts in the Academy of Seamanship. While the breadth of this art has diminished since the Golden Age of Sail, it still evokes an attitude that should never change, one that Joseph Conrad understood well: 'Of all the living creatures upon land or sea, it is ships alone that cannot be taken in by barren pretences, that will not put up with bad art from their masters'.

To become a sailor, you must learn the ropes.

141

Rope

MATERIAL

The greatest change in rope has been the introduction of man-made fibres. These have completely replaced natural fibres because they do not rot and have much higher breaking strengths. But they are slippery – making it harder for knots to hold – and prone to deterioration from ultraviolet light and abrasive grit held by the fibres.

Nylon is strong, elastic, and absorbs shock loads better than any other material. It is the most common of the modern ropes because it is so rugged. It is almost impervious to chemicals, able to withstand harsh handling, and has a pleasant, soft feel. It is ideal for docking, towing and mooring lines, and for anchor rodes.

Dacron (US) or *Terylene* (UK) are brand names for rope made of polyester. Not quite as strong as nylon, and about 15% heavier, it is more resistant to wear and chafe. It has minimum elasticity, particularly when pre-stretched during manufacturing. It is used for halyards, sheets and sail-control lines.

Polypropylene has one-third less tensile strength than nylon and the same ability to resist stretch as Dacron, but at half the price. It is easily chafed and, unless treated with UV inhibitors, degrades rapidly in sunlight. Cheaper commercial grades are very slippery and do not hold knots well. It is so light that it floats. It may be used for dinghy painters, man overboard equipment, sheets for light-air sails, and heaving lines.

Newer exotic materials include *Kevlar*, which is stronger than stainless steel for a given weight and has almost no stretch, and *Dyneema/Spectra*, which is lighter, slightly stronger, and more tolerant of flexing than Kevlar, but may elongate slightly under continuous strain. Both are easily abraded, susceptible to rapid degradation in ultraviolet light, and very expensive. They can be used as cores within braided ropes for halyards, sheets and sail-control lines.

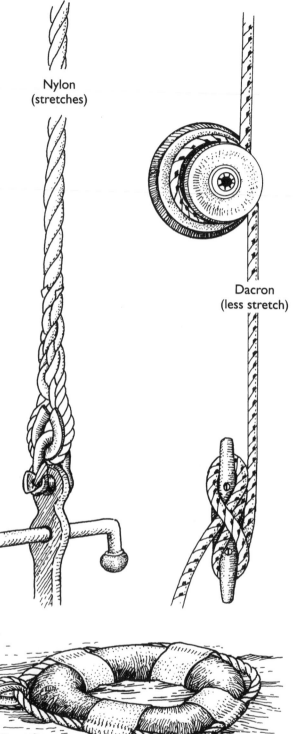

Nylon
(stretches)

Dacron
(less stretch)

Polypropylene
(floats)

142

CONSTRUCTION

The most common rope construction is *three-strand laid*. It is formed by twisting *fibres* into *yarn* and yarns into three *strands*, then laying the strands into rope. The next most popular is *double-braided* rope, which has an outer *sleeve* (cover or jacket) of braided fibres surrounding a similarly braided core. Less common are *single-braid*, which has no core and is often found in inexpensive rope that you might buy at a hardware store, and *parallel-core braided*, used for strong, ultra-low-stretch, high-tech materials.

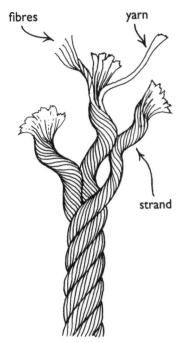

fibres   yarn

strand

Three-Strand Laid

THREE-STRAND LAID

+ Comparatively stiff and rigid
+ Makes a secure knot
+ Easy to splice
+ Maintains shape, runs through blocks easily
+ Shows wear and defects clearly
+ Costs less
+ Best for rugged uses such as anchor or docklines

DOUBLE-BRAIDED

+ Soft and pliable
+ Some knots may slip
+ Difficult to splice
+ Flattens under strain, holds better on winches
+ Hides defects of internal core
+ More expensive
+ Best for low-stretch uses such as halyards and sheets

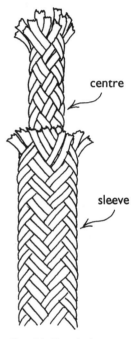

centre

sleeve

Double-Braided

SIZE

Rope is specified by its diameter. When measuring, don't compress the rope; it must be able to rotate slightly in the gauge. Rope that is to be handled often (such as sheets) should be ¼ inch in diameter or larger. Even if you don't need its strength, anything smaller will be too difficult to grasp and may cut flesh in a hard pull. *Line* (once a length has been cut from a bulk coil of rope it becomes line) that is less than ¼ inch is called *small stuff*, which is always handy to have about for odd jobs.

Diameter = Size

The Ditty Bag

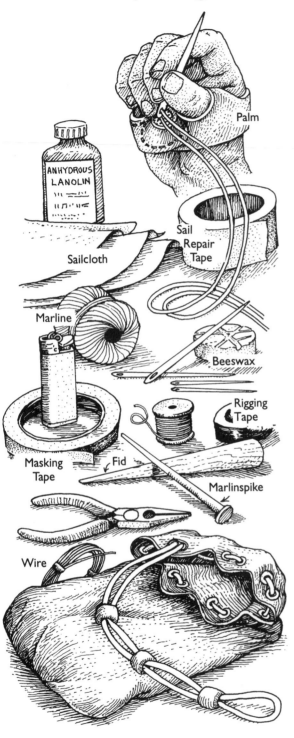

Palm

Anhydrous Lanolin

Sail Repair Tape

Sailcloth

Marline

Beeswax

Rigging Tape

Masking Tape

Fid

Marlinspike

Wire

For centuries sailors have kept their rope-working gear in small canvas drawstring *ditty bags*. Find a rugged bag that is about 12 inches deep and 8 inches wide. Within the bag are kept the basics for practising marlinspike seamanship. These should include:

Sailmaker's needles are graded by number, with the lowest being the largest in length and thickness. Purchase a full set, or have one needle that is big enough for heavy canvas- and ropework (#12), another fine enough for lightweight sail repair (#18), and a third for whipping and general stitching (#14 or #16).

A *palm* is used for pushing needles through heavy cloth or rope. Good ones are hard to find, most being stiff and roughly made. To improve yours, soak it in leather softener for a few days and adjust the strap so it just touches the back of your hand.

Thread for whipping or sail repairs should only be of nylon or Dacron, not cotton. If it can be found in sizes, use a #7 for whipping and #4 for most sailwork.

Beeswax should be a deep amber, soft, and resinous. Run doubled thread across beeswax to hold the separate strands together, making it easier to work with.

A *fid* is typically about 8 inches long and made of oak or hickory. It is used when splicing rope to push the strands apart and open a wide gap without harming individual fibres.

A *marlinspike* is made from steel, with a more gradual taper and smaller diameter than a fid. It is used in splicing wire.

A *lighter*, particularly a butane-powered one, can be used to temporarily heat-seal the end of a line in preparation for whipping (page 145).

To round out your kit you will also need ½-inch-wide *masking tape*, a pair of *needle-nose pliers*, some scraps of *sailcloth* and a wide roll of *sail repair tape*. *Anhydrous lanolin*, which can be found at any pharmacy, will give new life to leather and, when put on the threads of shackle pins, will keep them from freezing up. Also have a length of *Monel* or *stainless steel wire* for seizing shackle pins in place.

The most important tool in your ditty bag is your *knife*. A folding knife is convenient, but not absolutely rigid, while a sheath knife is stronger, and easier and safer to use.

The blade of a sailor's sheath knife should be short and stubby, gently curved along its edge, with a thick back and anti-slip finger grooves. It should have almost no point at the tip and, in cross section, a gradual taper towards the cutting edge. The blade should be made from a high-carbon steel. The handle must provide a non-slip grip in wet hands, have a hole for a lanyard that loops over your wrist, and be balanced where the forefinger touches the handle.

Dull knives are dangerous. Keep yours honed with a good two-sided sharpening stone of carborundum (silicon carbide). Use the smooth side for general sharpening and the rough for reshaping a damaged edge. To take the roughness from your edge, polish it on a natural Arkansas stone. Lubricate while sharpening with any light oil, such as 3-In-One Oil.

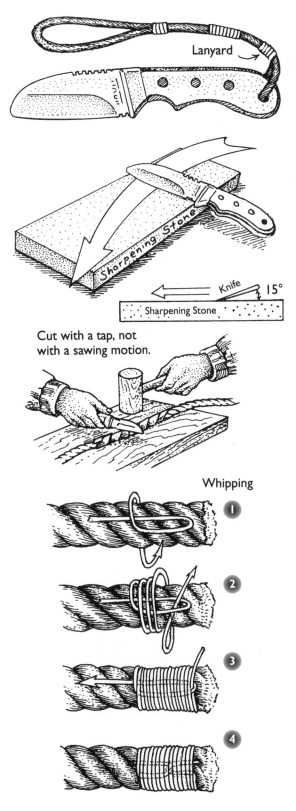

Cut with a tap, not with a sawing motion.

Whipping

CUTTING LINE

Tightly wrap the spot to be cut with tape covering a length four times the diameter of the rope. If the knife blade is sharp, and the line not too thick, pressure from the heel of your hand should be enough. If not, put the blade in place and hit its back with a piece of wood. Do not saw or hack your way through. The intent is to neatly sever the fibres without distorting or unravelling the strands. Once the rope is cut, heat-seal both ends with a lighter, remove the tape, and whip.

WHIPPING

The English used to refer to untidy rope-work aloft or frayed rope ends as either *Irish* or *Dutch pennants*, depending on the international ill winds of the moment. To prevent this embarrassment, and keep lines from unravelling in your hand, the ends must be finished off with a good, tight whipping.

1. Make a loop in a length of thread and lay it against the rope.

2. Wrap the thread as tightly as possible over the loop, working towards the rope's end.

3. After making enough wrapping turns so the whipping is at least equal to the rope's diameter, and going no closer than ⅜ inch to the rope's end, tuck the thread through the loop.

4. Pull firmly on the standing end of the thread to trap the working end midway underneath the turns of whipping. Cut off the exposed ends.

Knots

Using only the knots on the following pages, you could probably sail along without mishap for the rest of your life. There are others that are useful to know, but these few will be more than enough to get you started. They have proved practical, versatile and ideally suited to the jobs they do. As with all great knots, they are secure, so they will not slip or come apart; simple, so they are easy to tie; and will not jam, so they are easy to untie.

No matter how good a knot is, it can't do its job if it has been tied incorrectly. There are no partially correct knots. They are either completely right or all wrong. Follow the instructions, and match what you tie to the illustrations.

FIGURE-OF-EIGHT KNOT

Here's a knot that looks like its name. Since the knot creates a bulky mass, it is used at the ends of lines to prevent them from running out through blocks. Use this stopper knot at the ends of sheets, halyards, boom vangs, or any other line that passes through a fitting.

+ Loop the end of the line over itself, then pass it under, back over, and through the loop. Always alternate, over and under, to weave the knot into shape.

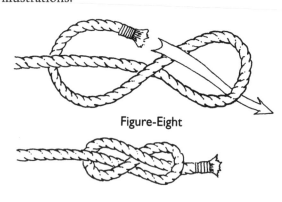

Figure-Eight

ROUND TURN & TWO HALF HITCHES

A *hitch* attaches a line to an object. Even if they've never tied anything before in their lives, most people instinctively use this hitch, and it will probably be the knot you resort to when you can't think of anything else. Use it to secure fenders to railings or docking lines to rings. Do not use it where there will be prolonged and extensive strain, as on anchor rodes, as it will jam.

1. Wrap the line around the object twice, so it completely encircles what you are tying to.

2–4. Make a half hitch around the standing part of the line, and then another in the same way. The two hitches should be identical.

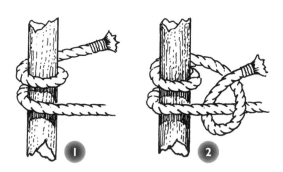

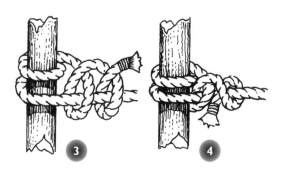

Round Turn and Two Half Hitches

BOWLINE

The bowline (pronounced 'bo-lin') is rightfully known as the king of knots. It is easy to tie and untie, increases its grip as tension is applied, and will never jam. It takes time and practice to learn, but the effort will be well rewarded. Use the bowline for attaching jibsheets and halyards to sails.

1. With your palm down, hold the working end between your fore- and index fingers, placing it over the standing part of the line. Grasp the standing part with your thumb.

2. Twist your wrist so your palm faces up and a loop has been formed in the line.

3. Pass the working end behind the standing part and then back through the loop. Remember, after the end passes under one part it must then pass over the next. Always alternating.

4. Before putting into service, snug the parts up to make sure they are set.

SHEET BEND

A *bend* joins two ropes. The worst way of doing this is with a square knot, which can slip or come apart. The best way is with the sheet bend. It is easy to tie, strong, secure, and works well with ropes of dissimilar sizes. If you are going to remember one bend, this is it.

1. Make a loop in the end of one rope. If one line is heavier than the other, make the loop in it. Pass the end of the other rope through and around the loop as shown.

2. The working end should exit the knot on the same side as the loop's short-ended side.

3. You may have noticed that the sheet bend is similar in construction to the bowline, so it can be tied in the same manner.

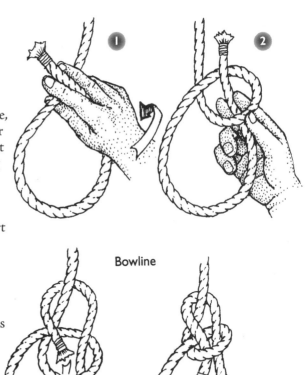

Bowline

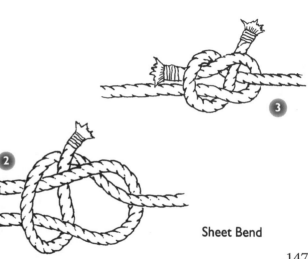

Sheet Bend

147

CLOVE HITCH

The clove hitch is for tying to pilings when there aren't any dock cleats. Its best feature is that it can be easily tied when there is strain on the line, as there might be when docking in strong winds. The first turn around the piling is usually enough to hold the boat, keeping everything in place while you finish tying the knot. This is essentially a temporary knot and may slip if the direction and strain on it changes.

1. Take a turn around a piling.

2. Take a second turn, this time crossing up and over the standing part of the line and the first turn. Tuck the end under and through the crossing you just made.

3. Pull both ends to snug up the knot. For a more permanent knot add two half hitches around the standing part of the line.

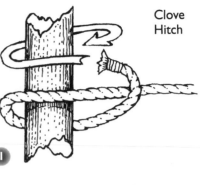

Clove Hitch

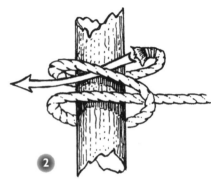

ROLLING HITCH

This knot is used when you need to apply a pulling force that is parallel, rather than at right angles, to the object you are tying to. It will hold on smooth surfaces like a mast or wire and can even fasten the end of the rope to itself when there is nothing else to tie to. Use a rolling hitch for adjustable guylines on a bimini top or dodger, a safety line on a bosun's chair, or transferring one rope's load to another rope or cleat.

1. Take two turns around the object. These turns go on in the direction from which the pulling force will be coming.

2. Cross the working end over the turns.

3. Pass the working end under the crossover and draw the knot into its final shape. Apply loads slowly to allow the knot to grab. To adjust, ease off slightly and reposition.

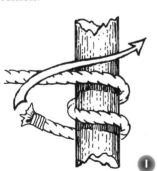

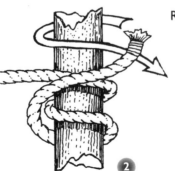

Rolling Hitch

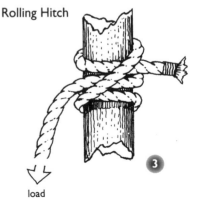

load

SLIPPED REEF KNOT

The reef (or square) knot should only be used to bind a line around something, such as tying off reef points or fastening gaskets around a furled sail. Never use it as a bend to join two lines. As a bend it is dangerous and unreliable, especially if the lines are of different size or material. A sharp jerk or a tug at an oblique angle can cause it to *spill* (collapse) unexpectedly, or it may jam completely from prolonged tension. When used as intended, it is just fine, especially in its *slipped* (quick-release) version.

1. Twist one line around the other in one direction.

2. Double an end back against itself and make a second twist around the line in the other direction. Draw up by pulling on the loop and the other end.

3. The finished knot looks like half a bow. The free ends must exit the knot so they lie flat and parallel to the standing parts, or you have a granny knot.

4. Give the doubled end a sharp pull to spill the knot.

TRUCKER'S HITCH

If you want to hold something in place, like a dinghy on deck or a boat to a car rack, you'll need a way of getting a mechanical advantage to increase the tension on the restraining lines. The trucker's hitch gives you this extra power and can also be used to tighten lifelines, halyards and outhauls, or to make a boom vang kicking strap.

1. Make a loop a few feet from the end of the line.

2. Pull some of the working end of the line through the loop.

3. Close up the knot so this most recently made loop is held in place.

4. Lead the end to a secure point, back to the loop, and through it. This makes a primitive tackle that multiplies your pulling force.

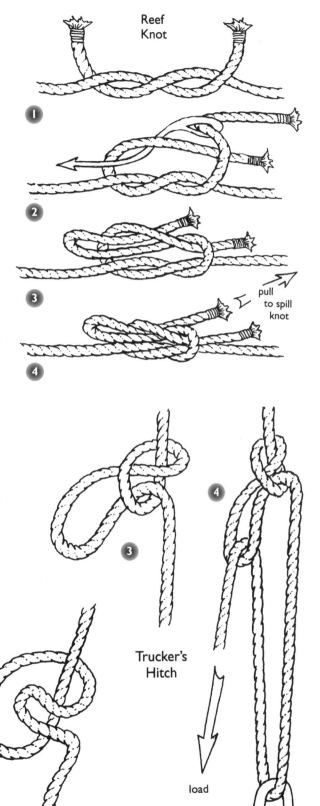

Trucker's Hitch

149

Cleats

The cleat is a blessing to mariners. It is inexpensive, simple to use, elegant in form and maintenance free. To get the most from a cleat it must be securely mounted and set at a 10-degree angle to the line's lead to prevent the turns from jamming. You can either *belay* or make a line *fast* to a cleat.

To belay a line, make a complete turn around the cleat's base and then two S-turns over the *horns* (the extended arms). This secures the line temporarily. It will hold, but is not permanent. Sheets are always belayed.

To make a line fast so it is permanent, finish the belay with a single hitch. The hitch must be placed so the exiting line lies beside, not over, the last belaying turn. This will prevent jamming and improve strength. Docking lines, anchor rodes and halyards are always made fast.

A *slippery hitch* makes a line fast while still retaining the ability to be immediately cast off. It is secure and a good choice for halyards on smaller craft. Alternatives to this are other types of 'cleats' that grip the line in different ways.

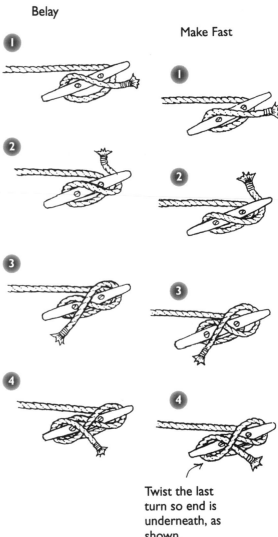

Belay

Make Fast

Twist the last turn so end is underneath, as shown.

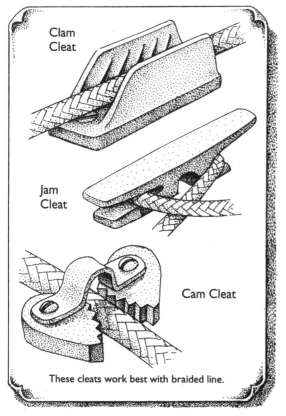

Clam Cleat

Jam Cleat

Cam Cleat

These cleats work best with braided line.

pull to spill knot

Make Fast with a Slippery Hitch

Eye Splice

A loop can be worked into the end of a line with a knot like a bowline. But knots, because they are made up of many sharp turns, reduce a line's strength. A bowline may weaken line by as much as 40% and most hitches by about 30%. This is acceptable for general usage, but not for hard service such as anchor rodes or towlines. These require an *eye splice*, which retains almost 95% of the rope's strength.

An eye splice is meant to be permanent. Unlike a knot, it will never be untied and therefore takes a little more time and craftsmanship to make.

IN DOUBLE-BRAIDED LINE

This requires specialised tools that are only supplied as a kit and can be found at almost any marine supply shop. The kit includes a set of *hollow fids* (one for each size line), a *pusher*, and full instructions. All you have to do is follow the directions to make the splice.

While the instructions are precise, they give no overview of the process, leaving you unsure of why you are doing each step. So, rather than go through the complete procedure (which the kit's instructions do quite well), here is the bigger picture.

Think of double-braided line as two ropes in one. There is a braided centre and a braided sleeve. When making an eye splice, the centre and the sleeve become like two snakes, each trying to swallow the other:

1. Separate the centre from the sleeve.
2. Put the sleeve into the centre.
3. Put the centre into the sleeve.
4. Feed the eye into the sleeve of the standing part so the crossover point disappears.

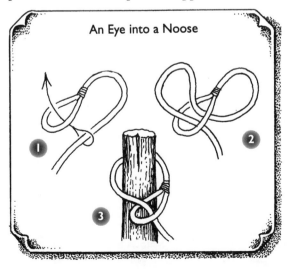

An Eye into a Noose

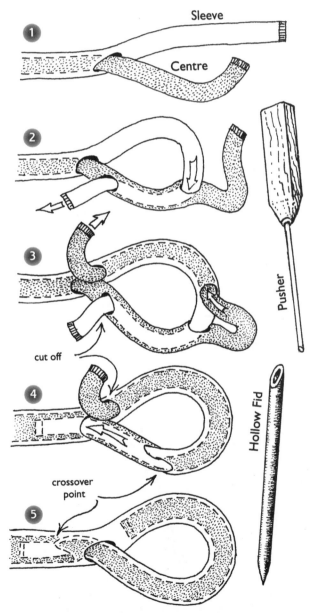

151

IN LAID LINE

It is easier to grasp the concept of an eye splice in laid line than in braided. The strands are partially *unlaid* (unravelled), then intertwined back into the line to form the eye.

Start by wrapping a strip of tape around the line 6 inches from its end. Separate the three strands, taping their ends so they won't come apart. Of these three strands one will be uppermost and between the other two. Take that strand and tuck it under an uppermost strand on the standing part. Note that the tuck is made *against the lay* of the standing part, from right to left. On old or tightly laid line you may need a fid to part the strands.

Tuck the left-hand strand under the next strand up on the standing part (and over the strand you previously tucked under). Then flip the eye over and tuck in the remaining (right-hand) strand, still working from right to left. After the first three tucks, stop and check what you have done. If the strands emerge symmetrically from the standing part, each coming out from under a different standing strand, you've got it right. Complete the splice by pulling the first tucks up tight, and then adding four more tucks done in the same sequence (centre, left, right) as the first. When finished, cut off and heat-seal the projecting ends to ⅜ inch.

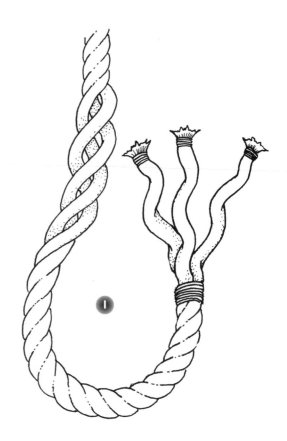

Unlay Strands

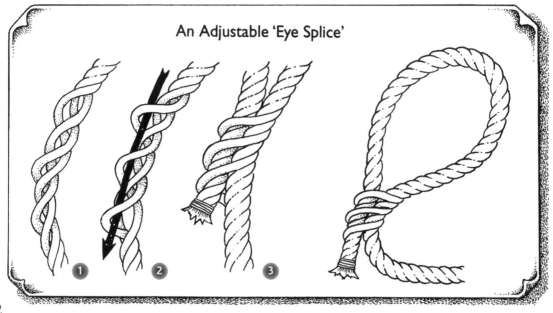

An Adjustable 'Eye Splice'

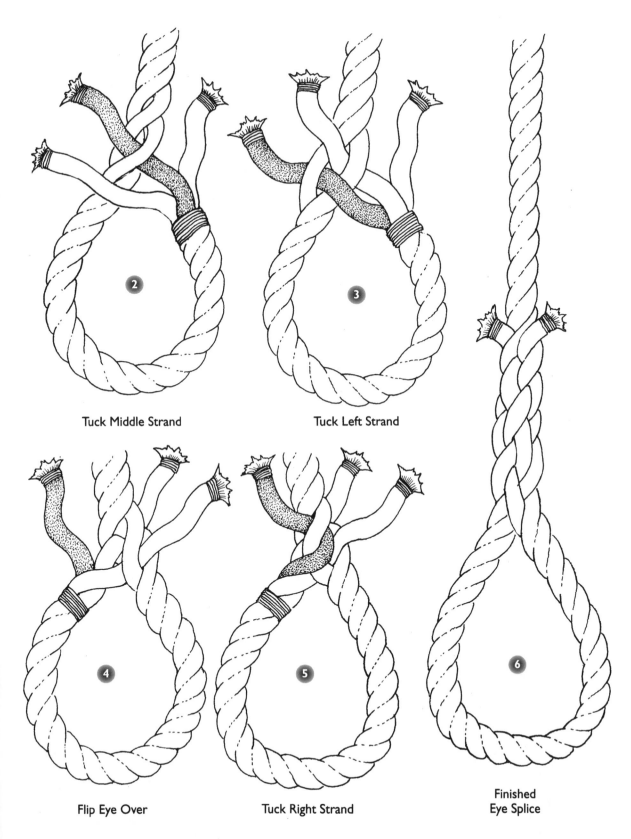

Tuck Middle Strand

Tuck Left Strand

Flip Eye Over

Tuck Right Strand

Finished
Eye Splice

Going Aloft

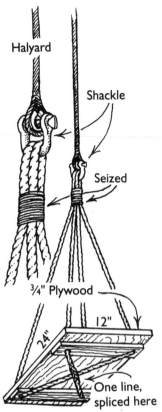

Halyard

Shackle

Seized

¾" Plywood

24" 12"

One line,
spliced here

**Traditional
Bosun's Chair**

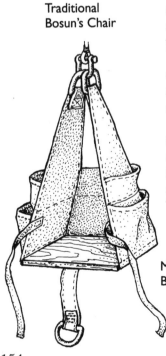

**Modern
Bosun's Chair**

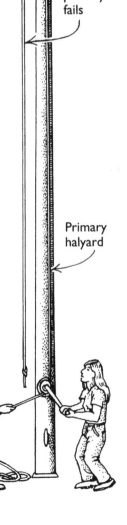

Backup
halyard
in case
primary
fails

Primary
halyard

On a small boat, when something goes wrong high up, you take the mast down. When something goes wrong on a larger boat, you go up. The experience should be nothing more than a routine drill, with as little resemblance to a circus act as possible.

Since a boat's motion is amplified with height, go aloft only in calm conditions. Attach the *bosun's chair* by securing the shackle (never use snap shackles) on the main halyard, or any other halyard going through a strong block or masthead sheave. Lead the halyard to a winch (that is not self-tailing) and then to a stout cleat. You will need a deck crew of two: one to crank, the other to tail. The person on the winch does nothing but crank. The one who is tailing leads the line low so none of the turns will jump the winch or jam, keeps an eye on the ascent, and stays ready to make fast.

The chair should be rigged with a ⅜-inch, 8-foot safety line eye-spliced to the bridle. Once aloft, secure the line to a solid fitting or around the mast with a rolling hitch. This will prevent you from swinging about and protect you from a sudden halyard failure. On the way up, stay close to the mast by gripping it with your legs and hands.

Most jobs take longer and require more tools than you'd expect. Take along everything you need (and more) in a deep *rigging bucket* (canvas bag) that cannot capsize and rain gear on those below. Anything carried aloft should be rigged with a lanyard that can be attached to you or the chair. Do your work slowly and deliberately.

To descend, let go the safety line. Then the deck crew casts off the cleat and, with plenty of turns around the winch, eases the line out while snubbing it, maintaining control at all times.

The best way to deal with lofty problems is to prevent them. Most trips up the mast can be avoided by paying extra attention to maintenance. Next time the mast is down, check wires, cotter pins, shackles, spreader attachments, sheaves, tangs and shrouds. Remember: The safest trips aloft are those that are never made.

Chafe

No matter where you look on a boat, there are lines slowly wearing away towards self-destruction. And if the lines themselves are not being destroyed, what they are in contact with is. Everything suffers from chafe, and the culprit is friction.

Blocks and fairleads must be wide enough to keep running rigging from binding, jamming or causing frictional heat build-up that degrades the strength of synthetic fibres. A block's sheave diameter must also be large enough – at least six times the rope's width – so the line does not make too tight a turn. And wire halyards should run over sheaves at least twenty times their diameter.

Cleats as well as chocks must be big enough for the line used. Allow 1 inch of horn length for each 1/16 inch of rope diameter. When docked or anchored during rough conditions or for long periods, provide chafing gear where line passes through chocks or over rails. Spirally split hose works well, as do stitched-on leather strips.

Internal chafe is another problem. At least once a year, hose down lines in fresh water, or wash in a machine using a mild soap, putting them in a mesh bag or pillow case to prevent tangles. Air-dry and stow away from sunlight.

Consider retiring line from service if its core is visible through the cover, if more than 50% of the surface strands on braided line are damaged, if friction-caused heat has fused a length of more than four diameters, if it feels stiff or brittle, if strands of laid line are elongated, or if there are any serious cuts or abrasions.

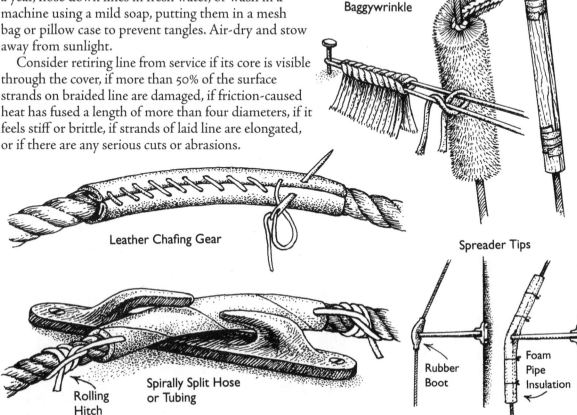

Turnbuckle Protecters

Unprotected   Tape   Boot   Hose

Shroud Roller (wood)

Tape or Seizing

Baggywrinkle

Leather Chafing Gear

Spreader Tips

Rubber Boot

Foam Pipe Insulation

Rolling Hitch

Spirally Split Hose or Tubing

Coiling

To prevent lines from becoming impressively convoluted Gordian knots, adhere to the golden rule: Keep lines in use, stowed away, or in the process of being coiled. Anything else means trouble.

Before you can coil a line, it has to be *overhauled* (cleared of tangles). Loosen everything and spread the line out on deck. Find an end and pull it, shaking out and untying the fouled parts as you do. As it is being cleared, put the recovered line in a separate loose pile on deck. When all the knots are out, the line will still have a lot of residual kinks that can be removed when you coil it.

Most lines prefer to be coiled clockwise. Hold the accumulated coils in one hand while feeding with the other. For laid line, the feeding hand must impart a slight clockwise twist to the line with the thumb and forefinger so it will form into a neat, flat coil. Braided line does not need the twist and naturally falls into a series of figure eights. Always coil towards the free end, the end not attached to anything, shaking or twirling the line to release accumulated twists as you coil.

Once coiled, line must be stowed in such a way that it will remain coiled. Use the *halyard coil* to stow line that has already been made fast to a cleat (like halyards). Start coiling about a foot away from the cleat. Reach through the coil and take hold of the line near the cleat. Pull the line through the coils, twist it three or four times, and slip it over the cleat's top horn.

A *gasket coil* is another way to hang a coil. It was originally used for coiling furling lines (gaskets) on the yards of square sails, but is now used for hanging the stowed mainsheet from the boom. Start coiling about 3 feet away from the secured end. Make four or five tight turns around the finished coil with the standing end. Take a *bight* (loop) of the standing end through the coil and then back over the top.

A *bight hitch coil* gives you a loop to hang the coil from a hook or cleat. Coil as usual. Double the remaining free end. Take one or two turns around the coil, and then pass the loop through the coil. Hang up, or stow in a locker.

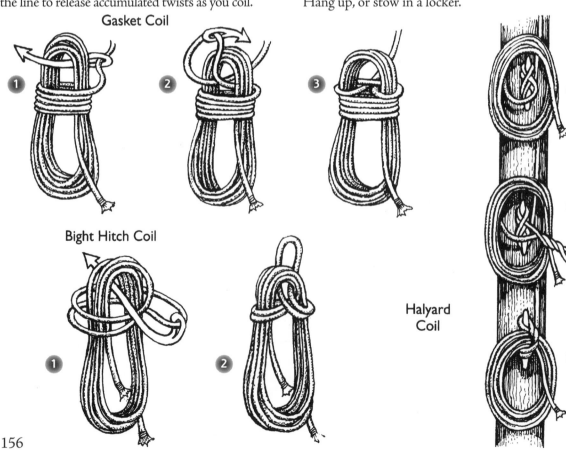

Gasket Coil

Bight Hitch Coil

Halyard Coil

156

Heaving Lines

When you need to get a line over to a dock or another boat, you can improve your heaving distance by adding a weight to the end of the line in the form of a knot, or (not as effectively) by tossing a tight coil.

A *heaving line* can be made up of a 50-foot length of ⅜-inch line with a *monkey's fist* at its end. The knot's name is a perfect description of its appearance. Picture small fingers intertwined to enclose a round object and you've got a monkey's fist.

Make three 3-inch diameter loops about 4 feet from the end. Put a second set of three loops around the first three at right angles to them, ending with a single pass through the first three loops. Put a third set of three loops around the second set, passing inside the first set of loops. Insert a rubber ball into the knot's middle if you want it to float. (The heavier

the insert, the further you can heave, but at the risk of damage to people and boats.) Carefully work out the slack, and splice the leftover end into the standing part as if making an eye splice. If there is no heaving line aboard, use a *heaving knot* to add weight to the end of a line.

To heave a line, coil it into two foot-long loops. Divide the coil, keeping the half with the knot in your throwing hand and the remaining half in the other. Swing the throwing coil in a low arc back and forth at your side. Let the coil go as an underhand toss, allowing the line to run free from the other hand. Before tossing, make sure the line's end is made fast to something, thus avoiding the anticlimactic feeling of seeing the end go flying overboard after you've just made a perfect toss.

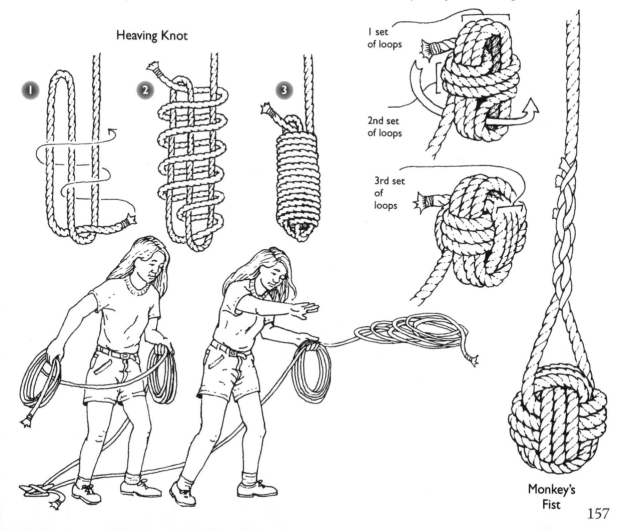

Heaving Knot

1

2

3

I set of loops

2nd set of loops

3rd set of loops

Monkey's Fist

157

EMERGENCIES

'And I would recommend to them . . . to keep the halyards clear for running, [and] to remember that "any fool can carry on but only the wise man knows how to shorten sail in time" . . .' Joseph Conrad, Letter to owner and crew of the *Tusitala*, 2 June 1923

We dream of endless broad reaches, calm seas and steady gentle winds. All anchorages are protected, waters deep enough for our keels, foul weather long foretold, winds and currents eternally fair and days warm and clear.

Alas, as you may have noticed, this is not the way things are. And that's just fine, because most of us head out under sail looking for a taste of adventure. A boat kept at its mooring is perfectly safe, but that is not what she has been built for, nor why we sail.

The risks of sailing need not be foolhardy. When problems come, you should be ready to meet them on their own terms and understand that they are your responsibility. There is a wonderful feeling of independence when you know you can handle whatever is thrown at you. In the beginning you will stumble into these adventures; there will be no avoiding them. Later they will be of your own making.

The wind and sea take nothing personally. If you are prepared and cautious, and always leave yourself an out, you'll do fine. Prudence and patience will be rewarded.

159

Avoiding Trouble

For starters, don't take unnecessary chances when the weather is expected to turn bad. Stay within easy reach of shelter or, if contemplating a longer voyage, hole up and wait it out. Too many mariners get themselves in trouble trying to adhere to a schedule when the weather goes against them.

Be patient, and whenever you do go out, put the odds in your favour. Have charts or cruising guides for harbours of refuge along your route, always leaving yourself with options. Know where you are, navigate with caution, keep a good lookout, and *never* follow another boat just because it seems to know where it's going.

Stop disasters before they start. Think of what can go wrong, how you would handle it, and ways you can prevent it. For example, have an alternative steering system in case your primary one fails. Practise redundancy – always have a backup plan or system. Keep an orderly boat. When gear, sails or lines are not in use, stow them. Have a place for everything and everything in its place. This way you will be able to find what you need, and anything that is not right will stand out. Get things down to a routine. If you are forgetful, have checklists so nothing gets overlooked. Turn preventive maintenance into an art. And be creative. Imagine how things can go wrong. Do what you can so they won't.

Be careful moving around the boat. Walk cautiously, with your weight low and feet well apart. Move from handhold to handhold, remembering the axiom, 'One hand for yourself and one for the ship'. Grab shrouds, stays, handrails and the mast. Do not look for support from the boom or lifelines. Watch where you step. Do not stand on hatch covers, sails or lines. Never put a foot in a coil or stand in the bight of a line under load. Don't try holding onto a line that wants to run – you could get rope burns or be dragged overboard. Go forward along the windward side to avoid thrashing booms, entangling sheets and whipping sails. In rough going, slide along on your rear or crawl. The safest areas are in the cockpit, by the mast, or within the pulpit. When working on a tossing deck, kneel or sit with your feet well braced. When lowering the jib, muzzle it in as fast as possible, watching out for the flailing clew. Once the jib is down, lash its head to the pulpit and cleat the halyard so you won't lose it up the mast.

Keep warm, dry and, on a long cruise, well fed and rested. Don foul-weather gear before it starts to rain or spray begins to fly. Wool clothing, along with those made with polypropylene and polyester, will keep you warm even when wet. Wear boat shoes for a better grip and to prevent mashed toes. And wear a hat to keep the sun off or stay warm. Avoid getting seasick if you can; it will weaken you and impair your judgement. Take preventive measures early. If you feel queasy, don't go below. Keep your eye on the horizon, and stay active. Make sure the boat has a well-stocked first-aid kit with an instruction manual.

Even on the most casual outings someone has to be captain, taking responsibility for the boat and the crew. In an emergency there must be only one decision maker. At sea one accident often leads to another, escalating along the way. So act fast to stop things before they get out of hand. But before you do, take a moment to size up the problem. Figure out how you will fix it, what can go wrong along the way, and what you will do then. Once you decide, let the crew know what has happened and what is to be done. In an emergency, chaos can be dangerous.

Be prepared, and don't panic.

Personal Safety

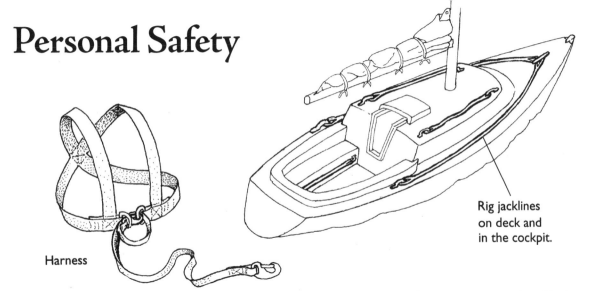

Harness

Rig jacklines
on deck and
in the cockpit.

Your first priority is to stay in the boat. In rough weather, or when you are offshore and on your own, wear a safety harness. This is mandatory for deck work and makes sense even when at the helm. A good harness must be able to withstand considerable shock loads. It should have secure clips at both ends of an 8-foot tether. One end attaches to the harness high on your chest (so you will be dragged with your head out of the water). The other end is attached to the boat. Run *jacklines* made of ⅜-inch line or 2-inch webbing so you can stay clipped on at all times. Other good clip-on points are shrouds, stays, stanchion bases (not lifelines) and any other solidly bolted fitting.

If you do go overboard, you'll appreciate having a *personal flotation device* (PFD). These are divided into five types. The Coast Guard says that sailing boats 16 feet or less must have one wearable PFD (Type I, II, III, V) for each person on board, and that sailing boats over 16 feet (and not a canoe or kayak) also have one throwable PFD (Type IV). In all boats, children under thirteen are required to wear a PFD while underway; however, some states have lower age limits. That's the law, but good seamanship demands more. All PFDs must be cared for and stowed in an accessible spot, and everyone on board must know where they are and how to use them. Each PFD should have a whistle to signal for help and, for night sailing, a small strobe light and strips of reflective tape. PFDs must fit snugly, and those for young children should have a crotch strap and a foam collar with a grab handle.

When to wear one? On small boats that capsize easily, wear a comfortable Type III or V at all times. On boats where the risk of immersion is less, you need wear your PFD only when abandoning ship or to feel more secure in a hard chance.

Type I, Offshore Life Jacket. Best when help may be delayed. Has at least 22 pounds of flotation and turns an unconscious wearer face up. Some are bulky although hybrid models can be comfortable.

Type II, Inshore Buoyant Vest. Use when there is chance of a quick rescue. Has at least 15.5 pounds of flotation. Some turn an unconscious wearer face up. Not as bulky as Type I. Available in inflatable models.

Type III, Flotation Aid. Same buoyancy as Type II. Made to be worn at all times, comfortable, and easier to swim in. Will not turn an unconscious wearer face up. Available in inflatable models.

Type IV, Throwable Device. Meant to be tossed to someone or held onto when help is nearby. Horseshoe buoys have at least 16.5 pounds of flotation; cushions have 18 pounds.

Type V, Special Use. Most comfortable, least restrictive. Some inflate automatically. Shown here is an automatic inflatable with a harness. Used for coastal or offshore sailing.

Aground

Even the best navigators run aground. Sail long enough and it will happen. The trick is to be prepared to get yourself off quickly, or if that can't be done, to minimise any damage.

The first thing to do after the boat comes to a grinding halt is check for leaks and broken gear. Next, try to determine where you are, how you got there, and which way to get out. Look at your chart, notice where the buoys or markers are, and take *soundings* (check the depth) with a boathook, spinnaker pole or lead line off the bow, stern and both sides. Note the state of the tide, currents, wind and waves. Are they working for or against you?

On small boats you may be able to raise the centreboard and rudder to get free. But check the wind direction first. If it is blowing onto the shoal, raising the board will only send you further aground. Moreover, with the board up you will not be able to sail to windward. Instead, you will have to paddle or pole to deeper water before you can lower the board and sail off.

In larger boats, or those with a keel, the typical first response is to use the engine (if there is one). Try powering out in reverse. If you can't get free right away, stop. Further use might draw muck into the cooling system, doing serious damage to the engine.

Your next alternative is to reduce the boat's draught so it can float free. Know your boat's underwater profile. Most are deepest aft, so sending the crew forward might raise the stern enough to get her unstuck. Or try heeling her over with the sails (backwind the jib, sheet in the main), with a weight swung out on the boom (reinforce the topping

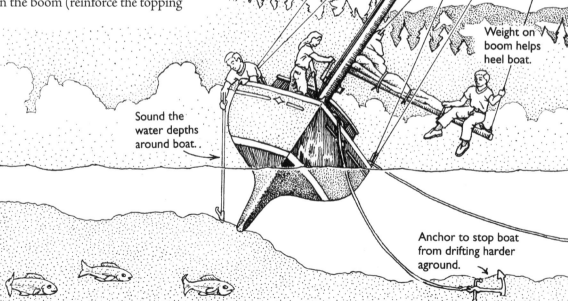

Weight on boom helps heel boat.

Sound the water depths around boat.

Anchor to stop boat from drifting harder aground.

lift with a halyard), with a halyard led from the masthead to an anchor, or by rocking the boat from side to side. You may also be able to spin her around and drag her to deep water by *kedging*. Carry out a lightweight anchor in the dinghy, or by wading or swimming (using a PFD to support the anchor). When rowing, put the kedge and its rode in the dinghy, making the bitter end fast to the boat aground. Set the kedge as far from the boat as possible to maximise scope. Haul away with a sheet winch or tackle. Try to swing the bow around, then the stern. If she won't budge, keep the rode taut and look for opportunities. A powerboat's wake may momentarily lift her enough to pull free.

On a falling tide, work quickly. If you can't get off, set out an anchor to keep the boat from sliding further aground and to help pull her off when the tide returns. Be sure to close all through-hull openings to keep her from flooding as she refloats. Make use of the time ahead of you. Clean the bottom. Go clamming. Be philosophical. There's more to sailing than just sailing.

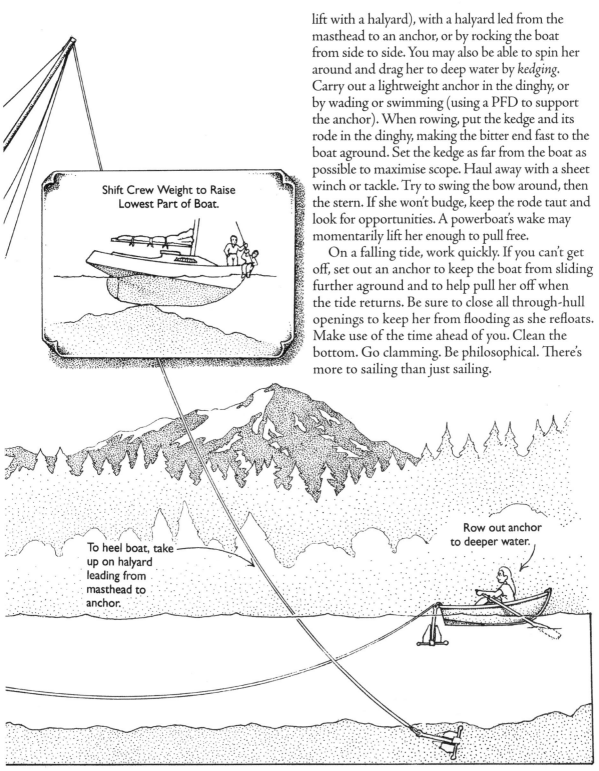

Shift Crew Weight to Raise Lowest Part of Boat.

To heel boat, take up on halyard leading from masthead to anchor.

Row out anchor to deeper water.

Man Overboard

As soon as someone goes in, call out 'Man overboard!' and toss a cushion or buoy to provide flotation and mark the spot. If you have a GPS unit, hit the MOB (man-overboard) button to do the same. Always keep a Type IV PFD at hand, ready to be thrown. Never lash it down. The skipper then assigns one crewmember to watch the person in the water and continually point to that spot. If possible, that crewmember should have no other responsibilities during the recovery.

On small, highly manoeuvrable boats in protected waters, the fastest way to make a rescue is by gybing. It is also the easiest to remember. As soon as someone goes over – gybe. In larger boats, when offshore in rougher seas, your primary objective is to keep the person in sight. In this case you should use the 'quick-stop' method. Immediately head up, let the sails luff to stop the boat, locate the person or the thrown marker, bear off on a run until just downwind of the victim, then come back on a close reach.

The further you get from the person in the water, the harder he or she is to see, and once lost from sight the chances of recovery diminish greatly.

If you have an engine, turn it on to help manoeuvring, being careful not to foul lines in the prop and to be in neutral when near the person in the water. Approach the pickup point on a reach, keeping your speed down. Aim to windward of your mark, coming to a dead stop with the victim in the protected lee of your boat. Have a heaving line ready in case you miss. Be sure there is a ladder or some other boarding aid rigged.

Hold frequent man-overboard drills on all points of sail so you and the crew will know what to do. Throw out a PFD to recover. Or when a hat blows over, treat it as if someone has gone in. Make a game of it, but take it seriously.

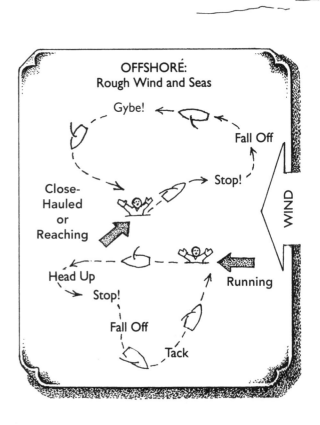

OFFSHORE:
Rough Wind and Seas

Gybe!

Fall Off

Stop!

WIND

Close-Hauled or Reaching

Head Up

Stop!

Running

Fall Off

Tack

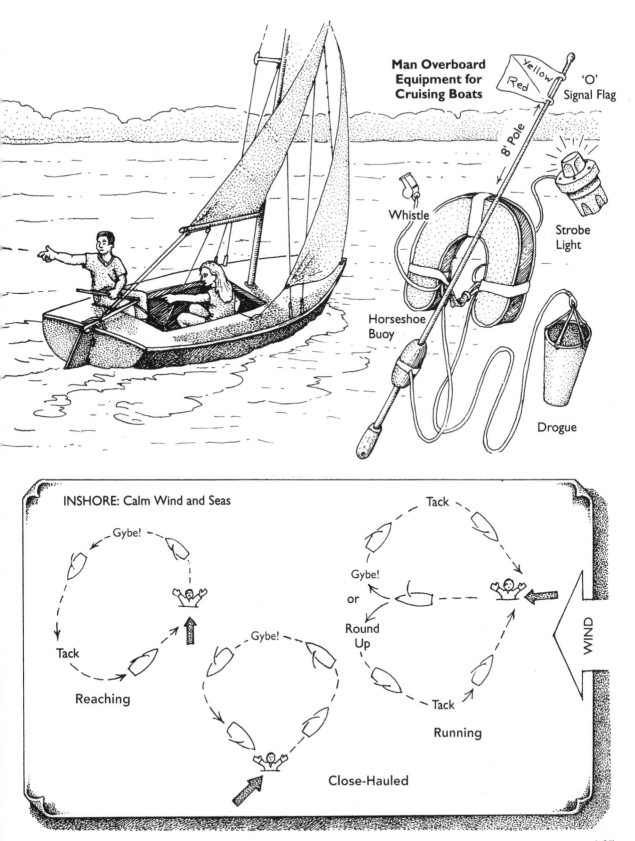

Man Overboard Equipment for Cruising Boats

'O' Signal Flag

Yellow
Red

8' Pole

Whistle

Strobe Light

Horseshoe Buoy

Drogue

INSHORE: Calm Wind and Seas

Gybe!

Tack

Reaching

Gybe!

Close-Hauled

Tack

Gybe!

or

Round Up

Tack

Running

WIND

Towing

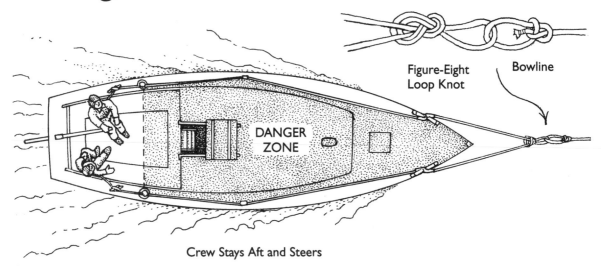

Figure-Eight Loop Knot

Bowline

Crew Stays Aft and Steers

There will come a day when all your resources fail. Your boat may be damaged, too firmly aground, or just becalmed. When this happens, your only alternative will be to accept a tow.

You will need a towline long enough to maintain about five boat lengths between you and the towboat in open waters, and one boat length in close quarters. Make the line fast to one substantial fitting, or spread the load over many. On most small craft, the foredeck cleat is not up to the job. A better choice would be a bowline made fast to the bow eye, or even better, a *towboat hitch* tied to a *keel-stepped* mast, see page 95). But do not hitch the line to a *deck-stepped* mast, for it is not capable of taking a pull. You may want to rig a bridle with its ends

led aft to the sheet winches and cleats. Whatever you make fast to, be sure that the towline is taken through the bow chocks, that there is ample chafing gear, and that the line leads fairly, avoiding sharp edges and tight turns.

Don't leave yourself at the mercy of the towing boat. Most people who offer help, even professionals, will tow you at excessive speeds (over 5 mph). Make them aware of your boat's natural speed limits. Stay in touch with the towing boat using hand signals or the radio. Use a knot such as the towboat hitch that can be adjusted or cast off while underway. When freeing a line, stay clear as it runs out. And never stand over, behind, or in the bight of a towline when it is under load.

Towboat Hitch

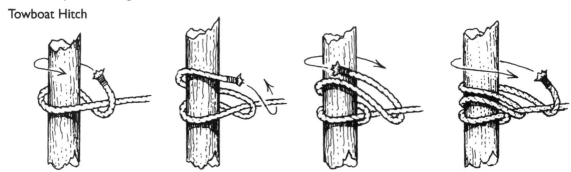

① Take a round turn to hold the initial strain. Lead the end under and back over the standing part.

② Bring the end around the bitt (or mast) in the opposite direction.

③ Repeat the 'under, over, back around' on the other side.

④ Keep adding turns in opposite directions until you feel there is no slippage.

166

Signalling for Help

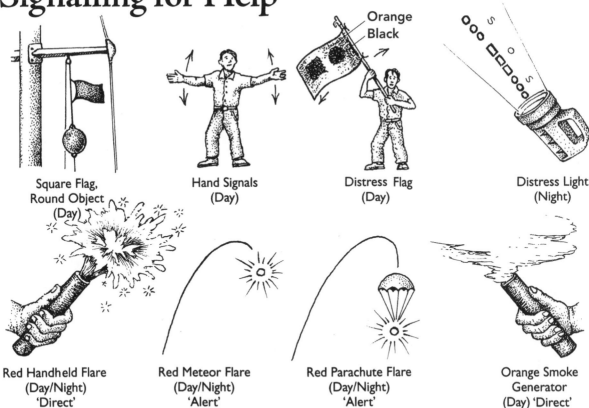

Square Flag, Round Object (Day)

Hand Signals (Day)

Distress Flag (Day)
Orange
Black

Distress Light (Night)
S O S

Red Handheld Flare (Day/Night) 'Direct'

Red Meteor Flare (Day/Night) 'Alert'

Red Parachute Flare (Day/Night) 'Alert'

Orange Smoke Generator (Day) 'Direct'

The most effective way of getting assistance is by calling the Coastguard on a VHF marine radio tuned to Channel 16 (the international distress frequency) or to use the VHF's digital selective calling (DSC) feature – press the emergency button and it sends a signal identifying who you are and, if connected to a GPS receiver, your location. To make contact, transmit on maximum power. If you are in grave danger and require *immediate* assistance, broadcast a Mayday (a phonetic of the French *m'aidez*, 'help me') three times. This will clear the channel of other traffic. When contact is made, describe your problem, the help you need, your boat, its location, and how many people are on board. The Coastguard will either take action themselves or coordinate efforts to assist you through commercial towing firms or nearby boats. For less dire emergencies, call the Coastguard without the Mayday preface.

When going offshore, or beyond VHF's reliable range of about 20 miles, you can transmit a continuous Mayday signal with an *emergency position-indicating radio beacon* (EPIRB, pronounced "ee-perb) or *personal locator beacon* (PLB).

PLB

EPIRB

Both are monitored by satellites to notify the authorities of your general area and provide a homing beacon. A GPS/EPIRB, or GPIRB, has the additional feature of giving your exact location.

All vessels should carry visual distress signals. The ideal is: an orange-and-black distress flag (for day), a light to flash an SOS (at night), and three hand-held red flares (day or night). Every boat regardless of size should carry these and it's wise to have more, as when trouble hits you'll feel foolish for skimping. Unofficially, anything that attracts attention will do the job.

Visual signals have two functions: to *alert* and to *direct*. Your first priority is to alert, to make people take notice of your plight. High-altitude flares are perfect for this as they can be seen beyond your horizon and make a loud noise. Once you've got their attention you will need to direct rescuers to your exact location. For this you can use hand-held flares or smoke generators. Do what you can to be seen.

SEA & SKY

'Whether the weather be fine, Or whether the weather be not; ... We'll weather the weather, Whatever the weather; Whether we like it or not!'

Traditional British school rhyme

Sailing boats are held captive within two elements, deeply immersed in each. Above, they are vulnerable to wind, rain, fog and storms; below, they are bound by the tides, currents and waves. And we sailors live in between, trying to orchestrate it all in our favour.

Take the time to study the language of sea and sky. Be receptive, and open your senses. This is the kind of knowledge acquired through experience rather than from the pages of a book. Every time you go out, keep track of what clouds precede what weather, or how the current interacts with the tide. In time, the pieces will come together and a broad, interwoven picture of cause and effect, air and water will emerge.

You may become fascinated with this part of sailing; many do. And this is good because it will enhance your enjoyment while teaching you humility and patience. If not, at least try to understand and temper your impatience with acceptance. To rail against the elements is futile. When Xerxes heard that a storm had just demolished years of work, he had the sea branded and whipped 300 times. 'Thou hast wronged me,' he said, 'albeit I did no wrong to thee.' He probably felt better afterwards, but the sea couldn't have cared less.

Weather

How many times on hearing a weather report have you wondered if the meteorologists bothered to look out of the window? But it's not their fault when the weather you see is not what they're describing. Their report may have been compiled from conditions far away from you and hours past. To obtain the very localised information that is important to sailors, you are going to have to become your own forecaster.

Still, a good local forecast starts with a knowledge of the broader weather systems, for which your best sources are the weather channels on VHF/FM (page 19) or inexpensive weather radios and reports on TV or online. The last two are especially helpful as you often get an up-to-the-minute weather map, time-lapse satellite imagery, and a radar sweep showing cells of bad weather. Being visual, they are also easier to assimilate than a radio report.

When you are out of touch with any of these electronic marvels, you'll have to depend on your own observations. The table on page 172 and a barometer will help. Enter in the wind direction and what your barometer has been doing for the previous 3 hours, and you'll be able to make some surprisingly accurate forecasts. This table has been derived from the typical weather patterns associated with areas of high and low pressure, so there's no mystery as to why it works.

To improve your forecasting abilities, you will have to train yourself to look closer at what is going on around you. On an open body of water, one of the most informative things you can look at are clouds.

Clouds are the harbingers of weather. Their shape, height, colour and sequence foretell coming events. There is no need to learn their scientific names, just which ones go with what weather patterns. There are, however, some generalities you should know.

High clouds are associated with the upper atmosphere and distant weather systems up to 6 hours away. If they are wispy and white, the weather will be fine. Lower clouds relate to the current weather or that which is soon to come. If they are dense and dark, change is imminent, usually for the worse. Notice if clouds are lowering or lifting, and if they are gathering or dispersing. Lowering or gathering usually brings wet weather. Lifting or dispersing means the weather will improve. A cloud's colour

> ## The Generic Forecast
>
> 'Probable northeast to southwest winds, varying to the southward and westward and eastward, and points between, high and low barometer swapping around from place to place; probable areas of rain, snow, hail, and drought, succeeded or preceded by earthquakes, with thunder and lightning.'
>
> Mark Twain

seems obvious: the darker, the more dangerous. And a sharp-edged dark cloud is the most dangerous of all. In shape, flat clouds are characteristic of stable air, while lumpy, well-rounded clouds live in unstable air. Watch which way the clouds are moving. Stand with your back to the wind and look up. If the high-altitude clouds are moving from left to right, the weather will worsen; from right to left, it will improve. And if the clouds are moving towards or away from you, things will stay the same.

There are other atmospheric effects to note. Until not too many generations ago, people heard, felt or saw signs that correlated to the weather, and what they observed they handed down as folk sayings to those who followed. Some were quite fanciful, but others were based on empirically gained knowledge. So, when all else fails, try looking around for some of these ancient indicators of weather.

The most famous bit of weather lore was spoken by Christ in Matthew 16:2. 'When evening comes, you say it will be fair weather, for the sky is red.' The old 'red sky at night, sailor's delight . . .' works. Most weather travels from west to east. The setting sun seen through the dust of dry air appears red, and fair, dry weather will arrive the next day.

Dew in the morning indicates a fair day, while a dry morning is a sign of rain. This is because the heat absorbed by an object during the previous day can be released only as dew (or frost) when the night and early morning are calm, clear and cool.

When far-off shorelines seem closer than usual, rain is usually less than a day away. During fair weather a great deal of salt haze evaporates and is held in the air. The mixing action of unstable pre-storm air clears this away, visibility improves, and objects seem closer.

A halo around the moon is another sign of rain. The halo is caused by the moon shining through ice crystals of moisture-laden clouds. If the halo is a tight fit, rain is still far off. If the halo forms a large ring, rain is near. If the clouds close in and the moon loses its outline, rain can be expected in about 10 hours. The same is true with the sun.

When smoke from a ship's funnel curls downwards and hangs by the water's surface, it means approaching rain. This is because the lowering air pressure is not dense enough to support the heavier particles in the exhaust. Another sign of rain is that a boat's engine exhaust, horn, or any other loud sound will have a hollow clarity, as if heard down a tunnel. This is caused by a low cloud ceiling bouncing sounds back. In fair weather, the clouds are too high to do this. Some old sailors insisted that they could smell an oncoming rain. This makes sense because the lowering air pressure encourages odours to emanate. Notice how much riper seaweed and low-tide muck smell before a rain. You may also notice that if the air is moist, and the air pressure already low, rain will come most frequently at low tide. This is nothing more than the air pressure being further reduced by the lowering of the waters. And an incoming tide often brings cooler water with it, which can chill the air and produce a breeze in a dead calm.

The wind changes its direction by either *veering* or *backing*. A wind that veers is changing its direction to your right as you face it. This is a sign of the clockwise wind common to high-pressure areas in the northern hemisphere, bringing fair or improving weather. A wind that backs changes its direction to your left. This is an anticlockwise wind from an area of low pressure, which brings a promise of foul weather. 'A veering wind will clear the sky; a backing wind says storms are nigh.'

All winds have a personality. The west wind brings fair, dry weather to the eastern shores of continental landmasses, because it has travelled over land. Yet it often brings rain to western shores, because it has travelled over water. West winds prevail in North America, but can be reversed by areas of low pressure. These bring east winds with cloudiness, a drop in air pressure, and a rise in humidity to eastern shores. When winds from the north and south encounter the prevailing westerlies, or each other, the colliding air masses can trigger all sorts of havoc, usually in the form of precipitation. The north wind brings snow, and the south, rain.

Hopefully the foregoing will help you predict what will happen next over your cruising grounds. In all fairness, though – and any honest meteorologist would agree with this – no matter how weather-wise you become there will always be an element of chance.

SEA AREAS FOR THE BRITISH ISLES

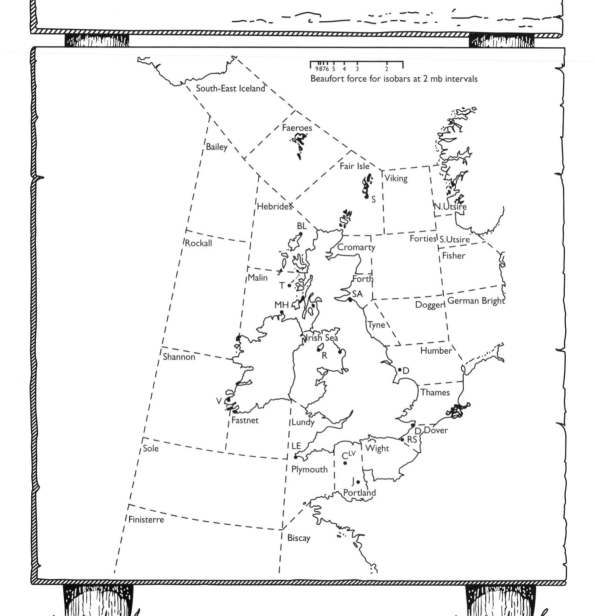

Beaufort force for isobars at 2 mb intervals

South-East Iceland

Faeroes

Bailey

Fair Isle

Viking

S

Hebrides

N.Utsire

Rockall

BL

Forties

S.Utsire

Fisher

Malin

Cromarty

T

Forth

SA

Doggel

German Bright

MH

Tyne

Shannon

Irish Sea

R

Humber

D

Thames

V

D Dover

Fastnet

Lundy

RS

Sole

LE

Wight

C LV

Plymouth

J

Portland

Finisterre

Biscay

Fog

For those who sail on the West Coast, the Great Lakes, or from Maine to the Chesapeake, fog is a fact of life. Even off the southern Atlantic coasts and on smaller inland lakes, you're bound to be enveloped by it sometime. Only on the Gulf of Mexico are the waters relatively fog free, but there you can get socked in by haze or blinding rain. Regardless of how your vision is restricted, there are ways of staying safe.

Just before the fog closes in and you find yourself running blind, determine where you are. Look to your chart, find landmarks, take bearings, pinpoint your position. Next figure out where you want to go. Check your compass, take frequent soundings, see if there are any currents, and set your course to cautiously creep from one marker to the next.

If you are heading towards a harbour or some point on a coastline, don't aim directly for it. Chances are you won't hit it, and then which direction would you turn? Instead, set a course well off to one side. Then when you close with the land, you will at least know which way to steer. If you're trying to find a buoy and miss it, don't worry; you're probably not more than half a mile away. Stop where you think it should be and then sail in a square pattern of half-mile legs with your starting point in the middle. When you can, set your course for a big, hard-to-miss target. Try not to hit anything along the way. At the same time, try to make sure nothing hits you.

Post a lookout on the bow, with instructions to listen as well as look. If you have your engine going, stop it once in a while so you can hear what's out there. Stay away from the traffic of main shipping channels, or think about anchoring and waiting it out. Get out your horn or bell and start letting people know where you are and what you are doing. Don't use a mouth horn – no one will hear it. A hand-held pressurised-air horn is more effective. Put up a radar reflector. Reduce speed so you can stop in less than half the range of your visibility. If you hear another boat's signal, slow down or stop. Don't proceed until you know what it is doing.

Fog plays tricks with sight and sound. An object seen in the fog could be something very big and far away, or small and close at hand. Sound is equally baffling. A far-off horn could sound as if it were next to you, while you may not notice a nearby bell buoy. Don't assume that you are near a signal because you hear it clearly. Consider the wind – sound travels further downwind than up. Or a sound could be blocked altogether by intervening land. Try cupping your hands around your ears to amplify what you hear. Listen for clues around you. The sounds of waves on a shore, the rumble of passing boat engines, car traffic on a bridge, all tell a story – the worst being the bells of a ice-cream van close aboard. This is always a bad sign.

Fog Signals

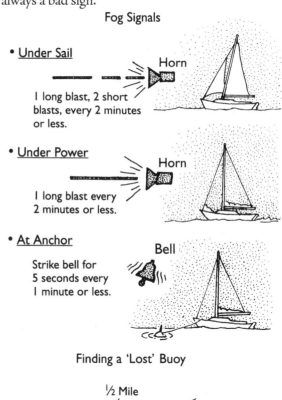

- **Under Sail**

  Horn

  1 long blast, 2 short blasts, every 2 minutes or less.

- **Under Power**

  Horn

  1 long blast every 2 minutes or less.

- **At Anchor**

  Bell

  Strike bell for 5 seconds every 1 minute or less.

Finding a 'Lost' Buoy

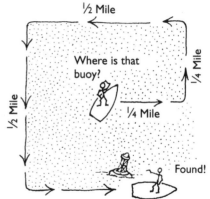

½ Mile

¼ Mile

½ Mile

¼ Mile

Where is that buoy?

¼ Mile

Found!

Squalls

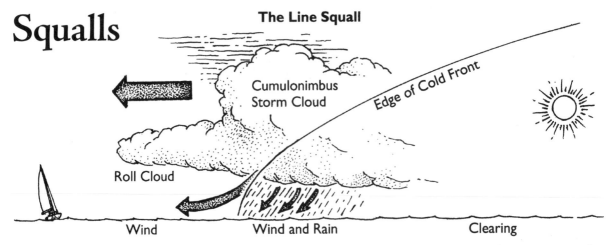

Cumulonimbus Storm Cloud

Edge of Cold Front

Roll Cloud

Wind   Wind and Rain   Clearing

Squalls are fierce, brief, highly localised storms whose most frightening aspects are their high winds and the speed with which they pounce. They come in two varieties: *line squalls* and *thunderstorms*.

A line squall is the penetrating first wedge of a cold front. It looks like a low line of boiling, sulphurous black clouds steamrolling towards you. When the first clouds arrive, you might experience a lull or a wind blowing towards the storm. After they pass, a few heavy raindrops may fall and the sky may lighten a little, tricking you into thinking that the worst is over. Then wham! You get blasted by the front itself – with rain, lightning, and a cold, powerful wind from a new direction. You can often predict this wind shift by facing the pre-storm breeze. The new wind will usually come from your right. Within 20 minutes or so it's all over, leaving you soaked, shaken, and sailing on a cool, dry wind.

Thunderstorms happen on their own, independent of any large weather system, and are created by the upwelling of warm, moist air that has been heated during the day. While they can strike at any hour, thunderstorms most often occur in the late afternoon or early evening. Signs to look for are a singular dark cloud of great height, terminating in an anvil-shaped top that points in the direction of travel. As with a line squall, there is a preceding line of low, rolling clouds. But these clouds bring violent winds, first from an updraught, then a brief lull, followed by even more brutal downdraughts that continue blowing outward until the storm has passed. Wind shifts in a thunderstorm are only temporary, with the prevailing wind returning after its passing.

A good early warning for squalls is lightning-caused static on an AM radio. If the first clouds are anywhere west to north of you in temperate climates,

you could be in trouble. The clouds may miss you if both their outer edges seem to be moving in the same direction. But if the edges are spreading apart like opening arms, prepare for the worst. You can tell how far off a squall is by timing the difference between the lightning and thunder. After seeing a flash, count the seconds until you hear the thunder. Multiply the number of seconds by 0.2 to get the distance off in miles. Squalls travel at 20 to 40 mph; the faster they advance, and the darker and lower the clouds, the harder the blow. You can judge what you are in for by the squall's first punch. A lot of rain before the wind hits means you're in for a long bout. But if there is a sharp gust first and then rain, it will be over shortly.

Before the squall hits, get an accurate fix of your position. Run for shelter if there is time; otherwise head for open water. Since your visibility and boat control may be severely limited, leave plenty of room for error. Next get the boat ready. Reef down, or get the engine warmed up if you plan to power through it. Take precautions against lightning by keeping the crew below or away from conductors such as the mast, stays and shrouds. Be prepared and you'll do fine.

The Thunderstorm

Cumulonimbus Storm Cloud

Roll Cloud

!?

Updraughts   Downdraughts and Rain

Currents

Any movement of water, no matter how slow, affects a sailing boat's progress. Four mph is a respectable speed for a 19-foot Lightning, but against a 1-mph current that speed will be cut by 25%, adding an extra hour to a 3-hour cruise.

Unlike the wind, a current's *set* (direction) is named for the direction towards which it is flowing. The Gulf Stream off Florida sets to the north. The speed of a current is its *drift*, and the time between *flood* (incoming tidal current) and *ebb* (outgoing) when there is no drift is *slack water*. A tidal current's set, drift and time of slack water can be found in the government's *Tidal Current Tables*, which are accurate but often affected by wind and weather.

The best current indicators are those around you. Pilings will have a bow wave on their upcurrent side and a V-shaped wake downcurrent. Buoys lean with the current, and the more they lean, the stronger the current. Anchored boats are not reliable indicators, since they swing to the wind as well as the current. The simplest method is to stop your boat's movement through the water and watch reference points on land to see which way you are being set. If you can't see signs of a current, there probably isn't enough to affect you.

If you know the wind's direction, you can also tell the current's. Look at the water's surface. Waves or a chop will form where the current is running against the wind, and the water will be relatively smooth where the wind and current are aligned. Where a strong wind blows against the current, as when an inlet's outgoing tidal stream opposes an onshore wind or incoming waves, a rough sea can result, often making the passage impossible. Look for current lines, usually marked by floating debris, where currents meet. Choose the side you want to be on by its wind-caused wave pattern.

Use currents to your advantage. When beating, favour the tack that puts the current on your lee bow. This is *lee bowing*, and if you keep her footing, the current will help push you to windward. Currents are strongest where the water is deep, and weakest over

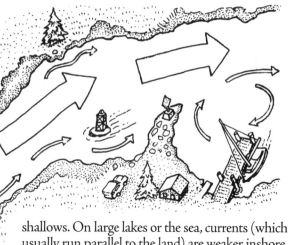

shallows. On large lakes or the sea, currents (which usually run parallel to the land) are weaker inshore than offshore. Tidal currents change direction along the shore first, with the ebb usually being stronger and lasting longer than the flood. So if you are sailing with a *foul* (on-your-bow) current, stay near shore or over thin water – the current will be weaker and of shorter duration. All currents speed up in restricted passages, and a bend in a channel has its deepest water and strongest currents on the outer curve. Water speeds up around points of land, piers and such, often with back eddies on the downcurrent side.

Check for currents when docking or mooring, because they can set you way off. In open water they have the ability to take you places you might not expect or even want to go. To prevent this, see page 205.

175

Tides

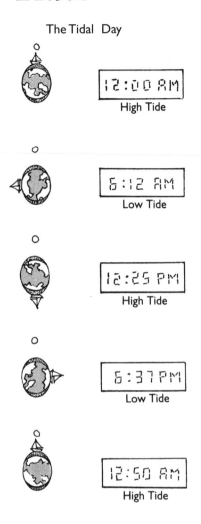

12:00 AM
High Tide

6:12 AM
Low Tide

12:25 PM
High Tide

6:37 PM
Low Tide

12:50 AM
High Tide

In times not all that distant, it was believed that tides were the respirations of a huge sea monster. And given the tide's regularity, it is not an inappropriate image. Over most of the world, tides are *semidiurnal* (twice a day), with two equal highs and lows. The West Coast of North America has *mixed* tides, with one higher high and one lower low. Along the Gulf of Mexico the tides are *diurnal* (once a day), with only one high and low per day.

Tides are caused by the gravitational pull of the moon and to a lesser extent (about half) the sun. The result is that the moon (helped or hindered by the sun) drags a bulge of water around the planet with it, with a complementary bulge caused by centrifugal force on the opposite side. We experience this bulge as tides. The relationship of the sun to the moon affects the tide's *range*, the difference between consecutive high and low waters. Greatest ranges, about 20% more than average, occur during *spring* (as in 'rising up') tides. The smallest ranges are during *neap* (from the Old English – without power of advancing) tides, and are about 20% less than average.

Think of tides and currents as separate entities. Tide is up and down, current in and out; and they are not as directly related as it might seem. For example, the tide's *stand* (period of no vertical motion) is not always in sync with the current's slack water. The current could still be flooding at the mouth of a river long after stand has passed and the water level has begun to drop. Always think of the two movements separately.

The duration of the tidal cycle follows the Earth's rotation. Semidiurnal tides change every 6 hours and 12 minutes, producing highs and lows 50 minutes later each day. The *Tide Tables* give you information about the tide's range, and the time and height of high and low waters to the minute. But local winds (an onshore wind can pile up water in a bay) and weather (a low-pressure area or heavy rains might raise tides) will have their way with these predictions.

The heights shown in the *Tide Tables* do not represent the depth of the water; they are figures to be added to or subtracted from the

The Tidal Month

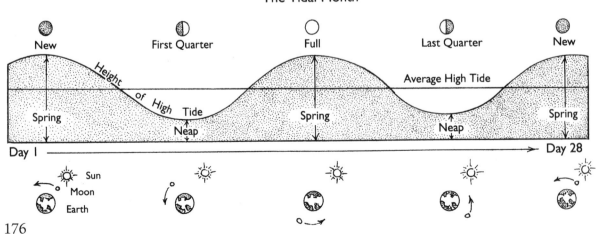

depths shown on the chart. These *charted depths* form a plane of reference called the *datum line*. On all charts drawn after 1987, charted depths are measured at *mean lower low water* (MLLW), the average height of the lowest low tides.

The easiest way to predict depths between high and low tides is to use the *Rule of Twelfths*. Tides do not rise or fall at an even rate. The water level changes more rapidly during the middle than at the beginning and end of each cycle. By dividing the tide's range by 12 and using the scale shown to the right, you get five intermediate stages of depths and times. To know the depth at any stage, take the figure you got from the rule and combine it with the depth of water found for the previous low or high tide.

The above-water heights given on charts use *mean high water* (MHW), the average high water level, as their datum line. Vertical clearance is important when dealing with bridges or overhead wires, and of course you should know the height of your mast above water before trying to squeeze under anything.

Stay in tune with the tides. Consider range when adjusting anchor scope or docklines. Cross shoals on a rising tide so you'll float if you ground. Expect tides on all waters joined to the sea. There are tides 100 miles up Florida's St. Johns River in fresh water. A good indicator of what the tide is doing is the high-water mark on beaches (a line of weeds and debris) or structures (barnacles or weeds). If it's dry between the water and the mark, the tide is rising. If it's wet, the tide is falling. And you might want to observe a moment of silence, for the receding tide is said to carry the souls of sailors to rest in the sea.

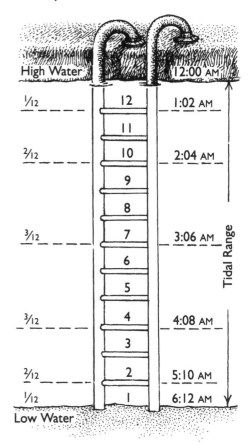

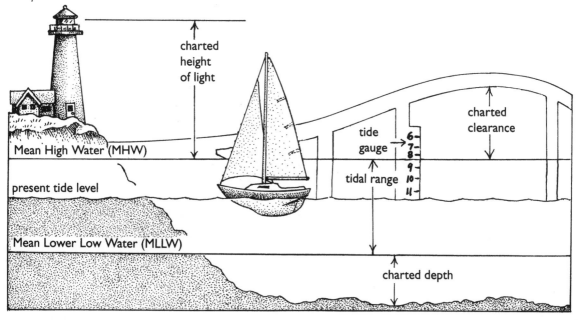

Waves

We need wind – it's what sailing is all about. Unfortunately, with the wind comes waves, which we don't need.

Waves are like mindless bullies roused into action by the prodding of the wind. The two are inseparable and, unless you sail in a seismographically active area, almost all the waves you'll encounter are born from and controlled by the wind.

Winds up to 6 mph generate waves by friction against the water's surface, with waves remaining small and angling out from the wind's direction by about 30 degrees. In stronger winds, waves become high enough for the wind to actually push on them, growing at a faster rate and following the wind's path.

The stronger the wind and the longer the distance the wind blows over open water (its *fetch*), the bigger the waves – up to a point. For any wind speed there is a maximum wave size that can be created.

The waves you sail on could be from a local wind and small, or from a wind hundreds of miles away and much larger, which are called *swells* and are not affected by local winds.

While waves are products of the wind, they are also easily manipulated by other forces. A current from either a river or tide running against the waves will cause them to steepen. Shallow underwater ledges or irregularities confuse them, narrow funnelling passages hasten them, points of land bend them, and steep shorelines or bulkheads bounce them around.

The first thing you'll want to know when dealing with waves is their size. A wave's height is the distance from its *trough* (the low point between two waves) to its *crest*, and it's not easy to judge.

We almost always overestimate their height because most of the time when you think you are looking out on a level line you are actually looking down on an angle, which can distort your judgement. The only time to make an accurate appraisal of the waves is when you are at the bottom of a trough. In general, though, waves are almost always smaller

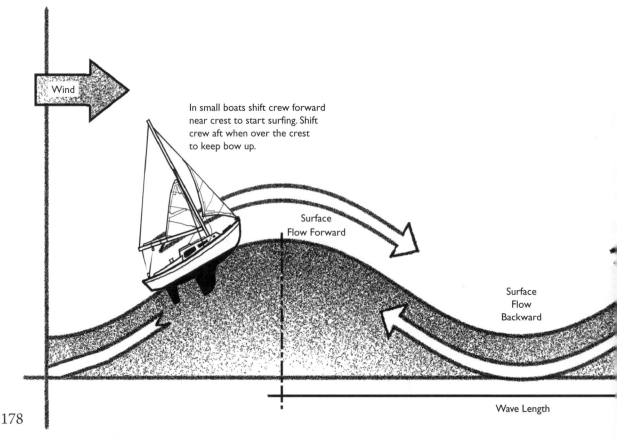

Wind

In small boats shift crew forward near crest to start surfing. Shift crew aft when over the crest to keep bow up.

Surface Flow Forward

Surface Flow Backward

Wave Length

than you think, and always seem calmer and less intimidating when you have your back to the wind. But turn and look into the oncoming wind and the waves suddenly seem a lot bigger and nastier.

Another confusing nature of waves is that once they are over 2 feet some of the water particles within them will be going along in the same direction, while others will be going backwards. You'll feel this mostly while sailing downwind. When a wave lifts your stern you'll not only pick up speed from sliding down its face, but the water in the crest is also moving forwards. For a few seconds you'll be flying. That is, until you hit the trough, where the water is moving against you.

As wind and waves build you may find your downwave speed increasing at an alarming rate. Your main concern now is retaining control. If the bow starts to dig in and begins to broach, you're going too fast and it's time to shorten sail.

There's not much to worry about when the waves are on your beam other than that they can roll the wind out of your sails if there's a big swell and not much of a breeze. The only solution is to head up until it stops. In fast light boats a beam sea can catch a hiked-out crew unaware by tripping the centreboard or keel so you suddenly heel to windward, or even capsize.

When close-hauled you'll find that widely spaced, deep-water swells are almost pleasant as they gently undulate past. More troublesome is the short chop found in shallow waters that have recently been whipped up. These short-*period* (the time between crests) waves can hit the bow hard and frequently enough to slow or even stop your progress. In light boats, this can be alleviated by shifting your weight aft to lighten the bow. In all boats try to sail full and by to keep your speed and momentum up, especially right before tacking. If you can, time your tack so you pivot at the crest of a wave. This gets the boat's ends out of the water, making it easier to turn, and gives you plenty of wind.

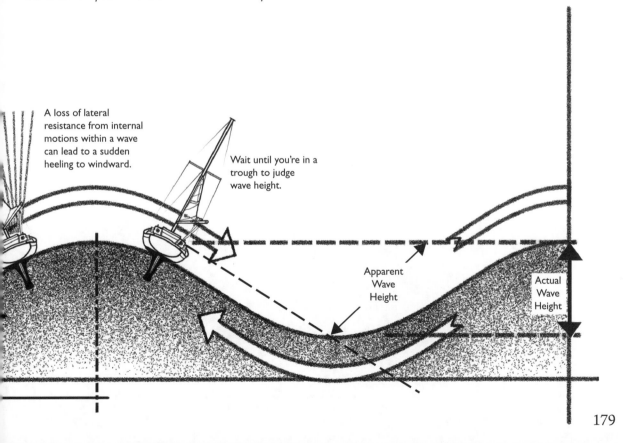

A loss of lateral resistance from internal motions within a wave can lead to a sudden heeling to windward.

Wait until you're in a trough to judge wave height.

Apparent Wave Height

Actual Wave Height

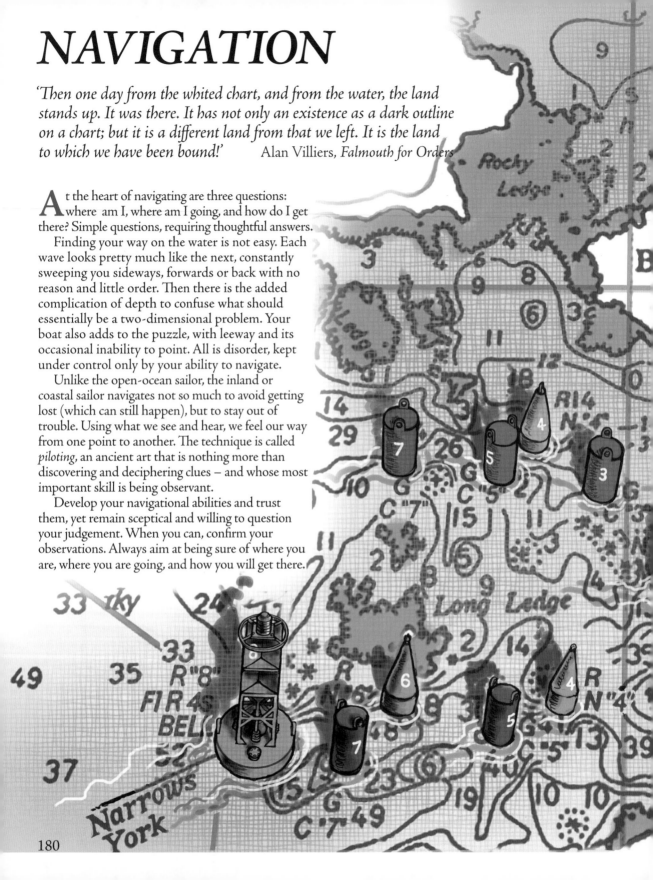

NAVIGATION

'Then one day from the whited chart, and from the water, the land stands up. It was there. It has not only an existence as a dark outline on a chart; but it is a different land from that we left. It is the land to which we have been bound!' Alan Villiers, *Falmouth for Orders*

At the heart of navigating are three questions: where am I, where am I going, and how do I get there? Simple questions, requiring thoughtful answers.

Finding your way on the water is not easy. Each wave looks pretty much like the next, constantly sweeping you sideways, forwards or back with no reason and little order. Then there is the added complication of depth to confuse what should essentially be a two-dimensional problem. Your boat also adds to the puzzle, with leeway and its occasional inability to point. All is disorder, kept under control only by your ability to navigate.

Unlike the open-ocean sailor, the inland or coastal sailor navigates not so much to avoid getting lost (which can still happen), but to stay out of trouble. Using what we see and hear, we feel our way from one point to another. The technique is called *piloting*, an ancient art that is nothing more than discovering and deciphering clues – and whose most important skill is being observant.

Develop your navigational abilities and trust them, yet remain sceptical and willing to question your judgement. When you can, confirm your observations. Always aim at being sure of where you are, where you are going, and how you will get there.

16 34 38 72 84

19

13 43

54 M 81

9

26 18 23 42

rky

30

50

10 27

9

33 RW "CB" 27

14 BELL

G 26

42 M 25 rky 39 38 Sh

CASCO PASSAGE

+9 G 55 62 71

C "1" 49

32 57

13 Wk 58

1 15

8 G 15

"1A" 8 12

2 3 Phinney 20 55

8 I 15

Orono I M Crow I

13 9 42

11 The 23

4 7 Triangles

35 9 22

56 6 9 15

Round I. 40 9

181

Language of the Chart

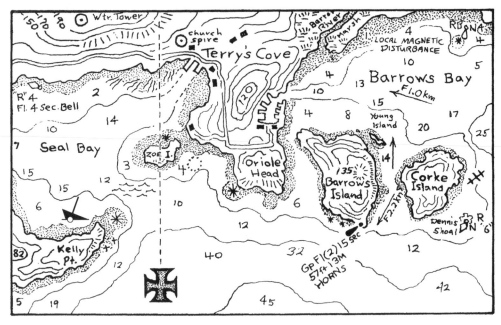

As seen on a chart

The most important tool the navigator has is the chart. In fact, navigation as we know it can't be practised without one.

A chart is like a guidebook to a foreign country – revealing what is not obvious, and loaded with facts that would take years to discover or are unknown even to locals. Charts show hidden obstructions, shoals, topography above and below water, *soundings* (depths), bottom characteristics, landmarks, buoys, wrecks, channels and much more. By showing you where to look and what to look for, your chart will keep you out of trouble.

When travelling, whether in home waters or abroad, use the most up-to-date chart available. Charts are constantly being revised – some every few years, others after decades. In the meantime, things change. Older charts can be updated with the *Local Notice to Mariners*, which is published weekly and put online by your regional Coastguard district, giving chart revisions and timely data.

To get the chart that shows the most information about your area, choose one with a *large scale* (1:50,000 to 1:15,000, or larger). For coastwise navigation and more generalised coverage of a wider area, choose a *small-scale* (1:50,000 to 1:150,000, or smaller) chart. The higher the second number in the ratio, the smaller the scale. The lower the number, the larger the scale. Small scale = smaller

This is what you see

⊙
Water Tower, Spire or Stack

∴
Obstruction

Cliffs

Kelp

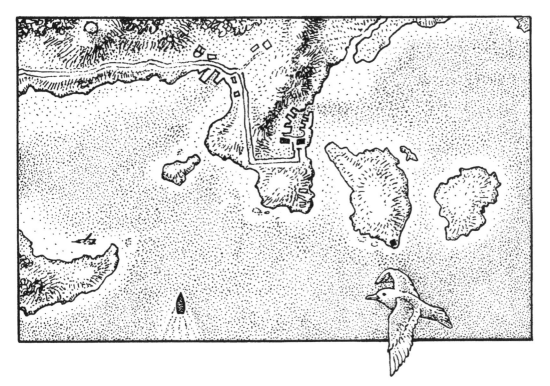

Seagull's-eye view

+|+ Sunken Wreck

≈≈≈ Tide Rips

⌐ Jetty

⊛ Rock Awash

+ Submerged Rock

Exposed Wreck

details over a large area. Large scale = larger details over a small area.

The language of the chart is written in symbols. A few are self-explanatory, but for most you'll need a translating dictionary. To learn the language get *Chart No. 1*, a booklet explaining all the colours, numbers, lines and symbols. It, and all other U.S. charts, are published by the National Oceanic and Atmospheric Administration (called 'Noah' for its acronym).

Before heading out on the water, compare what is on your local chart with what you see. At first what is represented on the chart will look nothing at all like the world around you. That is, until you learn to see. Start by picking out obvious and known landmarks, and find your position among them. Next judge the distances between the landmarks, and then between them and yourself, to get a sense of scale. Do the same each time you use a chart for a new area. It takes time to get the proper perspective, but it must be done or you'll confuse rocks with islands, islands with peninsulas.

Never be afraid to question a chart. Lighthouses fail, shorelines erode, and channels shift in storms. Charts are incredibly accurate, for people's lives depend on them; but they are not perfect and cannot predict the future.

Aids to Navigation

When nature leaves us none, we must provide our own landmarks in the sea. The most familiar is the buoy, from the Old French 'boye', meaning chained, in reference to the chains that hold the marker in place. Buoys indicate channels or underwater hazards.

The IALA Maritime Buoyage System has now been standardised throughout the world, differing only in the use of red and green Lateral marks. In Europe and the Mediterranean (IALA Region A), red buoys are kept to port (left). Somewhat confusingly, in Region B, covering North America, the opposite prevails. Everything else is essentially the same.

Lateral marks indicate channels, while Cardinal marks show dangers in relation to the compass. Two cones pointing upwards on a buoy, for instance, advise the yachtsman to stay to the north of the danger' cones pointing down, or south, indicate the opposite. Isolated danger marks, safe water marks and special marks are distinguished by their colour, shape or topmark by day, and light characteristic by night.

Buoys are only warnings or guides, not infallible sentries. They can be dragged under by strong currents, break loose from their moorings, sink, or have their lights fail. So don't follow them blindly. Channels do not always run in straight lines from one buoy to the next. Refer to your chart before boldly charging ahead. To give a few examples, if confronted by a red Lateral mark on entering harbour, keep it to port, and the green starboard mark that may accompany it to starboard, as the channel lies between the two. A spar buoy coloured black with a single horizontal yellow band and two black cones to base on top will tell the yachtsman to keep to the east. At night it will flash 3 white very quickly (VQ) every 5 seconds, or quickly (Q) every 10 seconds.

The buoyage system is a logical system based on the clock face. The west Cardinal mark flashes nine times, the south Cardinal six times and the north continuously. Isolated danger marks appear in black and red striped jerseys with two balls for a top mark.

Red and green channel marker posts are often used in shallow estuaries or creeks. Sometimes tricky entrances to harbours are given leading marks, or lights at night. When lined up these keep a yacht on course, in the safe channel. This is a very precise method of designating deep water. The principle is often used informally by yachtsmen picking their own sets of shore markers – two trees in line, etc. – to keep clear of obstructions.

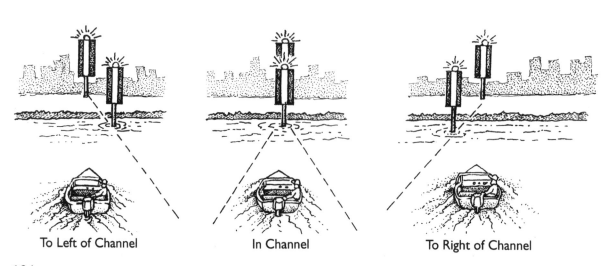

To Left of Channel   In Channel   To Right of Channel

Cardinal Marks

Used to indicate the direction from the mark in which the best navigable water lies, or to draw attention to a bend, junction or folk in a channel, or to mark the end of a shoal.

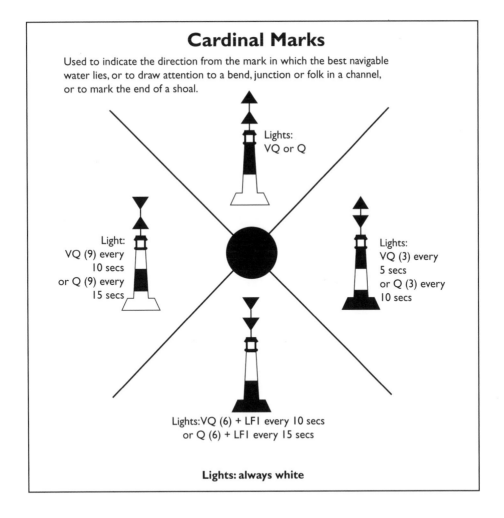

Lights:
VQ or Q

Light:
VQ (9) every
10 secs
or Q (9) every
15 secs

Lights:
VQ (3) every
5 secs
or Q (3) every
10 secs

Lights: VQ (6) + LFl every 10 secs
or Q (6) + LFl every 15 secs

Lights: always white

Navigation Marks

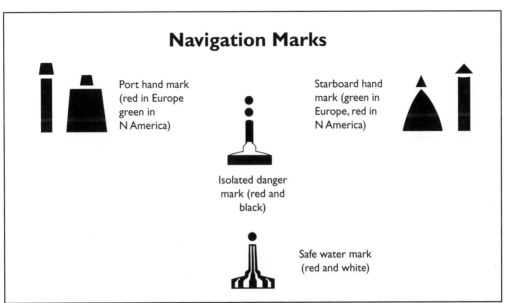

Port hand mark
(red in Europe
green in
N America)

Isolated danger
mark (red and
black)

Starboard hand
mark (green in
Europe, red in
N America)

Safe water mark
(red and white)

Lights

When the sun sets, fog closes in, or storms turn day into night – the lights go on, automatically.

The most prevalent lighted aids are buoys, each of which is distinguished from its neighbours by lights of different colours and *characteristics* (patterns). When looking for a light, first note its colour. Red lights are for red buoys and junction/obstruction buoys whose top band is red. Green lights are for green buoys and junction/obstruction buoys whose top band is green. White lights are only for midchannel buoys.

Next check the buoy's light characteristics against what is marked on the chart. Red or green buoys are either *flashing, group flashing, quick flashing, occulting* or *equal interval*. Junction/obstruction buoys showing the preferred channel are always *composite group flashing* (2 + 1). Midchannel buoys showing safe water flash a *Morse code 'A'*.

To further distinguish one navigational aid from another, their characteristics have a *period*. A buoy marked 'Fl G 4 Sec' has a period of 4 seconds between green flashes. Time the period with a stopwatch or learn to count seconds. Start when the pattern goes off, stop when it comes back on.

There are fewer *lighthouses* than buoys, but they make up for this with their grandeur. The earliest were simple fire platforms, built around 800 BC along the North African coast. Later, in 3 BC, the 200-foot light at Alexandria was the first of the true lighthouses, evoking as much wonder then as modern ones do today when approached from the lonely sea. In addition to lighthouses, there are now *light towers* (or 'Texas towers' because they look like oil rigs) offshore and smaller *beacons* on land. Their light characteristics are often more complex than those on buoys so you can clearly identify which light is which. Some lights can be further identified by their sound-making device or *radio beacon* (R Bn) signal. Their height (in feet above mean high water, MHW) and approximate range of visibility (in miles) are shown on the chart.

Lighthouses and towers often have *danger sectors*, a portion of their arc in which the light is seen as red, not white. The light's characteristic (flashing, fixed, etc.) remains the same, only the colour changes. Red sectors mark hazards or show that you have strayed from the channel. If you're seeing red where a light is normally white, check your chart to find out why.

Don't let sailing at night intimidate you. It can actually be safer than the day, with aids to navigation being easier to see at a distance. Knowing this, many sailors time their landfalls for early morning, homing in on a long-range light just before daybreak.

When you first see a light, note its colour, characteristic and period. Then refer to your chart. Don't insist that what you see is what you hoped would be there. Be flexible. It's very possible that you are not where you think, and that flashing red light is really a traffic light ashore.

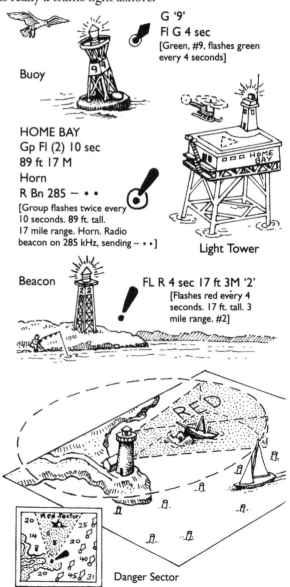

Buoy

G '9'
Fl G 4 sec
[Green, #9, flashes green
every 4 seconds]

HOME BAY
Gp Fl (2) 10 sec
89 ft 17 M
Horn
R Bn 285 – • •
[Group flashes twice every
10 seconds. 89 ft. tall.
17 mile range. Horn. Radio
beacon on 285 kHz, sending – • •]

Light Tower

Beacon

FL R 4 sec 17 ft 3M '2'
[Flashes red every 4
seconds. 17 ft. tall. 3
mile range. #2]

Danger Sector

LIGHT CHARACTERISTICS

These are the light characteristics for all *buoys* used in UK coastal waters and elsewhere. Some patterns are more complex, with sectors to denote danger areas, for example, hights are marked in magenta on Admiralty charts with their characteristics.

Pattern	Characteristic	Description
	Flashing Fl	A single flash of light at regular intervals of one in every 2 or more seconds.
	Quick Flashing Qk Fl	Flashes at least once per second.
	Occulting Occ	Periods of light are longer than period of dark.
	Equal Interval E Int	Equal periods of light and dark. Sometimes called isophase.
	Morse Code 'A' Mo (A)	Flashes Morse Code signal for the letter 'A'. For midchannel buoys only.
	Group Flashing Gp Fl	Flashes twice or more at regular intervals.
	Composite Group Flashing C Gp Fl (2 + 1)	Combinations of group flashes. Example: two flashes followed by one are for junction/obstruction buoys.
	Fixed F	A continuous light.
	Fixed and Flashing F Fl	A continuous light with flashes of greater intensity at regular intervals.
	Fixed & Group Flashing F Gp Fl	A continuous light with flashes of greater intensity in groups of two or more.
	Group Occulting Gp Occ	Two or more dark periods in regularly spaced groups.
	Composite Group Occulting C Gp Occ (3 + 1)	Combinations of group dark periods. Example: three dark periods followed by one.

Visibility

Each lighthouse, light tower and beacon on the chart has its height and range of visibility noted like this: '89 ft 17 M.' Height is measured in feet above mean high water, and range is the *nominal range* measured in miles.

Nominal range is how far the light can be seen in clear weather when it is not limited by the Earth's curvature. It is not how far away you can see the light, but rather a measure of its brightness. Of more practical use is the light's *geographic range*, which is determined primarily by its height.

Geographic range is also affected by the height of the observer. As with a light, the higher the observer, the further he can see and be seen.

To determine any object's geographic range, you need to know the height of the object and your height. The mathematical solution shown here is a practical approximation of a much more complex formula. It is a simple way to estimate range and accurate enough for general use. To make calculating easier, pre-compute the square root of your eye height at one spot in the boat. You can find a square root by squaring (a number times itself) a few good guesses until you get close, or use a calculator.

This formula will give maximum range, the point at which the light first becomes visible at night or the top of the tower pops above the horizon in the day. Of course, a light's geographic range cannot be greater than its nominal range. So get both, then use the lesser. There will be times when you can see a light's *loom*, its reflected glow, way beyond its range. Then again, atmospheric conditions can wipe out visibility completely.

When navigating at night, be careful not to blind yourself with bright lights on board. Keep lighting dim, or use red bulbs or filters. You are more likely to find what you are looking for if you scan a broad arc, rather than staring at the spot where it 'should' be. Scanning uses your peripheral vision, which is more sensitive in low light. Once sighted, it is often hard to tell if a light is a nearby buoy or far-off lighthouse. To judge, try *bobbing* the light by lowering your eyes to reduce geographic range. A far-off light will disappear; a nearby buoy will remain visible.

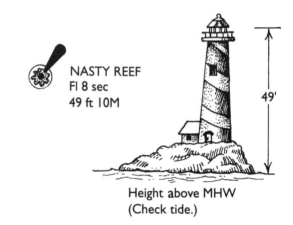

NASTY REEF
Fl 8 sec
49 ft 10M

49'

Height above MHW
(Check tide.)

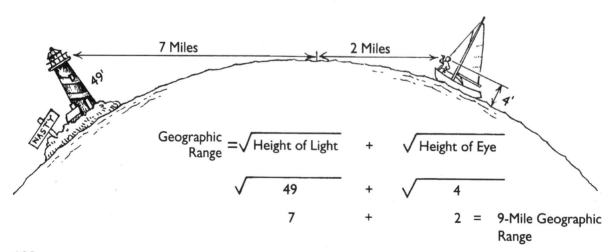

7 Miles   2 Miles

$$\text{Geographic Range} = \sqrt{\text{Height of Light}} + \sqrt{\text{Height of Eye}}$$

$$\sqrt{49} + \sqrt{4}$$

$$7 + 2 = \text{9-Mile Geographic Range}$$

Sound

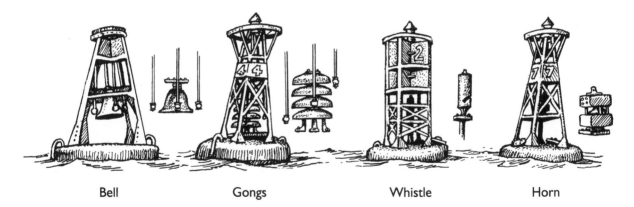

| Bell | Gongs | Whistle | Horn |

Sound is a relatively new feature for aids to navigation, the first bell and whistle buoys being installed around the late 1850s. And they make sense. On a sailing boat at night or in a fog, when there is nothing to see, you listen. You listen very carefully.

The chart always notes the type of sound-making device a buoy has. A *bell* uses many clappers to strike one bell, each producing a similar tone. *Gongs* have three or four small bells, each with its own clapper and each producing a different tone. A *whistle* uses the buoy's up-and-down motion to push air through an orifice, producing a sorrowful moan. A *horn* is the only sound-making device on a buoy that does not depend on the sea's motion. It uses electric power to make a tone that is similar to, but steadier than, a whistle.

Lighthouses, light towers and beacons also use sound to help identify themselves and are so marked on the chart. The type and characteristics of their sounds are different from a buoy's, and their range is greater. *Horns* use multiple horns (rather than a buoy's single horn) of different pitch to produce an almost musical tone. A *diaphone* gives a tone that starts with a higher pitch and ends on a lower. A *siren* may sound like a police siren but is usually an even tone similar to that of a single horn.

Charts tell only what sound-making device is used, with no information about the sound's characteristic pattern – the number and length of *blasts* per period. *The Admiralty List of Lights, and Fog Signals*, or an almanac such as the *Reeds Nautical Almanac*, will describe each light and buoy. They will also say if the sound-making device operates only during reduced visibility or at all times.

What they can't tell you, and no one can, is how the sound will travel. A foghorn's blast can go great distances downwind, while being inaudible just a short distance upwind. Range, loudness and apparent direction can all vary due to wind or atmospheric conditions. So give them a chance. Be quiet. And listen.

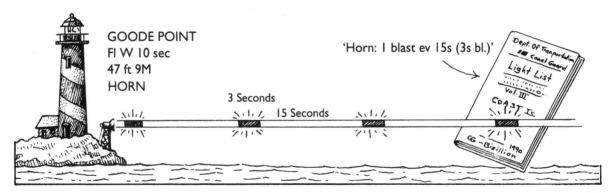

GOODE POINT
Fl W 10 sec
47 ft 9M
HORN

'Horn: 1 blast ev 15s (3s bl.)'

3 Seconds   15 Seconds

Plotting a Course

Before you leave familiar waters, heading over the horizon towards something you can't see, you have to be able to plot a safe course to steer by.

Start by finding where you are on the chart and choosing a point of departure, such as a buoy. Then find where you want to go and choose a point of arrival. Using a ruler and a soft lead pencil, draw a line connecting the two points. Now follow that line. Does it pass over shoals, hit land, or run through an anchorage? If it does, you will have to go around them, dividing the course into a series of short legs. Many sailors prefer making short jumps from buoy to buoy rather than one long haul, even if it adds extra distance, because it is easier to keep track of where they are throughout the run.

Once a course is laid down, you have to convert it into a compass heading for the helmsman to steer. No doubt you've heard that a compass always points to the north pole. Well, that's not quite correct. The Earth has two north poles: the *geographic*, which is one end of the axis of rotation; and the *magnetic*, which is at the northern end of the planet's magnetic core. While geographic (or *true*) north is fixed on top of the world, *magnetic north* is slowly wobbling

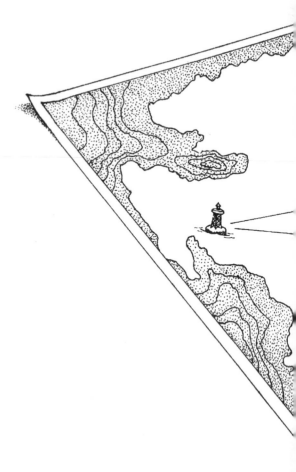

about somewhere to the west of Baffin Island. In navigation we are usually only interested in magnetic north, because that's where the compass points.

The difference between true and magnetic north is called *variation*, because magnetic north's position is constantly changing (varying). Variation could make plotting a course a complicated problem, but the chart's *compass rose* solves this for us. Each rose has an outer ring aligned to true north (which we can ignore), and two inner rings aligned to magnetic north – with the appropriate variation built in. The innermost ring is graduated in the antiquated system of *points* (such as NE by N). The middle ring is in degrees, and that's the one we use for navigation. The rose also shows annual increase or decrease of variation, which is usually small enough to be disregarded.

Compass Rose

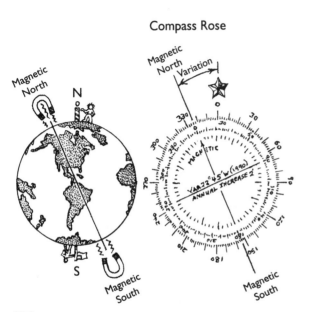

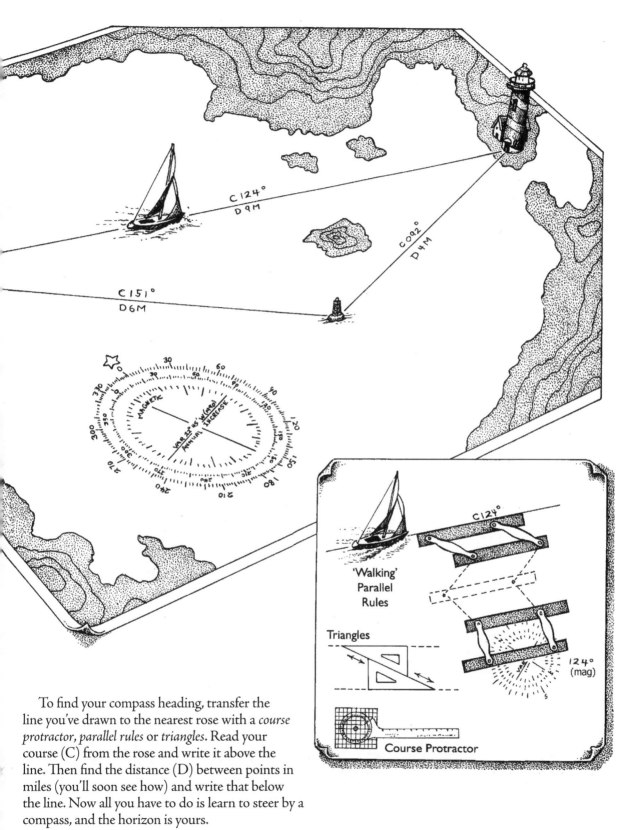

C 124°
D 9 M

C 092°
D 4 M

C 151°
D 6 M

MAGNETIC

VAR 12° 45' W(980)
ANNUAL INCREASE

'Walking'
Parallel
Rules

Triangles

C 124°

124°
(mag)

Course Protractor

To find your compass heading, transfer the line you've drawn to the nearest rose with a *course protractor*, *parallel rules* or *triangles*. Read your course (C) from the rose and write it above the line. Then find the distance (D) between points in miles (you'll soon see how) and write that below the line. Now all you have to do is learn to steer by a compass, and the horizon is yours.

The Compass

To steer a course you need a constant reference point, something that is always in the same spot; and if you can't see that spot, you'll need a gadget that will point to it. A compass indicating magnetic north does the job nicely, much better than what earlier sailors started with.

Back in an unknown time, someone noticed that one star in the northern sky – it may have been Draconis then and not Polaris – never moved. It was a constant, something to be steered against. When it could not be seen there were the winds, sun or moon, but these were not dependable.

Then came the north-seeking compass, although we don't know when. The Chinese are thought to have invented it around 2 AD, but there is little to substantiate this. We know for sure that Norse explorers used it to reach Iceland in the 9th century, and a true and accurate instrument, not just a sliver of lodestone floating on straw, was available by the 1300s.

The modern marine compass mounts its magnetised needle on a rotating circular *card*. Until well into the last century, the card was marked in points. Almost all cards today are graduated in degrees, with only the *cardinal points* (N, E, S, W) indicated. Regardless of how the boat turns, the card stays firmly aligned with magnetic north, with the boat's heading being read off the *lubber line*.

Sitting in a boat as it weaves through the sea, it may appear that the card is doing the moving. But it is locked in place, always pointing north, while the lubber line and the boat move around it. Without this concept you won't be able to steer or hold a course, so remember: Don't try to turn the card to the heading – turn the boat to it.

Specially made sailing boat compasses have *auxiliary lubber lines* at 45 and 90 degrees to each side of the centre lubber line. The 45-degree lines can be used as steering guides when the helmsman is sitting to one side and unable to see the centre lubber line. The 90-degree lines can be used to estimate tacking angles. When the next point you want to head towards can be sighted along this line, you tack.

Use and trust your compass even in clear weather. In crowded harbours where there is a proliferation of buoys, or where one landmark is much like the next, plot a course and steer it just to be sure.

When buying a compass, get one with a card that's easy to read at a distance. It should also be well damped so it doesn't swing about wildly. Check this by quickly turning the compass 30 degrees. The card should swing directly to the new course without wandering back and forth. Be sure to install it in a convenient place, and mount it so the lubber line is parallel to the centreline. Keep radios, knives, air horns, tools, anchors and chain well away. A good compass, properly installed and used, is an ally that can be trusted. Treat it well and let it work for you.

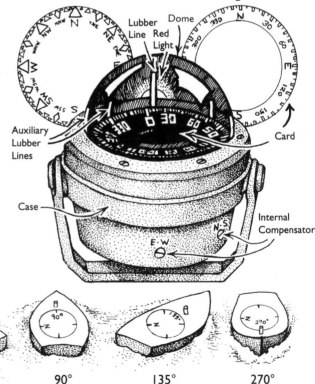

The card stays put as the boat turns.

STEERING A COURSE

Most compasses are *top reading*, with their lubber line on the forward edge of the compass case. These are read by looking down at them. If the desired heading is to the right on the card, you steer to the right. If it is to the left, you steer to the left.

Some compasses are *side reading*, with their lubber line on the aft edge of the compass case. These are read by looking horizontally at them. If the desired heading is to the right on the card, you steer to the left. If it is to the left, you steer to the right.

It's difficult to hold a straight course by staring at the compass. Put the boat on its heading and then look ahead for a temporary reference point: a cloud, hill, buoy, anything. Frequently recheck your heading on the compass. If need be, correct, and find another point to aim for. When there are no reference points, you will have to steer directly by the compass. Even then, look up once in a while, using the relative angle of the wind or waves as a reference before looking back at the compass.

Don't try to compensate for every little lurch and roll of the boat – go for a good average course. Make small, smooth corrections, not grand, bold ones. Accurate navigation depends on steering a straight course, not one that writes your name in the sea. A 1-degree error puts you about 400 feet off course after 4 miles. Only the best helmsman can steer within 2 or 3 degrees of the course, and if you can average 5 degrees over a long run, you're doing fine.

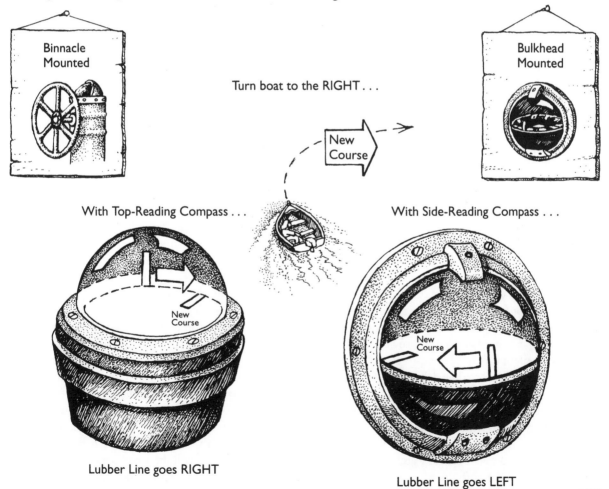

Binnacle Mounted

Bulkhead Mounted

Turn boat to the RIGHT . . .

New Course

With Top-Reading Compass . . .

With Side-Reading Compass . . .

New Course

New Course

Lubber Line goes RIGHT

Lubber Line goes LEFT

Deviation

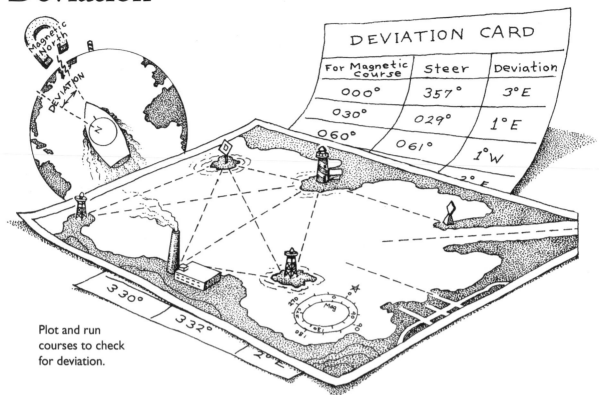

For Magnetic course	Steer	Deviation
000°	357°	3° E
030°	029°	1° E
060°	061°	1° W
		2° E

DEVIATION CARD

Plot and run courses to check for deviation.

A compass with nothing around it will search out the Earth's magnetic field and lock in. Put that same compass on a boat and its resolve weakens, as onboard magnetic forces make it deviate from magnetic north. The difference between what that compass reads and your actual magnetic course is *deviation*.

Your boat's compass may not have any deviation. On many small craft made with wood, fibreglass, and aluminium, there may be no local magnetic forces. But don't be too sure. Frying pans, outboard motors, ballast, wiring and electrical gadgets can all play tricks.

To check, plot courses that can be accurately held and then run them. Find natural ranges: two daymarks, a beacon and a water tower, long bulkheads, straight canals, or even streets on land. Never use buoys, because they drift about. Or locate yourself exactly and plot a course to a landmark at least 2 miles off. Since deviation changes with the boat's heading, plot as many courses as you can. Have some courses as close to the cardinal points as you can find. Pick a calm body of water with little wind, current, or boat traffic.

Make your first run towards the mark or range, and compare the compass reading to the plotted course. Then make a run away from the mark or range and get a compass reading on the *reciprocal* (180 degrees opposite) course. If the compass agrees with the courses in both directions, you have no deviation on those headings. If the compass is high (or low) by an equal amount in both directions, it needs to be realigned to the boat's centreline. If the compass is higher (or lower) than the plotted course towards the mark or range, and the opposite on the reciprocal, there is deviation.

Most marine compasses have small internal compensating magnets that can be used to eliminate deviation on the cardinal points. Once adjusted, these corrections should lessen or remove errors in the intercardinal points as well. Through compensation, it is usually possible to reduce deviation to within a single degree on all headings, which is thoroughly acceptable. For the remaining errors, make up a *deviation card* that will show compass error and the compass heading to steer for your desired course.

COMPENSATING FOR DEVIATION

Stow everything on board as you normally would. Bring along a marker float, a non-magnetic screwdriver (often supplied with the compass) to turn the compensators, and a helping hand. You will also need a daymark (less preferably, a buoy) with at least half a mile of deep water around it to use as a point of reference. Proceed as follows:

Steer a compass heading of 000 degrees (north) away from the mark. After about half a mile, drop the float to create a range. Turn wide to come back on the float, almost running it down, and steer towards the mark. Do not steer by the compass. On this course the compass should read 180 degrees. If not, slowly turn the N-S compensator screw to remove *half* the difference between your compass heading and 180.

Steer a compass heading of 90 degrees (east) away from the mark. After about half a mile, drop the float to create a range. Turn wide to come back on the float, almost running it down, and steer towards the mark. Do not steer by the compass. On this course

the compass should read 270 degrees. If not, slowly turn the E-W compensator screw to remove *half* the difference between your compass heading and 270.

Return your original compass of 000 degrees away from the mark, drop the float, and make the reciprocal run towards the mark. Recheck the difference between compass heading and 180. If any, remove half.

Return a compass course of 90 degrees away from the mark, drop the float, and make the reciprocal run towards the mark. Recheck the difference between compass heading and 270. If any, remove half.

Keep rerunning the course until you have removed as much error as possible.

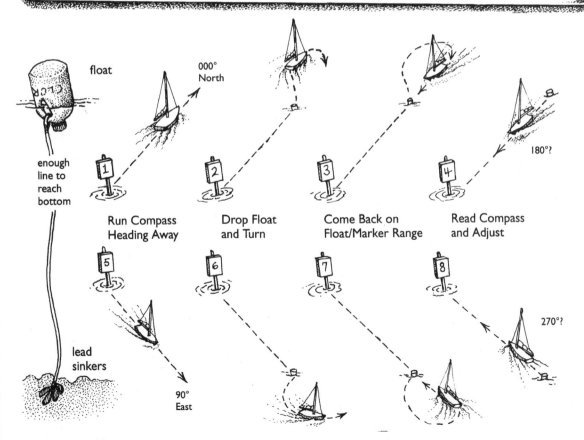

float

000°
North

enough line to reach bottom

lead sinkers

| 1 | 2 | 3 | 4 |

Run Compass Heading Away

Drop Float and Turn

Come Back on Float/Marker Range

Read Compass and Adjust

180°?

| 5 | 6 | 7 | 8 |

90° East

270°?

Lines of Position

You must be somewhere. But if you're not next to anything that can be picked out on the chart, where are you? A good place to start is by finding a *line of position*, or LOP. This is a line of reference, a visual line of sight upon which your boat sits. When drawn on the chart, you can say with assurance that your vessel is somewhere along that line. It's a way of estimating your position.

On land you might not know precisely where you are, but you could call someone and say, 'I'm on Mediterranean Avenue.' That's your LOP. On its own, a line of position does not tell where you are so much as where you are not, but that can narrow things down quite a bit. Now take that LOP and cross it with another, '. . . where it crosses Boardwalk.' You've provided a *fix*, and the person you called would be able to find you. There is no other place you could be. But to get a fix, you have to start with reliable and accurate LOPs, and one way to do that is by taking *bearings*.

All bearings (and there are many types) describe direction using angles. A *compass bearing* gives the direction to an object seen from your boat as an angle made with magnetic north.

Point your boat at a lighthouse and read the compass. If, for example, it says 90 degrees, the line connecting you and the lighthouse makes a 90-degree angle with magnetic north. We say that it 'bears 90 degrees magnetic'. Using the compass rose and parallel rules, draw a 270-degree line (the reciprocal of 90 degrees) through the lighthouse towards where you think you might be. That's an LOP, and you're somewhere on it.

Pointing the boat is an effective means of taking a bearing, but you can't always do that. An alternative is to sight over a top-reading compass, but this lacks precision. A better way that is both convenient and accurate is to use a hand-bearing compass. Just aim it and wait until the card steadies itself on the bearing. In rough weather, you may have to take a few bearings and average them out. They should all fall within 5 degrees of each other. When you can, take bearings of nearby objects. This keeps the LOP and area of probable error as small as possible.

You can get lines of position in other ways. One of the quickest and most accurate is to use naturally occurring ranges. A careful look at any chart will show

a wealth of ranges. Any two identifiable objects can become a range. Find them on the chart, draw an LOP through their two points, and extend the line towards your general area. When you see the two points line up, you are on that line. Simple and precise.

The 'line' in a line of position can be circular as well as straight. If you know the distance to an object, you can use that distance as the radius of a circle with the object at its centre. This circle then becomes a *circular line of position*. Distance can be found by determining geographic range (page 188), using a series of bearings (page 204), or employing other techniques (page 199).

Lines of position can also be curved or irregular. Depth contour lines, shown as dashed lines on the chart, make usable if not overly precise LOPs. Use underwater shelves where there is a drastic change in depth. Isolated shallows or sudden holes are also good, and if small enough can even provide a rough fix.

A Line of Position

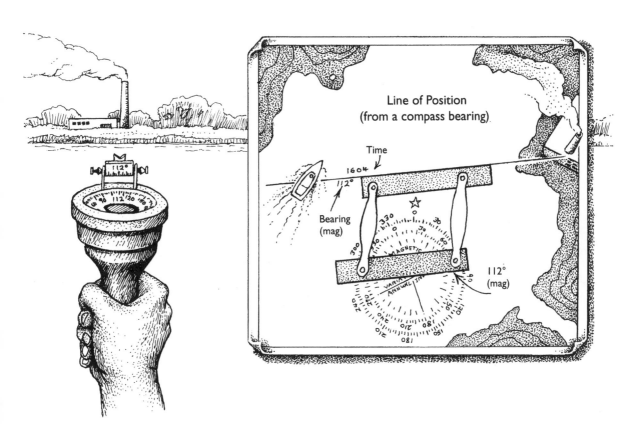

Line of Position
(from a compass bearing)

Time
1604

Bearing
(mag)

112°

112°
(mag)

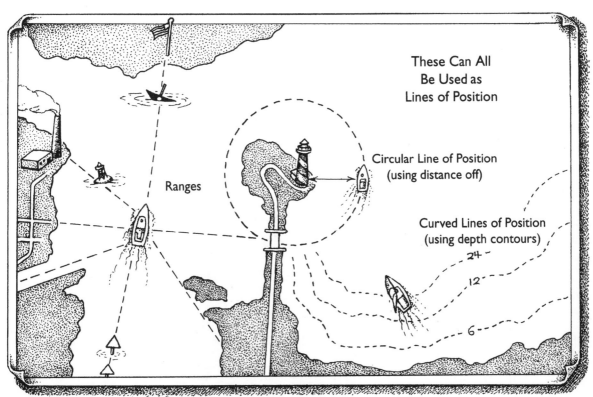

These Can All
Be Used as
Lines of Position

Ranges

Circular Line of Position
(using distance off)

Curved Lines of Position
(using depth contours)

24

12

6

Danger LOPs

Lines of position, when plotted in advance, can warn of danger and keep you out of harm's way.

An LOP made from a bearing can be used to avoid unmarked obstacles and assure your safe passage past them. Draw a line from a charted object (like a buoy) that lies along your course, skirting the edge of any danger you want to avoid. This line of position is your *danger bearing* – a safety barrier over which you must not cross.

Draw a second bearing, a *safety bearing*, that stands off from the hazard with a good margin of safety. This is the bearing you will steer by. Note the difference between the two bearings, and whether the bearings increase or decrease towards the hazard. This tells you that you can steer either higher or lower than a particular course and still remain safe. While sailing, continue to check your course until you are sure you have passed the obstruction. This will prevent current or leeway from setting you onto it.

Danger Bearing

Safety Bearing

45° 40° 35° 30° 25° 20°

Steering more than 30° is dangerous

Steering less than 30° is safe

Circular lines of position can also be used to keep you off the rocks. By drawing a circle around a charted object to enclose a piece of dangerous water, you create a *danger circle*. To use this circle, you will have to be able to estimate how far off you are from the object (next page). As long as you keep further away than the danger circle's radius, you will be safe. A circular line of position can also be used to help you *double* (go around) a point. Keep the charted object at a preset safe distance, and always keep it on your beam. In this way you sail along the circle's circumference, bypassing inshore dangers.

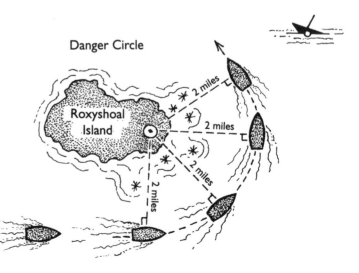

Danger Circle

Roxyshoal Island

2 miles
2 miles
2 miles
2 miles

Distance Off

'How far off is that?' It's a good question to ask in the interest of safety as well as finding out where you are. To help you, here are some rough-and-ready techniques that work well on a bouncing small boat, navigated by a skipper who already has his hands full. To be on the safe side, put their potential for error in your favour by assuming you are closer to, not further from, the object sighted.

You can get very reliable distances when you know the height of something and use the formula for geographic range (page 188). The same formula will give the distance to your horizon.

Another way of finding distance off from an object's height, or width, is to hold your fingers at arm's length to define an *angle of sight*. Plug that angle and the object's dimension into the formula shown below to get distance. Since height is rarely noted on charts, use width or a known distance between two points. Look for bridge spans, docks, islands, landmarks, or anything that can be measured.

You can also take sight angles for width by *winking*. With one eye closed, hold a finger at arm's length next to one point. Then close that eye and open the other. Multiply the horizontal length your finger appears to travel by 10 to get distance off. You may not be able to cover an easily measured length by winking. If so, try estimating: On a 500-foot-wide island, did you 'wink' halfway across, or a third?

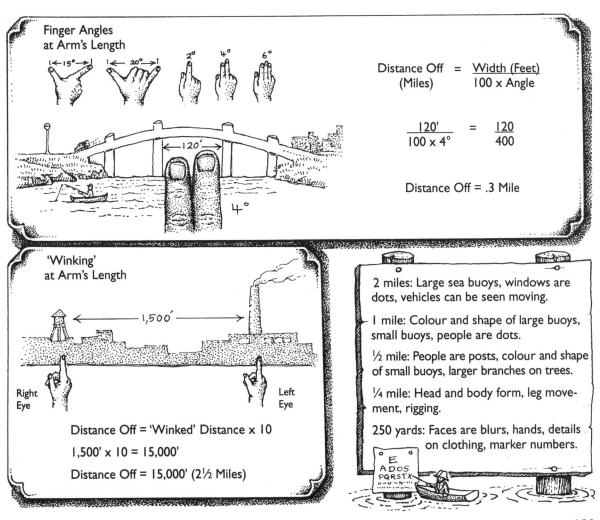

Finger Angles at Arm's Length

$$\text{Distance Off (Miles)} = \frac{\text{Width (Feet)}}{100 \times \text{Angle}}$$

$$\frac{120'}{100 \times 4°} = \frac{120}{400}$$

Distance Off = .3 Mile

'Winking' at Arm's Length

Right Eye   Left Eye

Distance Off = 'Winked' Distance x 10

1,500' x 10 = 15,000'

Distance Off = 15,000' (2½ Miles)

2 miles: Large sea buoys, windows are dots, vehicles can be seen moving.

1 mile: Colour and shape of large buoys, small buoys, people are dots.

½ mile: People are posts, colour and shape of small buoys, larger branches on trees.

¼ mile: Head and body form, leg movement, rigging.

250 yards: Faces are blurs, hands, details on clothing, marker numbers.

A Fix

While you were dozing contentedly in geometry class you may have missed the axiom, 'Two straight lines can intersect at only one point.' Something to yawn at back then, but a perfect definition of what happens when you cross two lines of position. You get a fix, the only spot on the chart where you could be.

An accurate fix depends on bearings taken at about the same time and intersecting as close to a right angle as possible. Angles of less than 60 or more than 120 degrees should be avoided. Accuracy can be improved by using nearby objects, and three bearings are better than two. When underway, fix your position at every opportunity – at least every 20 minutes on open waters.

Bearings or ranges can be combined with distance off to get a fix. They can also be combined with depth. The early Egyptians used *sounding poles* to check river depths, a technique that still makes sense for small craft in shallow waters. Sounding with a *lead line* is almost as ancient, being mentioned in the Bible. The lead is hollowed at its base and 'armed' with grease or wax to pick up bottom samples. It is tied to a line marked in *fathoms*, which the British Parliament once defined as 'The length of a man's arms around the object of his affections.' Today this is understood to be 6 feet. Even though compasses were available, sailors of the past often preferred to feel their way from port to port with soundings. An English *pilot* (nautical guidebook) of 1650 combines both: 'Find at 72 fathoms fair grey sand ... go north until you come into soundings of ooze, and set your course ENE.' Depths on U.S. charts are marked in fathoms or feet. The chart's title block shows the unit of measurement used.

Whether taking soundings with a lead line or modern electronics, doing it where the bottom changes rapidly will give better positions than on a gradual slope. Consider the tide, and be sure that there aren't several such depths along your LOP.

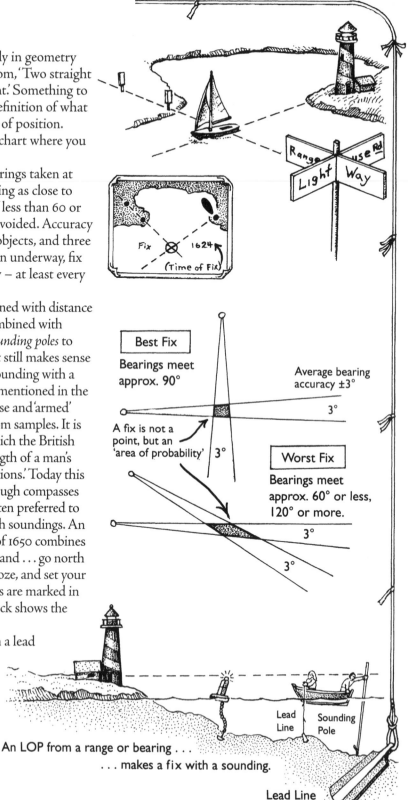

Fix 1624 (Time of Fix)

Best Fix
Bearings meet approx. 90°

Average bearing accuracy ±3°

3°

A fix is not a point, but an 'area of probability'

3°

Worst Fix
Bearings meet approx. 60° or less, 120° or more.

3°

3°

Lead Line

Sounding Pole

An LOP from a range or bearing . . .

. . . makes a fix with a sounding.

Lead Line

200

Dead Reckoning

An unfortunate combination of words. But dead is thought to have come from 'de'ed', a contraction of deduced. For this is *deduced reckoning* – you deduce your new position from a previous fix by using measurements of speed, time and distance. It is navigation without landmarks, and does not presage the impending doom its name might imply.

As with many things, where you have been determines where you are. If you start from a known point and run a precise course for a set distance you should (in theory) know exactly where you are. By keeping track of what the boat is doing you have deduced your new position.

The DR Plot

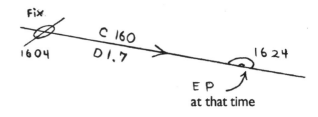

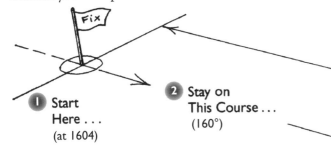

1 Start Here . . .
(at 1604)

2 Stay on This Course . . .
(160°)

3 For This Distance . . .
(1.7 miles)

4 And You're Here!
(at 1624)

Dead reckoning (DR) uses time (T) and speed (S) to find distance (D) along a course (C), giving you an estimated position (EP). Estimated because, while you may be able to compensate for currents (page 205), you cannot eliminate all effects of leeway, steering and plotting errors. Thus, we maintain a DR plot with these accepted limitations, starting clean after each new fix. The goal is not to fool yourself with a point on a chart, but to define a reasonably small area where you ought to be. The difference between good and bad dead reckoning is the size of that area of uncertainty.

When away from aids to navigation, actively maintain your DR. Start at your last fix. Keep track of the course steered and distance run. If you can't find distance directly, calculate it using speed and time. In this formula, time is measured in hours and tenths of hours. Remember that every 6 minutes is one-tenth of an hour. Since you need accuracy only to one tenth, this should get you through nicely.

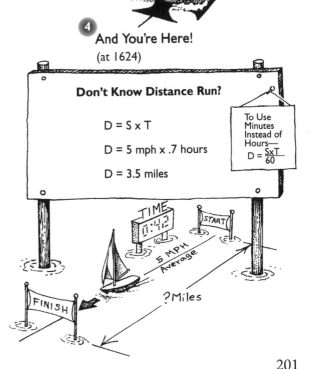

Don't Know Distance Run?

$D = S \times T$

$D = 5 \text{ mph} \times .7 \text{ hours}$

$D = 3.5 \text{ miles}$

To Use Minutes Instead of Hours—
$D = \dfrac{S \times T}{60}$

Distance Run

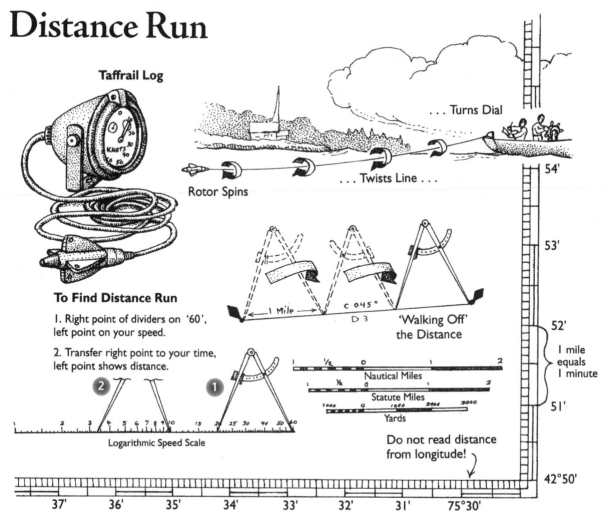

Taffrail Log

Rotor Spins ... Twists Line ... ... Turns Dial

To Find Distance Run

1. Right point of dividers on '60', left point on your speed.

2. Transfer right point to your time, left point shows distance.

'Walking Off' the Distance

Nautical Miles

Statute Miles

Yards

Do not read distance from longitude!

Logarithmic Speed Scale

I mile equals I minute

In a fit of wild optimism and creative geography, Columbus convinced the Spanish monarchs and himself that Cipangu (Japan) was one-quarter of its actual distance to the west. Which proves that poorly calculated distances can lead to confusion, or the Bahamas.

Distances on charts of the Great Lakes, Western Rivers, Intracoastal Waterways and other inland waters are measured in *statute miles* of 5,280 feet. This is the distance a Roman soldier covered in a thousand (*mille* in Latin) steps. Rather arbitrary. All ocean and coastal waters use the *nautical mile* of 6,076 feet. This is the length of 1 minute of latitude, a much more rational measurement than a soldier's stride.

On charts with scales of 1:80,000 to 1:15,000 or larger, there are *graphic scales* measuring statute miles, nautical miles and yards. On charts with smaller scales, distance is measured by the latitude

found on the right- and left-hand borders. A degree is divided into 60 minutes (each a nautical mile), and the minutes are divided into increments of 10 (each a tenth of a mile). Remember, for nautical miles it's *'a mile, a minute'.*

Dead reckoning is a lot easier if you can find distance run without having to compute speed against time. You can do this with an old-fashioned *taffrail log*, which needs to be periodically checked for errors against a pre-measured mile, or with a modern GPS receiver.

If you have to compute, do so without resorting to maths by using the *logarithmic speed scale* found on charts with scales of 1:40,000 to 1:15,000 or larger. Set the right point of the dividers at 60 and the left point on your speed. Then, without changing the spread, put the right point on your time. The left point will show distance.

Speed

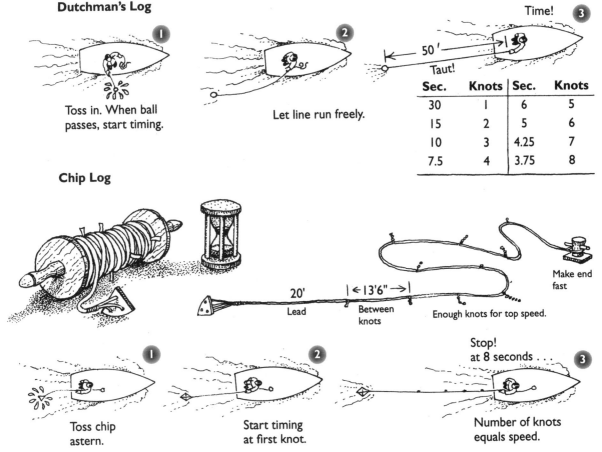

Dutchman's Log

1. Toss in. When ball passes, start timing.

2. Let line run freely.

3. Time!

50' Taut!

Sec.	Knots	Sec.	Knots
30	1	6	5
15	2	5	6
10	3	4.25	7
7.5	4	3.75	8

Chip Log

20' Lead

|←13'6"→| Between knots

Enough knots for top speed.

Make end fast

1. Toss chip astern.

2. Start timing at first knot.

3. Stop! at 8 seconds . . .
Number of knots equals speed.

If you cannot measure distance directly, you must deduce it by using time and speed. Time is easy – any good watch will do – but speed is a bit harder.

In simpler times, before GPS, there was the *Dutchman's log*. This consisted of an accurately measured distance along the ship's rail, a timer, and a float (the log). The float was thrown ahead and timed as it passed between the two marks on the rail. Speed was then calculated using time and distance. The results – plus courses steered, wind and weather – were recorded in a logbook to maintain the DR. You can make your own Dutchman's log with a tennis ball as a float and 50 feet of light line. Hold the line, toss the ball over and start timing. When the line goes taut, stop the clock and read your speed from the chart shown here.

An improvement over this was the *chip log*. A small triangular chip that acted as a drag was attached to a line that was knotted every 47 feet 3 inches. The chip was thrown overboard aft and allowed to run out for 28 seconds, timed by a sandglass. When the time was up, the number of 'knots' fed out were counted to get speed. Hence the term *knot*, which is a nautical (not statute) mile per hour. In experienced hands, chip logs can be surprisingly accurate and were still in use up to the 1920s.

Speed used in dead reckoning is the *average speed* during the measured time. Once known, enter this into the D = ST formula, or use the logarithmic speed scale on your chart, to find distance.

Knowing your speed is not only important for navigation. Seeing it constantly changing on your GPS receiver is like having a built-in sailing coach, showing you how to trim or adjust sails for maximum performance.

Running Fix

A running fix gives a position that is more accurate than a DR but not as good as a fix. It is useful for avoiding unmarked hazards along shores where there may be only one landmark for bearings.

Two bearings and a run uses any charted object. Take a bearing and plot it. Continue on a straight course until the bearing of the object has changed by at least 30 degrees. Take a second bearing and plot that. Estimate the distance travelled between bearings. Open dividers to that distance and, using parallel rules and trial and error, find a line parallel to your course where the points of the dividers fall on the bearing lines. These points indicate the positions of your boat at the times of the two bearings. Use the last one for your running fix.

Doubling the bow angle gives distance off from any object, charted or not, by taking two consecutive bearings along a set course. Upon taking your first bearing note how many degrees it differs from your course. This difference is the *relative bearing* to the object. Hold a straight course until the relative bearing (the angle between your course and the object) is twice (doubled) the first. Calculate the distance travelled between the two bearings. That's also how far off you are from the object at the second bearing. The only conditions are that the first bearing must be 45 degrees or less, and that angles of less than 10 degrees introduce a chance for error. You can take this information as is – 'I'm 3 miles off' – or plot the second bearing's LOP and distance off to get a running fix.

A handy version of the doubled bow angle is the *bow and beam angle*. If the first relative bearing is 45 degrees, the doubled angle is 90 degrees, or directly abeam. As before, the distance you travelled between the two bearings is equal to the distance to the object.

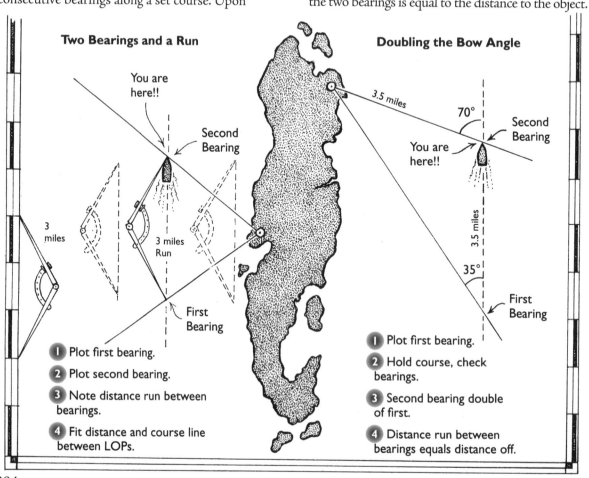

Two Bearings and a Run

You are here!!

Second Bearing

3 miles

3 miles Run

First Bearing

1 Plot first bearing.

2 Plot second bearing.

3 Note distance run between bearings.

4 Fit distance and course line between LOPs.

Doubling the Bow Angle

3.5 miles

70°

Second Bearing

You are here!!

3.5 miles

35°

First Bearing

1 Plot first bearing.

2 Hold course, check bearings.

3 Second bearing double of first.

4 Distance run between bearings equals distance off.

Correcting for Currents

Your compass heading only tells which way you are pointed, not which way the boat is moving. When there is a current the water carries you along with it, and there can be a big difference between the course you steer and the course the boat actually travels.

If the current is directly ahead or behind, only speed is affected. But when the current is off to one side, even slightly, it alters your course as well. To compensate for this, you have to head slightly into the current. But how do you know what course to steer?

To find the course, you need to know the current's set and drift from the *Tidal Current Tables* or personal observations, and an estimate of the boat's average speed. With these you create a *current triangle* – a graphic representation of how the current's strength and direction affect your boat.

First, measure the distance from your point of departure to your destination (3 miles). Then, using your estimated average speed (6 mph), calculate how long it will take to travel this distance (0.5 hour). Draw a *current line* out from the destination in a direction opposite to the set. Current tables show set in true, not magnetic, readings, so current direction must be plotted using the outer circle of the compass rose. All other directions here are magnetic. The length of the current line is drift (4 mph) multiplied by time (0.5 hour). This is the distance the boat would be pushed off course (2 miles). By drawing a line from the point of departure to the end of the current line, you get the course to be steered (10 degrees) to compensate for the current. While sailing this course, your compass will read 10 degrees, but the boat will be moving crabwise on a line of 50 degrees, directly towards your destination.

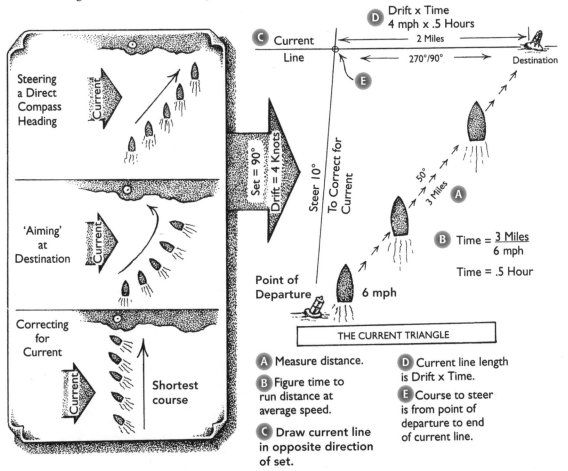

THE CURRENT TRIANGLE

A Measure distance.

B Figure time to run distance at average speed.

C Draw current line in opposite direction of set.

D Current line length is Drift x Time.

E Course to steer is from point of departure to end of current line.

GPS Navigation

Officially it's known as the *global positioning system*, but to you and me it's plain old GPS, the gadget we use to tell us where we are and how to get to where we're going. They're everywhere, and even the smallest boat will usually have one on board. Which is good, as it is a handy tool to use along with your other navigating skills. But never depend on it alone.

It's far too easy to be lulled into a sense of security as the GPS receiver displays your position down to what appears to be a few feet. Don't become like the skipper of a famous ocean racer who, not knowing his GPS wasn't providing an accurate fix, ran right into an island.

As with traditional navigation, to get a good fix you need plenty of widely separated lines of position. So it is with GPS, which uses satellites to provide the lines of position. To have an accurate GPS fix you want as many satellites as possible spread out around you. Something the ocean racer's captain didn't have.

All he had to do was check the *satellite page* to see what was going on in the sky. The centre of the circles represents what is directly above you, the inner circle is at an elevation of 45 degrees, and the outer circle is your horizon. Each satellite has a number that corresponds to a bar graph showing its signal strength. For optimum accuracy you want four broadly dispersed satellites with signal bars reaching the top line.

On this same page you will often see a box labelled 'Accuracy' or 'EPE' (estimated position error) – which is a more realistic way to think of it. The numbers shown are in feet (or metres) and should be used as a guide, not an absolute indicator. When in a channel it's best to have an assured accuracy of 15 feet or better, which is not always possible. That's why, when things get tight, take your eyes off the screen and keep a good lookout instead.

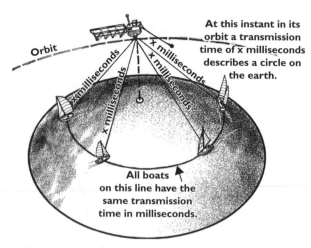

At this instant in its orbit a transmission time of x milliseconds describes a circle on the earth.

All boats on this line have the same transmission time in milliseconds.

You are somewhere on this circular line of position.

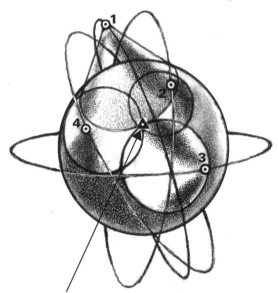

Your position is where the circles meet.

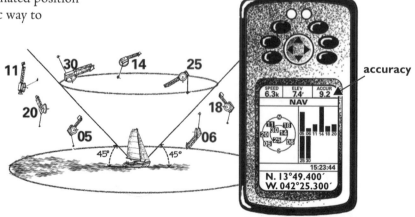

Satellite page.

Getting a Fix with GPS

The first thing you'll want is your location on a chart – a good thing to have as you can't get anywhere unless you know where you're starting from.

If your GPS uses *electronic raster charts*, which are derived from standard paper charts, an icon representing your boat will appear at your current location. If your GPS unit does not display charts, go to the *position page*. You'll find that it's made up of boxes filled with numbers. Right now you can ignore most of these, what you're interested in is the box with your *latitude* (distance north or south of the equator) and *longitude* (distance east or west of the *prime meridian* that runs through Greenwich), which should look like:

N 13° 49.400'
W 042° 25.300'

This means you are 13 degrees, 49 and 4/10 of a minute north of the equator; and 42 degrees, 25 and 3/10 of a minute west of the prime meridian.

Your GPS unit can also display a position in a notation using seconds, instead of tenths of a minute, if so it would look like this:

N 13° 49' 26"
W 042° 25' 18"

Check your printed chart to see which format it uses. Typically, charts with a scale of 1:50,000 or larger use minutes and seconds, while smaller scale charts are usually in minutes and tenths. Once you know this it's easy enough to transcribe the coordinates onto a chart.

First, find your latitude on the side of the chart. Using a parallel rule draw a line outwards level with the nearest *grid line* (printed lines of latitude or longitude). Now find your longitude along the bottom or top of the chart and draw a line upwards to meet your latitude line. Where they cross is where you are ... well, sort of.

The problem is that your GPS receiver can locate your position with greater accuracy than the accuracy that was used to survey most charts, which means that soundings and features might be slightly off. Yet another good reason why, once you've plotted your position, you should take a look around to see if your location on the chart matches what you are seeing from the cockpit.

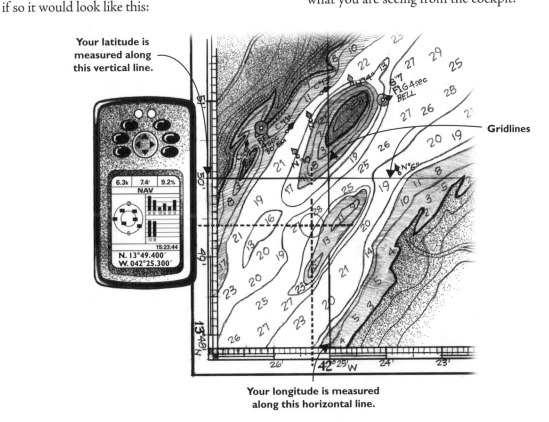

Your latitude is measured along this vertical line.

Gridlines

Your longitude is measured along this horizontal line.

Waypoint Navigation

As we've seen, in traditional navigation you find a precise spot on a chart where you'd like to go, such as a buoy, and draw a line to it that indicates your course (see Plotting a Course, page 190).

With GPS that precise spot is called a *waypoint*. While it can be a marker or buoy, it doesn't have to be. Think of it more as a virtual aid to navigation that can be anywhere you like, and to which the GPS calculates your bearing and course – no chart work required.

To create a waypoint all the GPS receiver needs is a latitude and longitude, which you get from the chart, and you then enter this information into the unit's memory. (On some GPS units you can simply push the 'Add Waypoint' function and it records the latitude and longitude of your current location – say, your mooring – as a waypoint.)

Before heading off to that waypoint remember always to *prequalify your course* by reviewing the entire route and plot it on a chart to make sure that it doesn't take you into dangerous waters. Once you've mastered entering a single waypoint you can add several of them – say, for instance, in addition to your mooring waypoint you add the buoy that marks the harbour channel entrance and the second buoy beyond that marking the middle of the bay outside your harbour – you can then link them into a *route*.

Once you've entered and selected a waypoint, and got underway, your GPS unit will start giving you a lot of information – most important are the bearing and distance to the waypoint. Some of the information – track and cross-track – will be in a new language.

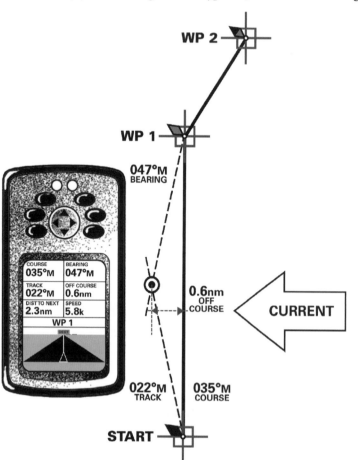

Bearing (BRG)—direction to waypoint from current position

Course—planned course line from start to waypoint

Track (COG, course over ground)—current heading of boat

Distance (DIST)—distance to waypoint

Off Course (XTE, cross-track error)—distance left/right of course line

Speed (SOG, speed over ground)—speed in mph or knots

VMG (velocity made good)— speed toward waypoint

ETE (estimated time en route)— how long until you arrive at waypoint

ETA (estimated time of arrival)— time you will arrive at waypoint

Staying on Course with GPS

You checked your course to the waypoint on a chart to be sure it clears any dangers. But if you use your GPS unit to just aim at the waypoint as if it were a homing beacon it's possible that you could stray from the course without knowing it and drift into the dangers you are trying to avoid. To stay on your plotted course you have to keep an eye on your track and bearing numbers, making sure they match the course number – which isn't easy to do. If your GPS has a chart, all you have to do is keep the boat's icon on the course line. If it doesn't, you can use the *highway page* to help you visualise what's going on.

The highway page is easy to use; at a glance you'll intuitively know if you are on course, and if not by how much. Steer so the boat icon on the bottom of the highway screen stays in the middle of the 'road' and you'll arrive safely.

But what if your waypoint is upwind, and you have to keep tacking? Not to worry. Just plot a straight course to the waypoint and note how far to each side of the course it is safe to go when tacking. While underway use the off-course (or XTE) function to monitor how far off the line you are and still staying out of danger. Don't exceed the limits and you'll be fine.

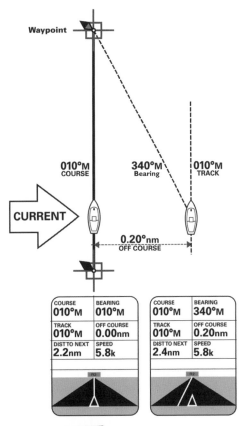

COURSE	BEARING
010°M	010°M
TRACK	OFF COURSE
010°M	0.00nm
DIST TO NEXT	SPEED
2.2nm	5.8k

COURSE	BEARING
010°M	340°M
TRACK	OFF COURSE
010°M	0.20nm
DIST TO NEXT	SPEED
2.4nm	5.8k

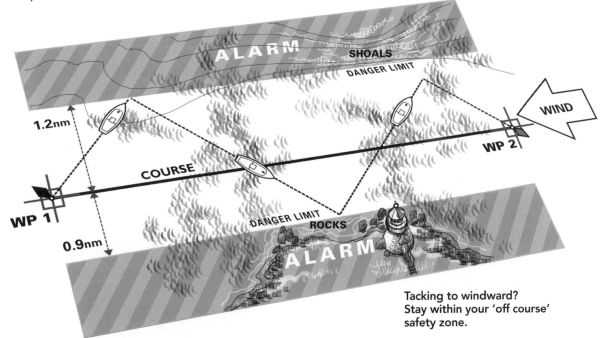

Tacking to windward?
Stay within your 'off course' safety zone.

RACING

'Once you race, every fault is pointed out in the way other boats sail away from you, and when you do anything well this too is revealed as you start pulling away from the rest of the fleet.'

Uffa Fox, *According to Uffa*

The first recorded race under sail was in 1661 between King Charles II and the Duke of York on the Thames River. The duke beat the king on the first leg, but had enough sense to let the king win on the return.

For the thousands of years before the history of racing was being written, sailors were not always so polite when their ships met. Going faster than another vessel was, and is, not just a reflection of human competitiveness; it's a matter of pride – demonstrating in no uncertain terms who is the better sailor.

Then, as now, the only way to measure how well you sail, and at the same time learn to become the best sailor possible, is to go up against others. And that means racing.

While much of the sport is about the clever use of rules, we'll focus on the actual sailing – getting where you want to go as quickly and efficiently as possible.

To start, try crewing and learning on someone else's boat. If you then decide to give racing a try, don't be put off by those first attempts, as it will seem like chaos with crews yelling and boats going everywhere. But soon it will make sense and you'll start working your way up the fleet. Even if you never win, when away from the course you'll have learned how to get the most out of your boat and how the joy of sailing can be increased by sailing well.

Now when you trade tacks with some unsuspecting craft, it will be you who gets home first, you who are the better sailor.

How It's Done

When you race a sailing boat, there's no track, no lanes, or even a set route, only an undulating surface with a few points you have to get around any way you see fit while adhering to a specialised set of rules. It's not just about speed either. This is a mind game of tactics, strategy, psychology and wind changes.

Sometimes it is done offshore, taking days and covering hundreds of miles, such as the Newport–Bermuda Race that starts in Rhode Island, and the Sydney–Hobart Race from Australia to Tasmania.

The type of racing most of us learn in takes place inshore aboard smaller boats, but can also be on a grand scale such as the America's Cup. There are three basic types of inshore courses, all with one thing in common – you start by going to windward. An old favourite is the *triangle course*, a beat upwind followed by two reaches back to the start. It's fun and fast. The *windward/leeward course* is more challenging. wAt the windward mark you turn dead downwind, providing plenty of opportunities for blocking and passing, and then you go around again. The *Olympic course* combines the two, making for a protracted battle.

Most likely you'll learn to race in a *one-design* class, where each boat is exactly the same to highlight the crew's skills. One of the first, and oldest, fleets is the One-design fleet. When boats race that are not exactly alike, a handicapping system is used. The most popular is the *PHRF* (Performance Handicap Racing Fleet), which applies a preset time correction to each boat at the end of the race. This way a variety of dissimilar racer/cruisers, such as a light stripped-down Melges 32 and the more comfortable Catalina 320, can sail against each other.

When starting out, remember: It's not only the boat that's important; the fleet you race in counts, too. Some are laid-back, others are cut-throat; some are conveniently local, others are scattered all over. Choose carefully.

Water Wag

Finish

Windward Mark

Leeward Mark

Finish

Start

Windward/Leeward

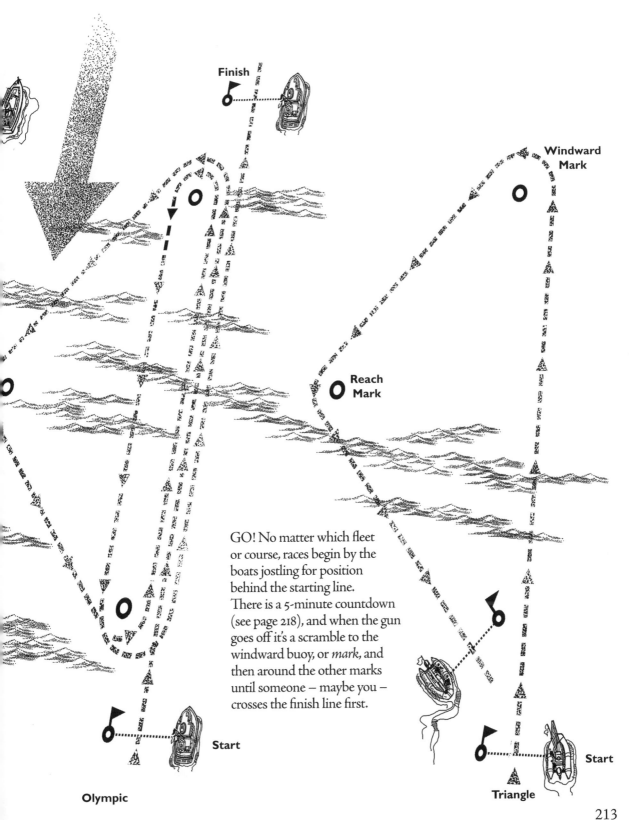

Finish

Windward Mark

Reach Mark

GO! No matter which fleet or course, races begin by the boats jostling for position behind the starting line. There is a 5-minute countdown (see page 218), and when the gun goes off it's a scramble to the windward buoy, or *mark*, and then around the other marks until someone – maybe you – crosses the finish line first.

Start

Start

Olympic

Triangle

Racers

LOCAL FAVOURITES

A North Haven dinghy: The oldest continually raced class in the United States. These 14-foot open boats started racing in 1888 and were built by local builder J. O. Brown & Son in North Haven, Maine.

B Inland lake scow: This A-class boat is one of the oldest one-designs, dating back to 1901. At 38 feet it's a spectacular racing machine capable of 25 mph.

C Bermuda fitted dinghy: Started in the 1880s, these 14-foot open boats can pile on a massive amount of sail. They are 'fitted' with a metal plate to their keel to help them stay upright.

ONE-DESIGNS

D Rhodes 19: A salty-looking, heavy-weather sailer designed by Philip Rhodes back in 1947. Available with a fixed keel or centreboard, it is a forgiving daysailer and spirited racer.

E J/24: Started in 1977 and now the largest one-design keelboat class in the world. It is simple to sail, responsive, fast to windward, and has a cabin for weekend cruises.

F Optimist pram: Designed by Clark Mills as a father-and-son project, this little 80-pound, 7-foot 6-inch boat is an excellent first racer for youngsters and makes up one of the world's largest fleets.

G 420: A basic 13-foot (4.20-metre), two-person dinghy for younger, more athletic sailors that is popular as both a trainer and racer, especially among collegiate programmes.

H Etchells: This 30-foot boat started as a prototype to become the Olympic three-person keelboat. The Soling won out, but the Etchells lived on to become a popular international class.

OLYMPIC CLASSES

I Laser: A one-person, 13-foot boat that emphasises simplicity and high performance. Over 200,000 have been built with strict regulations concerning construction and sails, making it a highly competitive class.

J Star: A classic 22-foot, two-person boat that has been an active international class since 1911. In 1921 the rig changed from gaff to marconi, keeping its fin keel with an iron bulb.

K RS:X: A high-tech windsurfer with a carbon fibre mast and boom that is the most portable Olympic boat, allowing sailors to easily and economically compete in races all over the world.

L 49er: This 210-pound 16-footer is so wildly overpowered that it takes a crew of two hiking out on trapeze beyond the boat's 'wings' to keep it upright. Definitely not for the timid.

PHRF BOATS

M Catalina 22: This trailerable pocket cruiser started life in 1970 and, with minor modifications, over 16,000 boats later is still going strong. A non-threatening sailer with good room below.

N Pearson Flyer: The most distinguishing feature on this 29-footer is its wide-open uncluttered deck with no raised cabin, yet it is still a good weekend cruiser.

O C&C 35: Introduced in 1969 it, and others like it, came to be known as a new type of boat – the cruiser/racer. Comfortable for long journeys, yet fast enough to be competitive.

Rules

The International Sailing Federation publishes the standard book of racing rules that is revised every four years after the Olympics. Get it and read it. There are only a few rules describing what boats must do when meeting. Luckily, you already know the first three – the most important ones in racing – from the basic navigation rules on page 125.

1. Starboard tack has the right of way over port tack.

2. When on the same tack, the leeward boat has the right of way.

3. The overtaking boat must stay clear of the boat ahead.

The next four basic rules (shown here) are specific to racing. Knowing these seven should be enough to get you around the course without causing trouble. But remember, even if you have the right of way you're still required to avoid collisions. Race with sportsmanship, not using the rules to argue your way around the course. Those who do are not sailors, but sea lawyers. Steer clear of them.

Besides the standard rules, before each race *sailing instructions* describing the course, signals, starting times, number of laps and other information for that specific race are posted or delivered at a skippers' meeting.

As no judges follow the boats, when racers feel a rule has been broken they can hoist a protest flag, with a judgement made after the race. If it's obvious that you've committed a foul, you must immediately do two complete turns, each with a tack and a gybe, well clear of others before resuming the race. The other flags shown here are hoisted by the committee boat (see next page).

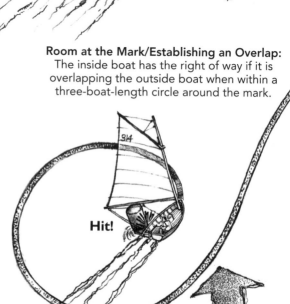

Room!

OVERLAP

Room at the Mark/Establishing an Overlap: The inside boat has the right of way if it is overlapping the outside boat when within a three-boat-length circle around the mark.

Hit!

Touching the Mark: If you hit it, sail well clear, perform a tack and gybe, and continue on. No penalties if forced into the mark by another boat.

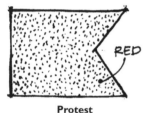

Protest
Hoist on starboard
shroud or backstay

RED

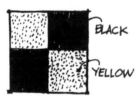

L Flag
Come within hailing distance,
or follow me (**raised: one blast**)

BLACK

YELLOW

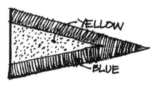

1st Substitute Pennant
General recall of all boats (**raised:
two blasts; lowered: one blast**)

YELLOW

BLUE

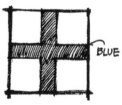

X Flag
Individual recall
(**raised: one blast**)

BLUE

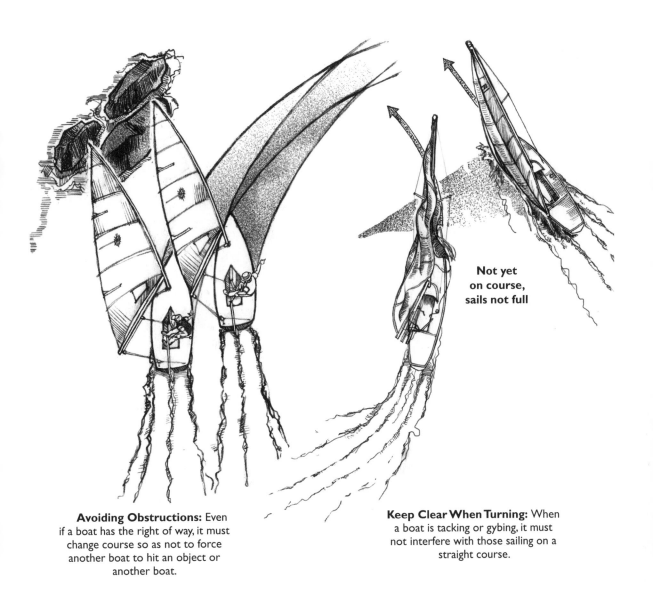

Avoiding Obstructions: Even if a boat has the right of way, it must change course so as not to force another boat to hit an object or another boat.

Not yet on course, sails not full

Keep Clear When Turning: When a boat is tacking or gybing, it must not interfere with those sailing on a straight course.

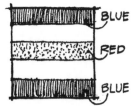

C Flag
Next mark moved, usually due to a wind shift (**raised: multiple short blasts**)

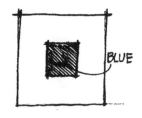

S Flag
Course shortened, usually if wind has died (**raised: two blasts**)

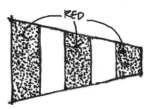

AP Pennant
Races not started are postponed (**raised: two blasts; lowered: one blast**)

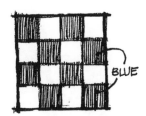

N Flag
Races already started are abandoned (**raised: three blasts; lowered: one blast**)

The Start

The fleet begins its thrash to windward by crossing an imaginary line that is roughly perpendicular to the wind marked by the *committee boat* at one end and a buoy at the other called the *pin*. Since no wind is steady, one side of the line will be the *favoured end* – being closest to the wind and the best place to start from. To find this, luff directly into the wind and your bow will point to the best side. If no difference, try to leave from the starboard side so you start off on a starboard tack with the right of way.

You are given plenty of notice as to when the starting gun will go off. Use that time to make sure you position yourself to hit the line at the best end, with plenty of speed, and in *clean air* – wind that is undisturbed by the other boats' sails. There are many strategies to making the perfect start; four are shown here. To execute them successfully, you need to know how fast your boat sails, accelerates and turns so you don't jump the gun or lag behind the fleet.

No matter how you start, be aware of the *barging rule*. Everywhere else on the course, the outside boat must give way to the inside boat at a mark. But when starting, if a boat tries to sneak in, or *barge*, between you and the committee boat you need not give way and can block its passage.

The Countdown

Use a watch timed to these signals so you cross the line on time.

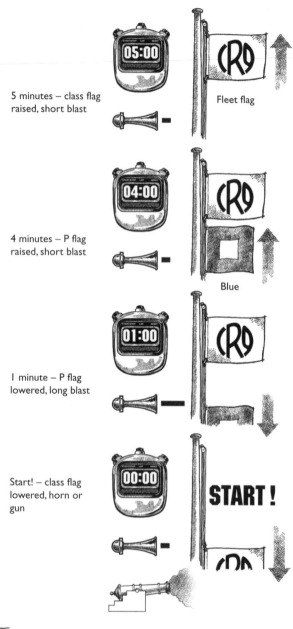

5 minutes – class flag raised, short blast

Fleet flag

4 minutes – P flag raised, short blast

Blue

1 minute – P flag lowered, long blast

Start! – class flag lowered, horn or gun

START !

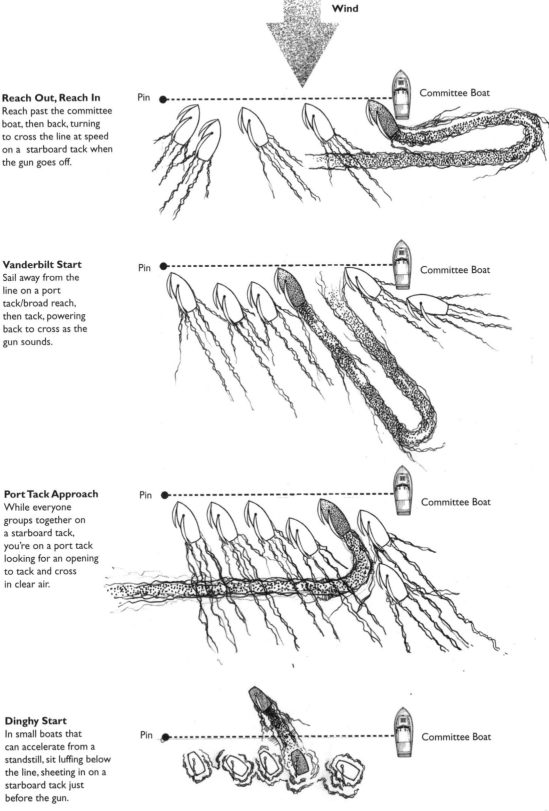

Wind

Pin • — Committee Boat

Reach Out, Reach In
Reach past the committee boat, then back, turning to cross the line at speed on a starboard tack when the gun goes off.

Vanderbilt Start
Sail away from the line on a port tack/broad reach, then tack, powering back to cross as the gun sounds.

Port Tack Approach
While everyone groups together on a starboard tack, you're on a port tack looking for an opening to tack and cross in clear air.

Dinghy Start
In small boats that can accelerate from a standstill, sit luffing below the line, sheeting in on a starboard tack just before the gun.

Playing the Wind

The wind is your source of power. But unlike a racing car's engine, a racing sailing boat's power plant is neither steady nor dependable. The wind twists and turns, and sometimes disappears, not only by itself, but when affected by the sails of other boats and your own. You can use this phenomenon to slow a competing boat's passage, block it completely, or give yourself a lift to point higher or go faster.

Each boat in the fleet exerts its influence on the performance of nearby boats by interfering with the wind. Sails can cause eddies and turbulences known as *dirty air*, which weakens the wind and makes it unpredictable, or creates downwind areas of almost dead air known as *wind shadows*. Since sails also redirect and accelerate the wind, they can hinder – or help – the boats around you.

Your sails not only drive the boat but can be used as tactical weapons. Wield them well.

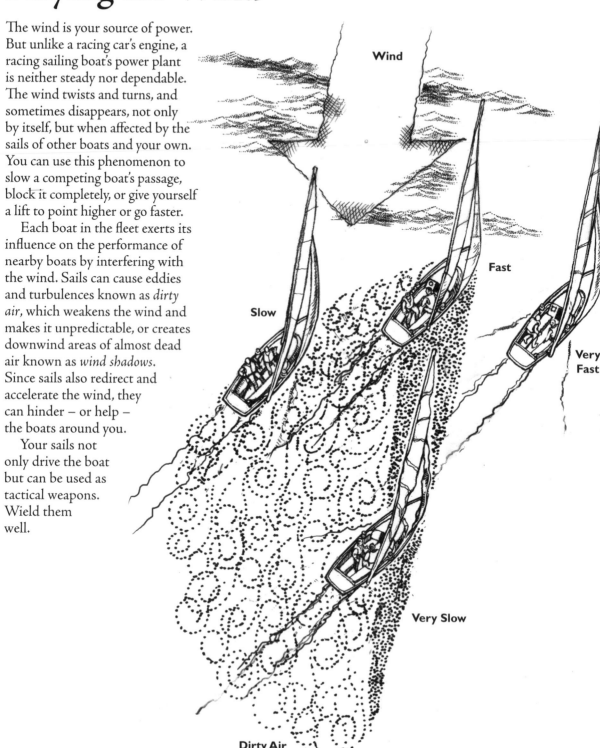

Wind

Fast

Slow

Very Fast

Very Slow

Dirty Air

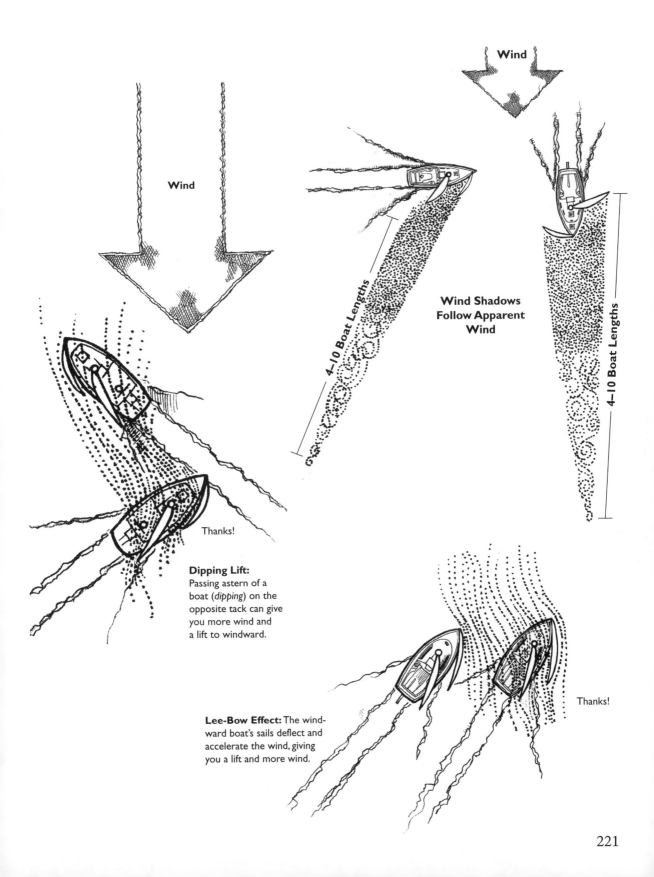

Wind

Wind

Wind Shadows Follow Apparent Wind

4–10 Boat Lengths

4–10 Boat Lengths

Thanks!

Dipping Lift: Passing astern of a boat (*dipping*) on the opposite tack can give you more wind and a lift to windward.

Thanks!

Lee-Bow Effect: The windward boat's sails deflect and accelerate the wind, giving you a lift and more wind.

Windward Leg

You'll constantly be trying to claw your way to the first mark without losing speed, all the time working to get the most out of the wind and waves.

Since the wind's direction is never steady, use its lifts and headers. Point higher when the wind comes aft in a lift, tack when the wind heads you. Watch your compass to see if the wind is *shifting*, going back and forth around one mean direction, or *bending*, moving further and further off to one side.

The wind's speed is also always changing. Take advantage of gusts to point higher, and bear off in the lulls to gain speed – or maintain it in choppy seas. When a puff hits, the apparent wind moves aft, which means the sails are momentarily overtrimmed, so let them out a bit or steer a slightly higher course.

Waves are a hindrance when sailing to windward, forcing you to maintain your momentum by sailing full and by, never pinching. Bear away in troughs and point up to cross the crests. Waves can also help. Time your tacks so the waves will help push the bow around. Make tacks quickly and cleanly, sailing through them rather than coasting.

While doing all this, never lose track of the *lay lines* – the two imaginary lines on which you can get to, or *fetch*, the mark without making any additional tacks. Stay well inside these lines until the end of the leg so you can continue to take advantage of any wind shifts. Also, try to stick to the *favoured side*, the one that gives the best slant to the mark with the fewest tacks. If you don't know which is favoured, stay near the middle and focus on working the wind to sail the shortest distance.

As a beginner, concentrate on getting to the windward mark as fast as you can without being distracted by other boats. Don't get caught up in tacking duels, as they make it easier for other boats to sneak by. And don't go out on your own – there's probably a good reason why the pack is headed the other way.

Gusts = Lifts

When the true wind suddenly increases, it changes the direction of the apparent wind so you can sail higher.

Occasionally head up to test the wind's direction.

222

If a header holds, tack so it becomes a lift.

Use gusts for a lift; when one hits ease the sheets, hike out, trim back in, and point up.

Place your weight forward when sailing to windward in a dinghy – these 420 sailors could also be hiking and on the trapeze to flatten the hull further, thereby increasing their boatspeed.

Turn towards a wave; once over bear off to regain speed.

Layline

Layline

Safety Zone

Risky

Risky

Stay away from the lay lines until near the mark so you can play the shifts.

A Racer's Tack

When a sailing boat tacks it loses speed, taking more time to reach the windward mark. To offset this, dinghy racers have come up with the *roll tack*, a faster way of coming about in light boats where the crew's weight affects how much it heels. If done right, the boat sails rather than coasts through the tack, picking up speed as it turns.

Approach the manoeuvre as you normally would, sitting to windward with some speed on. But when you put the tiller over to tack, stay put. Don't start climbing over to the other side. As you pass through the eye of the wind, you'll find yourself on the new leeward side with the boat heeling way over. You'll feel insecure being so far over to leeward, but it helps flop the sails over fast without luffing, and it's only for a few seconds.

Now, with the boat pointing on its new tack, dive for the new windward side to roll the boat back upright. As the boat comes up, it pulls the sails through the air, increasing the wind's speed over them. This artificial wind acts like a gust, giving you a nice push forward to accelerate out of the tack.

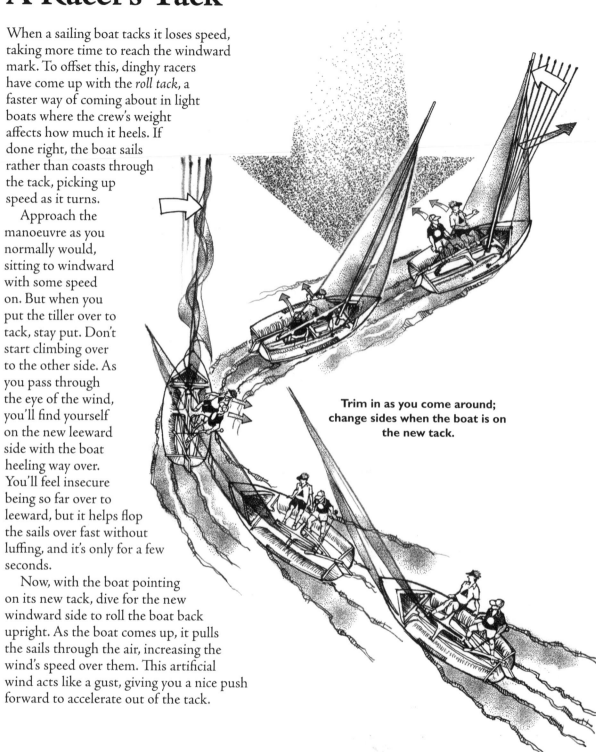

Trim in as you come around; change sides when the boat is on the new tack.

Offwind Legs

When on a reach, sail the straightest course you can towards the next mark. At the beginning of the leg, get a couple of boat lengths to windward of the fleet to give yourself a better chance of passing boats later on.

While reaching legs offer few opportunities to pass and use tactical manoeuvres, the real action after the beat to windward is when heading downwind. Here, getting maximum boat speed is difficult and wind shadows become harder to escape.

First, you have to make a decision. Do you want head up slightly to gain speed but travel further? Or do you want to run directly downwind towards the mark, covering a shorter distance but at a slower speed? In 8 mph of true wind or less, consider tacking downwind, going as far as 30 degrees from the direct course. In winds over 15 mph, you'll be close to hull speed anyway, so head straight for it. In between, the best approach is a gentle serpentine track.

Wind

Head up slightly to gain speed.

WINDSPEED

Going directly to the mark is slower, but a shorter distance.

WINDSPEED

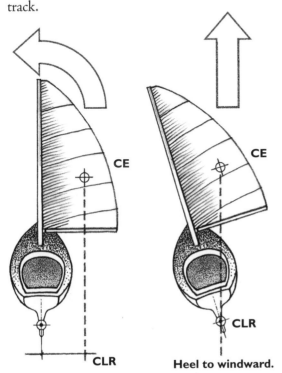

CE

CE

CLR

CLR

Heel to windward.

Always be on the lookout for wind shadows. If a nearby boat's masthead fly is pointing at your sail, your wind will be blanketed. Do what you can to get away.

Keep the boat heeled to windward to bring the sail's centre of effort closer to the boat's centre of balance so you'll have to use less drag-inducing rudder motions to stay on course. It also gets the sail area slightly higher into better air. The danger of this is that you are susceptible to rolls to windward, which can bring on an accidental gybe. If you feel a roll coming, give the mainsheet a quick hard tug to change the airflow and straighten the boat up. For a big roll, head up.

At the Mark

It all comes together here – literally. There's a mad crush as lay lines and various reaching or downwind tactics funnel boats towards this one point.

No matter where you are in the fleet, your goal at the end of the windward leg is to approach the mark on a starboard tack to maintain right of way. But be careful not to tack too close to the buoy. While you'll want to stay in close so the outside boats are forced to give you room, the rules say that if you go onto a starboard tack within three boat lengths of the mark you can't force other boats already on a starboard tack to point higher so you can sneak in.

When within ten boat lengths of the buoy, get to windward of the lay line by at least one boat length to eliminate the chance of not reaching the mark on your final tack because of currents, wind shifts or dirty air. If there's a crowd around the buoy, let them fight it out while you take the high road and go around them.

When you finally reach the mark, try to swing onto the next leg without losing speed. You want to turn in gradually at the buoy so you can exit fast, not turn quickly and exit slowly. If changing a headsail or hoisting a spinnaker, get the crew off the foredeck as soon as possible. In light air extra weight in the bow will slow you down; in a stiff breeze losing weight from the windward rail could cause a capsize.

At the leeward mark, or any mark where you have to gybe, keep your speed up by coming in more on a broad reach than a run. This will force you to approach wide and leave close – which is the fastest way around. The natural tendency is to steer straight for the mark and make a tight speed-killing turn when you get there. A much better approach is to aim for an imaginary point one or two boat lengths to the side of the buoy, then turn in gradually and smoothly so you exit close to the mark. Think of making a 'J' rather than a 'V'.

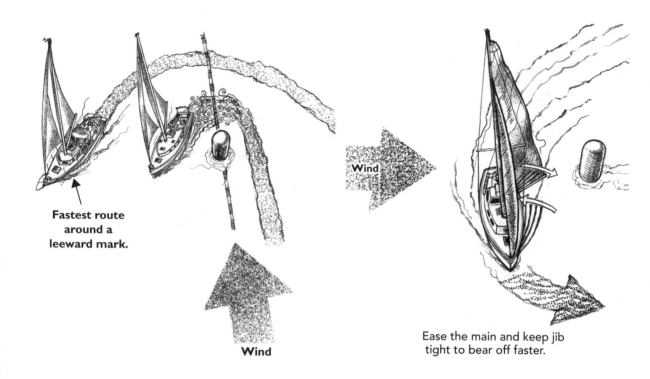

Fastest route around a leeward mark.

Wind

Wind

Ease the main and keep jib tight to bear off faster.

Racers' Secrets

Racers like to talk about their sport and share information. You'll learn a lot this way. But there are some secrets of winning that no one will tell you and might take years to discover. Not wanting you to wait so long, here are a few tips from the masters:

- Check the tide and current tables. The slower the boat, the more effect a current has on it. Study where the currents are strongest and weakest, and what their direction is.
- Look at the landscape. You may have a forecast for the wind's strength and direction. But that can all change according to how the surrounding land blocks and twists the wind.
- Practise accelerating. Go out early near the starting line and experiment getting the boat up to speed, remembering how long it takes in terms of time and distance. This will be a big help at the race's start.
- Go for a sail near the line well in advance of the starting sequence to get a feel for the conditions and to fine-tune your sails before the gun sounds.

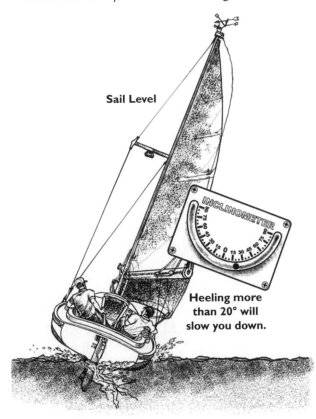

Sail Level

INCLINOMETER

Heeling more than 20° will slow you down.

- Get your head 'out of the boat.' When the starting gun goes off, get to maximum speed as soon as possible. Then look up and begin concentrating on what is going on with the other boats.
- Watch your masthead wind indicator. The wind often changes aloft before it does close to the water.
- Ease the sheets when hit by a gust, then use the rudder. This will keep you going faster and cause less drag from the rudder.
- Build up speed before making big course changes – manoeuvring is easier when sailing fast.
- Stand when steering with a wheel. This gives you greater height so you can see further and be able to predict upcoming situations. Keep two hands on the wheel, and don't be tempted to sit to leeward as you'll be sailing blind.
- The natural tendency is to overtrim sails. Occasionally ease the sheets and bring them back in to make sure you're well trimmed. When in doubt, ease out. Keep your telltales streaming.
- Reducing weather helm reduces rudder drag. Try shortening sail in strong winds, easing the sheets, flattening the main, or getting the crew to the windward side of the boat.
- Adjust sail shape. Maximum draught is usually about 40% aft of the luff. To point higher, move the draught aft; to sail faster, move it forward.
- Understand the rules. Besides helping you prevent collisions or avoid getting a penalty, they can also be used as an offensive and defensive tool against other boats.
- Don't be fooled. Other skippers may try to bluff you into giving way by yelling out a rule that isn't. Study that rule book.
- Know where the finish line is. Sounds silly but it's easy to get confused. As with the starting line, one end will be favoured – closest to windward. Aim for that end.
- Never give up. Sailing boat racing is a dynamic sport; things change all the time and it's possible to recover from a bad start or a mistake.
- Give clear commands. Don't just yell for someone to 'pull that!' Give the name of the line you want trimmed and exactly what you want done with it.
- Work out crew assignments before the start so everyone knows what to do when tacking, gybing and rounding marks.

TRAILERING

'... most boat trailer owners quickly come to realize that the tail is quite capable of wagging the dog.'
David R. Getchell, Sr., *Outboard Boater's Handbook*

At a top speed of 5 or 6 mph, sailing boats allow you to be a part of the world you are passing through and not just be a high-speed voyeur. Unfortunately, it is this same leisurely pace that limits just how much of that world you can actually be part of.

Most of us are restricted to brief vacations and compressed weekends. How frustrating, then, to be confined to a small cruising radius, spending most of your time going and returning. How much better to reach a cruising ground quickly, using your time for exploring and relaxing.

Trailers can make that possible. When trailering there is no need for the discomforts of a long passage to expand your horizons. Somewhere down the road there are mountain lakes, back bays of cities, foreign countries, and escapes from winter to warmer seas.

Even if you're staying near home, trailering eliminates marina costs and provides access to areas with limited dockage. Keeping your boat at home also lets you work on it yourself, thus avoiding yard bills and making maintenance more convenient (which means it will get done).

For a boat on a trailer, the song of the open road is at one with the call of the sea (or bay, or lake, or river ...).

The Trailer

Does the trailer fit your boat? Check its *weight capacity plate* to see if it can carry the boat's weight plus the outboard, anchors, chains, water (8 pounds per gallon), fuel (6 pounds per gallon), and gear. Do not load a trailer to more than 85% of its capacity. Make sure that hull supports (*rollers* or *support pads*) are under reinforced areas such as the keel, bulkheads, transom and chines, to distribute the load with no localised pressure points. Support pads provide the best support, while rollers make launching and retrieval easier. The boat must sit on the trailer so that no more than 10% of the boat/trailer weight is on the hitch. This *tongue weight* can be adjusted by moving gear in the boat, or by shifting the *bow post* and boat forward or back.

Corrosion is a major problem. Steel trailers can be painted, but live longer if hot-dipped galvanised. Aluminium trailers weigh about 20% less than steel and will never corrode. Fenders should be plastic not painted steel, and wheel bearings should be protected from water incursion by a pressurised grease system. Choose LED lights over incandescent as they can be waterproofed.

The winch pulls the boat onto the trailer and keeps the bow secure against the *bow stop*. For boats less than 2,000 pounds, use a gear ratio of 3:1 (the crank turns three times for every one turn of the drum); for those over 4,000 pounds you'll need at least 5:1. Webbing used on winches should have a breaking strength of 150% of the boat's weight; for wire cable, 125%. Place *tie-downs* over the aft end of the boat to prevent shifting and bouncing. Use straps with buckles that let you cinch them down tight. Don't use rope.

Trailer tyres should have stiffer and stronger sidewalls than a car's tyre. If the trailer's gross weight exceeds 3,000 pounds it's best to have brakes on all wheels and a *breakaway brake* that stops the trailer if it gets separated from the vehicle. Over 3,500 pounds, consider having two axles to share the load rather than one. Maximum trailer width is 7½ feet, and a maximum height of 12 feet will get you under almost everything.

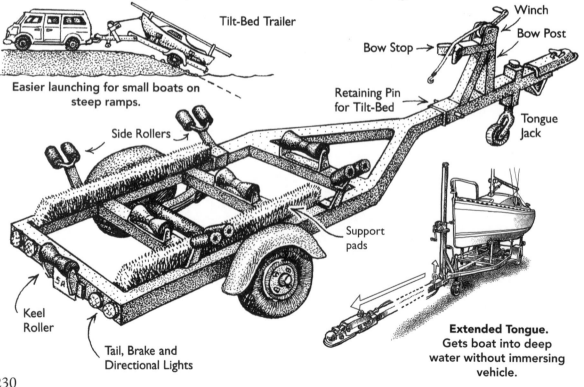

Tilt-Bed Trailer

Easier launching for small boats on steep ramps.

Winch

Bow Post

Bow Stop →

Retaining Pin for Tilt-Bed →

Tongue Jack

Side Rollers →

Support pads

Keel Roller

Tail, Brake and Directional Lights

Extended Tongue. Gets boat into deep water without immersing vehicle.

On the Road

Hitch Class	Towing Weight
I	To 2,000
II	2,000 ~ 3,500
III	3,500 ~ 5,000
IV	5,000 ~ 10,000

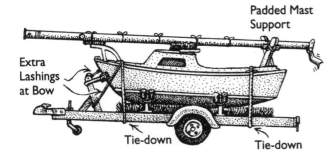

Padded Mast Support

Extra Lashings at Bow

Tie-down

Tie-down

Your boat is more likely to sustain damage while being trailered than when sailing, so give your rig a careful look over before hitting the road. Inflate tyres to the pressure indicated on the sidewalls, and be sure their tread is more than ⅛ inch deep. Check wheel bearings. If too hot to touch after 10 minutes of highway driving, they need to be greased or replaced. Have a spare tyre and a jack that works with the trailer (not all car jacks do). Look over the wiring for chafe-worn insulation and loose connections. Are frame and support bolts tight? Is the locking pin in place for the tilt-bed or extended tongue? Chock and lash down the mast with line, not elastic bungee cords. Tie the rigging to the mast. Stow gear so it won't slide, bounce or blow away. Put the trailer's winch in its locked position with the bow in the bow stop, and the tie-downs cinched tight, with padding where they come in contact with the hull. If needed, tilt up the outboard for extra clearance, or dismount it and stow it in the boat. Close all hatches and ports. Turn ventilators aft so they won't scoop up bugs or rain. Lower and secure canvas tops. Drop the centreboard so it rests on one of the trailer's cross frames to take the strain off the centreboard's lanyard and pivot bolt.

When all checks out: Back up to the trailer, lower the *coupler* over the *ball* and push the *coupler-lock* lever down, checking that the *ball clamp* is under, not riding on top of, the ball. Try pulling up on the tongue. If it is solidly connected, put a retaining pin in the coupler-lock, crank the *tongue jack* up, connect the chains making sure there is enough slack in both for tight turns, attach the wiring, check the lights and test the brakes.

Towing a trailer means driving slower and more deliberately. Signal early and start turns later than normal – making them wider and further from the curb. Trailers do not follow the car's path, but track closer to the inside of the turn. It will take longer and further to stop, so brake gently and sooner. It will also take longer to accelerate, requiring more room and time when passing or when entering a highway.

On long trips, pull over every hour to check that everything is tight, in place, and the bearings are staying cool. If the rig starts to sway in a crosswind, don't hit the brakes – that will only increase the motion. Slow down gradually. If the problem persists, the tongue weight may be too light, requiring the load to be redistributed before you continue.

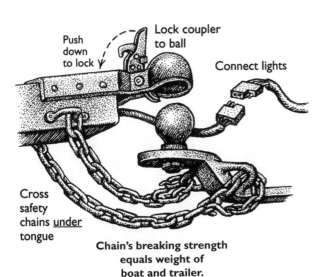

Push down to lock

Lock coupler to ball

Connect lights

Cross safety chains <u>under</u> tongue

Chain's breaking strength equals weight of boat and trailer.

Ramps

Choosing the ramp or slipway where you will launch and retrieve your boat is just as important as choosing the right spot to anchor you want the slipway you use to make things as easy as possible so you can get on with your main purpose of being there – to go sailing.

First, make sure your tyres will have plenty of grip. Check that the ramp is free of algae, moss, seaweed and debris. Then make sure that the slipway extends far enough into the parking area to allow your trailer's wheels to clear the sloped portion before the tow vehicle's rear wheels leave the concrete.

Ideally, slipways should extend far enough into the water so there is enough depth to accommodate deep-draught boats at low tide. Many slipways are too short and the concrete abruptly ends with a drop-off of a few inches onto the seabed. This can damage a trailer's wheels and suspension, and make it difficult to pull a trailer over this drop when retrieving your boat. The best slipways are finished off with a solid concrete *pillow*. This gives you plenty of depth, and protects the underwater part of the slipway from being eroded away by the prop wash of boaters *power-loading* (using the boat's engine to drive it all the way up the trailer).

Avoid slipways that have too gradual an incline, as they will force you to back your car's wheels (or more) into the water to get the boat deep enough to float on or off the trailer. Conversely, avoid ultra-steep slipways that can place a heavy burden on your tow vehicle.

There should be at least 40 feet between the top of the slipway and the parking area to give you enough room to get both the tow vehicle and trailer into alignment, which will make backing down the slipway a lot easier.

A good facility will also provide a breakwater in areas of heavy boat traffic or wave action to keep the water around the slipway calmer. Avoid slipways that are perpendicular to a fast-flowing (over 3 mph) river or tidal stream. In these cases the slipway should be angled downstream to reduce the sideways force of the current on your boat.

You'll also want properly built docks. If there's only a single pantoon, it should be on the car driver's side to provide a better view while backing. Check that the pantoon you are about to use has recessed bolt heads and nails so there

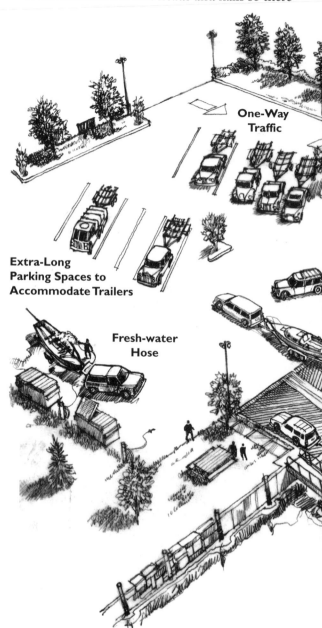

One-Way Traffic

Extra-Long Parking Spaces to Accommodate Trailers

Fresh-water Hose

is no chance of them scratching your boat. A nice touch is rubber rubrails along all exposed edges, as are raised wooden *curbs* along the outer sides of the pantoon that provide a handhold for passengers getting on and off the boat and to prevent items from getting knocked off the pantoon.

Back on land, the facility should provide a large *staging area* where you stop to load up, check the boat and rig the mast. This area encourages boaters to get their boat ready here, rather than doing it on the slipway where they slow everyone down.

As with the staging area, a designated *loading area* should be clearly marked off to the side of

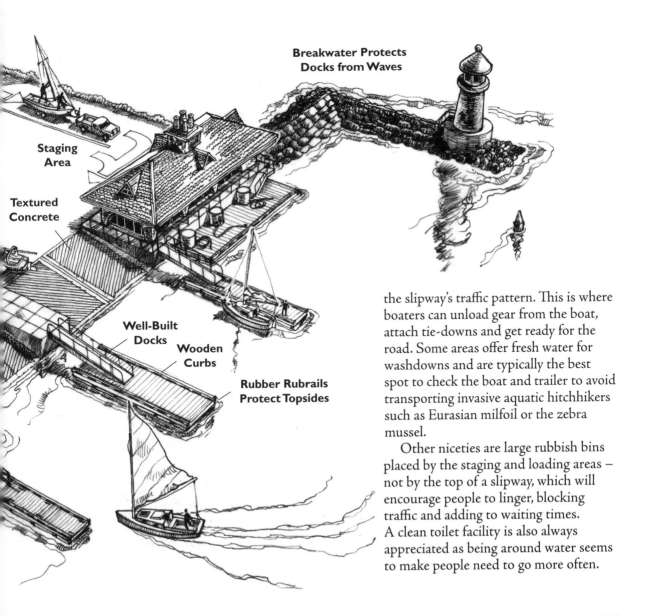

Breakwater Protects Docks from Waves

Staging Area

Textured Concrete

Well-Built Docks

Wooden Curbs

Rubber Rubrails Protect Topsides

the slipway's traffic pattern. This is where boaters can unload gear from the boat, attach tie-downs and get ready for the road. Some areas offer fresh water for washdowns and are typically the best spot to check the boat and trailer to avoid transporting invasive aquatic hitchhikers such as Eurasian milfoil or the zebra mussel.

Other niceties are large rubbish bins placed by the staging and loading areas – not by the top of a slipway, which will encourage people to linger, blocking traffic and adding to waiting times. A clean toilet facility is also always appreciated as being around water seems to make people need to go more often.

Backing Up

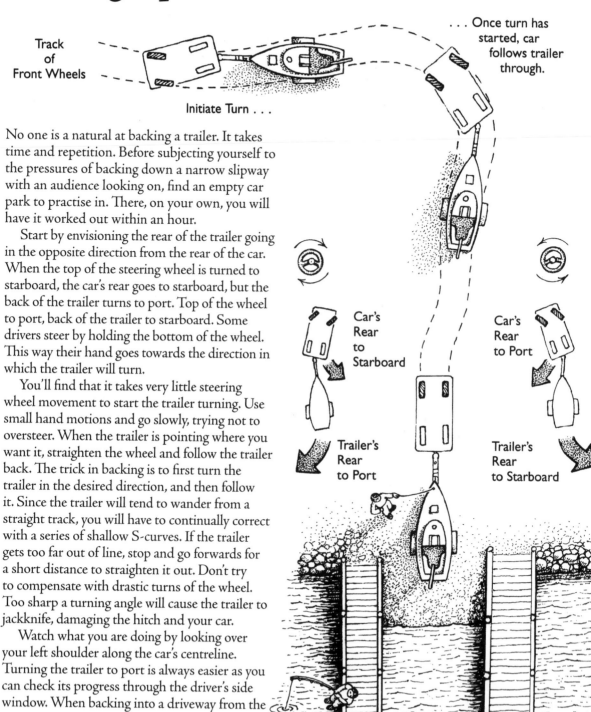

Track of Front Wheels

Initiate Turn . . .

. . . Once turn has started, car follows trailer through.

Car's Rear to Starboard

Car's Rear to Port

Trailer's Rear to Port

Trailer's Rear to Starboard

No one is a natural at backing a trailer. It takes time and repetition. Before subjecting yourself to the pressures of backing down a narrow slipway with an audience looking on, find an empty car park to practise in. There, on your own, you will have it worked out within an hour.

Start by envisioning the rear of the trailer going in the opposite direction from the rear of the car. When the top of the steering wheel is turned to starboard, the car's rear goes to starboard, but the back of the trailer turns to port. Top of the wheel to port, back of the trailer to starboard. Some drivers steer by holding the bottom of the wheel. This way their hand goes towards the direction in which the trailer will turn.

You'll find that it takes very little steering wheel movement to start the trailer turning. Use small hand motions and go slowly, trying not to oversteer. When the trailer is pointing where you want it, straighten the wheel and follow the trailer back. The trick in backing is to first turn the trailer in the desired direction, and then follow it. Since the trailer will tend to wander from a straight track, you will have to continually correct with a series of shallow S-curves. If the trailer gets too far out of line, stop and go forwards for a short distance to straighten it out. Don't try to compensate with drastic turns of the wheel. Too sharp a turning angle will cause the trailer to jackknife, damaging the hitch and your car.

Watch what you are doing by looking over your left shoulder along the car's centreline. Turning the trailer to port is always easier as you can check its progress through the driver's side window. When backing into a driveway from the street, start in the centre of the road, not off to one side. The car needs that extra room to swing around.

Launching & Retrieving

Before backing down the slipway, park off to one side and get the boat ready for launching:

+ Put the drain plug in.
+ Release all tie-downs, except the line to the winch.
+ Load gear aboard now, rather than when in the water.
+ Step the mast, set up standing rigging, attach the boom, rig running rigging, and bend on sails (but do not hoist).
+ Be careful of overhead electric wires when raising the mast. Aluminium is an excellent conductor, as are stainless steel shrouds and stays.
+ Make a long dock/control line fast to a forward cleat.
+ If you are tying up to a dock after launching, get a stern line ready, some fenders, and a boathook.
+ If you have no motor, keep a paddle ready.
+ Put the centreboard, rudder and outboard in their 'up' positions.
+ Disconnect the trailer lights from the car's system to prevent blown fuses.
+ Recheck that the drain plug is in.

When the boat is ready, walk over and check the ramp. Make sure it is clear of debris and the water is deep enough to float the boat. Back the trailer in, keeping the hubs out of the water if you can. If this can't be avoided, let them cool for at least 15 minutes after you get off the road, as a sudden cooling from immersion can crack the bearings. The trailer must go far enough in so the boat will slide off the rollers or float off its bunks. You do not want to get the car's wheels in the water. Put the car in gear and Park, set the emergency brake, and place chocks behind the rear wheels. Release the winch lock, unhook the cable from the bow eye, grab the bow dock/control line, and push the boat into the water. Restrain drift with bow and stern lines. Make her secure to the dock. Reel in the winch cable, and drive off the ramp to the parking area. Hose down any submerged parts of the trailer with fresh water.

To retrieve the boat, you may have to immerse more of the trailer than when launching. Back down the ramp, pull out a trailer length or more of cable from the winch, make sure the bunks are wet and slippery, bring the boat squarely to the trailer, and attach the cable to the bow eye. Guide the boat to the first set of rollers or bunks. Start winching in, standing off to one side to watch the boat's progress and to stay out of the cable's range in case it snaps. If the boat seems to be coming up with difficulty, don't keep cranking. Find out what is wrong, and if there are any doubts, push off and start over before damaging the boat. Once up to the bow stop, pull off the ramp and get things ready for the road.

Make sure the boat is properly seated on its supports, the trailer's lights reconnected into the car's system, all gear stowed, tie-downs in place, and the drain plug removed. When you are sure that all is secure and Aunt Edna is back from the ladies', get in the car and head home. It's been a long sail.

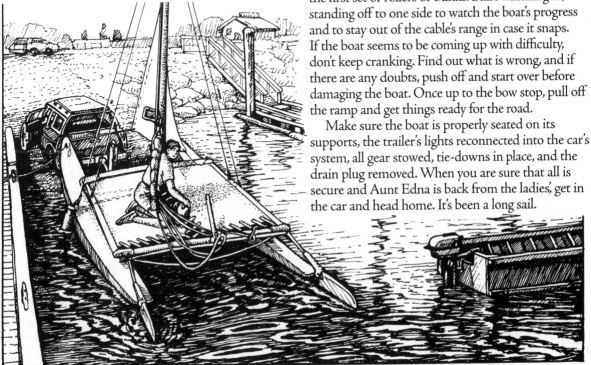

Index